The Human in Bits

the HUMAN *in* BITS

Graphical Computers, Black Abstractions

Kris Cohen

DUKE UNIVERSITY PRESS
Durham and London
2025

© 2025 DUKE UNIVERSITY PRESS
All rights reserved

Printed in the United States of America
on acid-free paper ∞

Project Editor: Ihsan Taylor
Designed by A. Mattson Gallagher

Typeset in Arno Pro and Cronos Pro
by Copperline Book Services

Library of Congress Cataloging-in-Publication Data
Names: Cohen, Kris, [date] author.
Title: The human in bits : graphical computers, black
abstractions / Kris Cohen.
Description: Durham : Duke University Press, 2025. |
Includes bibliographical references and index.
Identifiers: LCCN 2024059239 (print)
LCCN 2024059240 (ebook)
ISBN 9781478028857 (hardcover)
ISBN 9781478032090 (paperback)
ISBN 9781478061076 (ebook)
Subjects: LCSH: African American art. | African
American art—Themes, motives. | African American
artists. | Computer art—Social aspects. | Technology
in art—Social aspects. | African Americans—Race
identity. | Aesthetics. | Art and technology. | Race in
art. | Art, Modern.
Classification: LCC N6538.B53 C64 2025 (print) |
LCC N6538.B53 (ebook) |
DDC 776/.2092396073—dc23/eng/20250511
LC record available at https://lccn.loc.gov/2024059239
LC ebook record available at
https://lccn.loc.gov/2024059240

Cover art: Alma Thomas, *Mars Dust* (detail),
1972. Acrylic on canvas, 69¼ × 57⅛ in. (175.9 ×
145.1 cm.). Whitney Museum of American Art,
New York. Purchase, with funds from the Hament
Corporation. Inv.: 72.58. © 2025 Estate of Alma
Thomas (Courtesy of the Hart Family) / Artists
Rights Society (ARS), New York. Digital image
© Whitney Museum of American Art / Licensed
by Scala / Art Resource, NY.

CONTENTS

ACKNOWLEDGMENTS

The acknowledgments are the best part of every book. They're where the gratitude and love that is implicit in footnotes and mostly hidden in the main text get made explicit, where the individuating work of the author function is shown to have always been a lie.

This research for this book started in the summer of 2014 with Eli Coplan at the Stanford University archives, a trip supported by the Ruby-Lankford Grant Program for Faculty-Student Research in the Humanities. Thank you, Eli, for starting this project with me and for taking it in your own directions over the years.

Another instigating push: thank you to Heather Love and *Public Books* for the invitation to review Stephen Best's book *None Like Us*. That book turned out to be formative, so thank you as well to Stephen, for that book and for your friendship.

I met Stephen when I was a fellow at the Research and Academic Program of the Clark Art Institute in the winter and spring of 2019. Thank you to the Clark and the Andrew W. Mellon Foundation for funding my position there. Thank you to William Hernandez, my research assistant while I was in residence. And thank you to fellow fellows and fellow travelers, Celeste Olaquiaga, Jennifer Bajorek, Julia Bryan-Wilson, Jill Casid, Philippe Cordez, Susan Sidulkaus, and Robert Wiesenberger. I hope you remember me as the one who knew how to work the industrial dishwasher.

My friendship with Zirwat Chowdhury extends beyond that time at the Clark, but I was lucky to have her so nearby for those months. You were the liveliest part of that lively winter landscape. Your unabashed and scintillating formalism helps prop up my life, not just my writing.

Later in 2018, I got to test out the Alma Thomas chapter with University of Virginia faculty and students. Thank you to everyone who came out, and especially to Meaghan Walsh for help thinking about the ligatures in Thomas's work. And, of course, thank you to my host and friend Christa Robbins. You have always been my best editor, even if I didn't make you read every chapter of this book.

Thank you to Brooke Belisle and your class at Stony Brook University for letting me float a version of my Charles Gaines chapter in the quiet days of late book editing.

In October 2023, I got to test out a late-stage version of the Jack Whitten chapter for students, faculty, and community at the University of Louisville. Thank you everyone for the encouragement, and especially to Tiffany Calvert and Jennifer Sichel for being such easy, warm, fun hosts. Having been born in Louisville and raised as a Cardinals fan (as Jennifer said, the bird with the teeth), it was a real thrill.

I have had four research assistants at Reed. Thank you to Nita McDaniel for your help with the Charles Gaines research, and to Francesca Michel for your help with Jack Whitten. Thank you to Priya Narain for your help with bibliographic research and for starting the image-permissions process, and to Safi Zenger for your help completing that process. I will help any of you with your research anytime.

I have had access for the last couple of years to an on-demand writing retreat, and I've used it at key moments in the writing. Thank you, Brooke O'Harra and Sharon Hayes, for sharing your home with me. I'm writing these sentences from your kitchen table.

Ianna Hawkins Owen helped me with a crisis-read of the introduction. But more than that, the way you write and the way you live are inspirations to me. Thank you for staying close.

Thank you forever to the Media Aesthetics crew: Brooke Belisle, Stephanie Boluk, Jacob Gaboury, Jim Hodge, Patrick Jagoda, Patrick Keilty, Patrick LeMieux, and Scott Richmond. Our retreats are the highlight of my year. I do hope you can see your various contributions to this book. I love you all.

Some friends have a strong presence in these pages, whether they know it or not. Thank you to Anjali Arondekar, Jennifer Bajorek, Venus

Bivar, Kate Bredeson, Emily Godbey, Tere Harrison, Michele Matteini, Sarah Miller, Ben Read, Amanda Windle, and Damon Young.

Some debts can only be underdescribed by citation. Stephen Best's book, mentioned above, belongs in this category, as does the work of Saidiya Hartman, Jacob Gaboury, Jodi Melamed, and Grace Hong, as well as Richard Shiff's work on art and technology. Richard also provided a generous late read-through of my chapter on Jack Whitten. And thank you to Sun Ra and the Arkestra, who get no citation but whose music propelled, lulled, and prodded me while I wrote almost every part of this manuscript.

Thank you unendingly to Laura and Leo, for your lightness and love. And thank you to Mustache, Pickle, and Motor: you were pure distraction, which is why you were so helpful.

And, finally, to two of my closest friends who passed in 2021 to be with us in other ways: Paul Ratliff and Lauren Berlant. I dedicate this book to you. I wish you could read it. The book is all about the diminishment of the self in ways that are both chosen and not, experimental and impoverished, radical and difficult, pointing the way to other forms of gathering. You teach me about that every day.

Introduction:
The Human in Bits

Point, line, diagram; bit, field; grid, raster: this is the idiom of Howardena Pindell's work in the 1970s. Maybe one finds this austere as a description or a modality of artistic practice, but then, in relation or opposition to what? That will become a key question in what is to follow—which forms of personhood, particularly racialized personhood, rely on, and even need certain cordons to be drawn around technical vocabularies, technologies, and technologized forms of being? The visual forms that correspond to the idiom I've given them span Pindell's punched paper work and her video drawings, otherwise separated by the biographical fact that the latter began as her relief from the bodily tedium and strain of the former. The television she purchased and then photographed to make the video drawings was at first intended simply to vary the focal length of her eyes in relation to the strenuous work she had been doing with dots, points, thousands of bits that were no larger than one-eighth of an inch and that she often marshaled to populate massive canvases—in the case of *Untitled* (1973, plate 1), 17½ inches tall and 90⅜ inches long.[1] A paper collage, *Untitled* is a vast field of hole-punched dots, each dot inscribed with a handwritten numeral. The numerals span one to twenty thousand, but are not arranged in any discernible order.[2] So the numerals and their medium evoke an order without being themselves ordered beyond their existence in a particular and consistent numbering system and their inscription on the strictly gridded dots. As with anything that exists at two such extremes of scale, the dot field appears highly ordered from a distance, and far more chaotic up close.

The video drawings, such as *Video Drawings: Swimming* (1975, plate 2), are more modest in size. *Swimming* is 14 × 16 in. Here, too, we find system without order or systematicity, implied but not given. Arrows and numerals diagram the field of an image photographed from the TV screen, a process that makes the screen's own scan lines palpable as so much interference, or so much medium. In *Swimming*, the top fourth of the field is obscured or blotted out by something that obstructed the camera lens. Just below that, as though the figure had just fallen out of this obscure top fourth, a diver unfolds out of a pike, just starting to direct their own fall. The lane lines of the pool sit askance the scan lines of the screen—two systems, uncollated, except by their copresence here in this image. There is no sense in which the body with perfectly pointed toes exists free of any of the systems invoked here. The body is multiply embedded, multiply mediated, multiply transcoded.

Both sets of works give a formal delimitation to a social problem that requires a technical vocabulary: what could it mean to be a bit in a field? The question applies as much to the act of making these works as to the scene of dwelling with them. What could it mean to exist for all those hours *with*, if not *as*, points in a grid, at least insofar as one is willing to conform one's labor to those constraints? Were they constraints? If so, on what? What form of collectivity *is* a field stratified as bits? What are its histories, and how black or blackened were they? How were those histories related to the history of whiteness and its need for more flexible genres of control in the seventies?[3]

Of course, to watch television in the seventies on a bulbous cathode-ray tube (CRT), itself a raster field composed of bits called pixels, or even to trace from that field at a distance, is not automatically to become a bit in that field. That was a fear from previous eras of white power, when heterogeneity—forms of difference as light as the shade of khaki and as heavy as an identity—might feel like shelter from an imposed homogeneity. The move from *viewing* to *being* in the video drawings was Howardena Pindell's play, effected in her willingness, maybe desire, to let her labor take form through the raster of a gridded field, to meticulously, minutely occupy the life of bits, to scan bodily from bit to bit across that field, to accede to those currents, to alter (even damage) her body in the exacting movements this required, all of it forcing Pindell to seek relief from one set of screens in another. How are Pindell's diagrammed televisions and dot matrices, the forms of collectivity they offer and enforce, part of a black desire for freedom—not just freedom from the violence of whiteness, but freedom from the entire surround of whiteness seen together with its tawdry offers of inclusion? What was the collectivity of bit and field in relation to the long American history of, on the one hand, racist collectivisms (delimited by biology or skin and, later, in diversity), and, on the other, the collectivities of the black radical tradition that wanted nothing to do with either those racist enclaves or that which they would exclude?[4]

Pindell was not the only one sitting with such questions. Why did so many black artists in and after the sixties start to work with the grid and gridded structures? Alma Thomas's organicist plots, Adrian Piper's early permutational algorithms, William T. Williams's shattered screens, Peter Halley's circuit boards, Tom Lloyd's eight-bit pixel maps, Jack Whitten's "digital abstraction," Lorna Simpson's photo-textual systems, Charles Gaines's transpositional rasters, Lisa Corinne Davis's elastic grid landscapes, Julie Mehretu's massive networked paintings, American Artist's *Black Gooey Universe*.[5]

As with Pindell's work, it is the willingness, the consent to dwell inside the problem of the gridded field, that should caution us against assuming we know who the enemies are here—technology, on one side, and life, on the other. But that is how the lines have been drawn . . . when, that is, the question of race is left unspecified. In Rosalind Krauss's defining, if ambivalent, take on the grid, that structure sits at the fulcrum of an epochal antagonism between aesthetic expressivity and the rationalizing technologies that have, for critics who share Krauss's commitments, overscripted modernity.[6] There, two distinct possibilities hang in the balance: that modernism would find a way to defeat deadening rationalism on rationalism's own turf, or, that modernist rationality would claim art for its own, too.

The grid has always had other and longer histories, of course.[7] But by the sixties in the United States, and certainly by the late seventies when Krauss published her essay, the technology of the grid had already quietly slipped out of Krauss's defining antagonism to take up its place in another scene altogether. This escape was facilitated by military funding that aimed to transform the computer from a simple and brute tool of computation, at best a sophisticated servant for crunching numbers, to something that would come to take up a position in proximity to, even inside of, the human: a personal computer, a computer of the person-form. There, it would redefine the terms by which that human form can be known and lived while reimagining the kinds of labor and work that the computer user could be incentivized to produce. And it is this proximity, this intimacy fused to this "extimacy," that eventually makes race itself come to be legible as a technology.[8]

The history of the personal computer *is* a history of the desire to transform what a human was by way of a transformation of how and in what environments humans were to exist—whether working, playing, or idling. To accomplish this, the personal computer collapsed screen and computation in multiple ways, across multiple registers of meaning (from the visual to the logical). The enabling technology of this powerful collapse was the grid or raster of the screen made graphical. It was the screen's grid, turned immanently computational, that made it an infrastructure for information and, in what would become a near synonym, for life. The aims of this platform, the rastered screen or graphical field, were expressly to be the reorganization of personhood, now to be seen as augmented by or made symbiotic with information, and thereby with the computer.

The densest concentration of this *graphical* history has been in the field of the graphic user interface, or GUI—that ensemble of icons and windowed space, extended within pull-down menus, enveloped within an encompassing desktop metaphor, navigable by the prothesis of mouse and pointer, and all arranged in space meant to feel open, even free, not despite the raster but because of it. The GUI is most often associated with Apple Computers, although Apple is not where it was born, nor does Apple's interface design, however iconic, mark the limits of its influence. This particular graphically organized space will be intimately, muscularly, even painfully familiar to anyone who has ever used a personal computer.[9] That space has become the very site for the elaboration of personhood in computational and networked contexts. Contestatory, ameliorative, complicit . . . the mode or spirit of that elaboration barely matters (input alone was what mattered), even though it is tempting to want will, choice, decision (those technologies of liberal personhood) to matter, even to matter anew in that space. And the designers of the graphical interface of the personal computer were certainly driven to make those technologies matter anew, which is one of the reasons that their efforts were an investment in and reimagination of whiteness as well as an updated disavowal of that very fact.

Computer history knows this story as the invention of the personal computer, computer graphics, and eventually the GUI, and it has told this story in some detail.[10] Art history hasn't cared much about this history, although it has cared intermittently about certain abstractions it calls "screens" or "windows" and about a certain visual culture of computing and new media.[11] Media studies has returned to this history again and again, but, when loyal to a set of supercharged materialisms, it has sometimes dismissed it all as part of a fetishistic focus on the screen and visuality at the expense of other, supposedly more materialist aspects of computation. I'll refer to it as a *history of the graphical*. That phrase, describing not an invention so much as a slow process, gestures at the centripetal, but also centrifugal, expansion of the logics of the graphical interface out toward cultural and political spaces and the politics of the human.[12] Where the centrifugal and centripetal forces of the graphical intersect, there we find experimentation on the boundaries and capacities of the human itself. And so this is the place where a history of the graphical comes to intersect with a history of aesthetic experimentation in and around black abstraction and black abstractionists.[13]

For black artists working in parallel with these developments, the grid could never have comfortably fit Krauss's antagonism. Their history within the surround of whiteness, however they chose to live and reconceive it, had always wanted to violently situate them on the side of the deadening techno-rationalism that the human—the hero for Krauss and others of an embattled modernist art practice—was tasked with resisting.[14] Katherine McKittrick teaches us how to see this defining antagonism as itself a technology of racialization: "This is where we begin, this is where historical blackness comes from: the list, the breathless numbers, the absolutely economic, the mathematics of the unliving."[15] McKittrick considers the long entanglement of black life with numbers, with numeracy, with what she calls data—the ledgers of slave ships, police records, sociological data about "bad neighborhoods," digital videos of police violence coded with the metadata of hashtags, the foundational technologies of the digital computer. These are the various technologies for recording black life in order to extinguish that life.[16] As such, data, or mathematics, the quantification of life itself, has been one of the particular constraints on and scenes of possibility for blackness.

This means, of course, that mathematics, seen as the encoding of life in numbers such that life can be managed unto or in proximity to death, has also been one of the specters *of* blackness that haunts a white imagination (whiteness has always been haunted by the products of its own violence): that is, one of the various conflations through which blackness has been apprehended, misrecognized, violated.[17] But to return to, by way of one last move away from, the antimonies that structure Krauss's grid, this threat of becoming data is importantly distinct from one of the more iconic threats that has organized various discourses of postwar modernity: the threat of anonymity, becoming a mere cog, the erosion of self-possession and individuality in becoming part of a vast machinery.[18] The defenses arrayed against anonymity, facelessness, or getting lost in the nonindividualized address of television or of any mass address—assertions of autonomy, exhortations to individuality, an entire technical and psychological apparatus dedicated to shoring up the boundaries of individualistic self-possession—do nothing to protect against the threat of becoming data, which thrives precisely on quiddity, on heterogeneity, and especially on public attestations to the uniqueness of one's life.[19] This might not have been obvious to people who committed themselves to an American discourse of individuality in the immediate postwar period; or maybe it was, under the spell of a rush to the postracial. Now, it is obvious enough that social media has monetized individuality itself. No one who ever once entertained the fantasy of exhibiting their individuality online now knows how to escape that vaunted individuality.

McKittrick's account of modernity's other threat—the threat of mathematics, of data—helps us see how the history of the personal computer, and of the graphical field as a space for a labor of self-elaboration, needs to be seen as a technology for the recuperation of whiteness. Here, a driving anxiety of modernity is the fear of becoming numerical: not just a number among others, but a number in itself, a bit in a field. This is a story, in other words, about the fear of fungibility, not anonymity, of being interchangeable as well as endemically available to be read, to be understood from the outside, given as so much information.[20] I will address fungibility most directly in chapter 4 because Charles Gaines's work with systems aesthetics has long contended with the problem of freedom seen not in relation to the faceless mass but to fungibility, that other American "origin story." From the perspective of an embattled whiteness, seeking new footing after the world wars, in an American state that was itself seeking new footings for democracy and liberalism in the wake of World War II, those are fears not just about the computer and computation, but about blackness and its long historical enmeshment with data, with math, with encodings of life that make it both immanently available and extensibly interchangeable.[21]

The graphical field of the personal computer is a space in retreat from that threat, and so it is shaped by it. This story matters now precisely because of the proliferation of fantasies of autonomy, individuality, and liberal freedom that are fostered in and in proximity to the graphical field. Think here of Apple's famous 1984 advertisement. In airing its Cold War allegory during Super Bowl XVIII, Apple set the stage for the personal computer to go to war with the authoritarianism of television, of mass spectatorship: the personal (computer) against the mass (television). The athlete's body—its femininity indelible, but butched up to signal its autonomy from such social norms—wages a war where creative expression is the only weapon that mattered. This is what Apple offered to host in its newly graphical screens: life itself, so long as that life embraced difference as its platform. The graphical field doesn't cause these fantasies; there are myriad mechanisms for that. The entirety of America's nationalistic machinery often seems committed to sustaining the fantasy of individuality, rehabbing it whenever the fantasy grows tired (as we've seen so virulently during the COVID-19 pandemic, which has sent those machineries of individualism into hypertrophic death drive). But the graphical field was a crucible. It is now a host, the literal site where the labor of those fantasies gets elaborated, substantiated, recuperated, renewed . . . lived . . . for the benefit of some, still requiring the slow death of others.[22] But we will also have to note the ways that graphicalization changes the valences of that otherness.

A broader story here is the shift in the politics of race from a representational to a nonrepresentational matrix. This book generates a few idioms for the nonrepresentational logics that we find wherever humans and computers tend toward indistinction: *operational*, in the language of the first chapter, there adapted from art historian Leo Steinberg and computer historian Jacob Gaboury; but also, more simply and more overarchingly, *graphical*, itself a kind of synonym for, because an operationalization of, nonrepresentational logics. As we'll see more clearly in the pages to come, the graphical is nonrepresentational because of its commitment to fostering the self in its "ongoingness"; tethered not to what was but to what can be.[23] In this privileging of futurity over what has been, of what can be made over what can be re-presented, the graphical accommodates the representational as so much content. The work of Ramon Amaro, Louis Chude-Sokei, Grace Kyungwon Hong, Jodi Melamed, Christine Goding-Doty, Katherine McKittrick, W. E. B. Du Bois, and others lays the groundwork for thinking about race in a nonrepresentational matrix.[24] The graphical field of the personal computer makes such a matrix a space for life, including of course representations of life viewed and lived in all of their complexity.

Part of this story is told by Jodi Melamed, Grace Kyungwon Hong, and the feminists of color on whose work they build. Together, they have allowed an understanding of the late twentieth and early twenty-first centuries that revolves around the new palatability, and even popularity in some liberal circles, of an official antiracist stance that recognizes, in order to monetize, difference—when and only when difference is understood through the corralled representational logics of diversity and inclusion.[25] Melamed calls the 1940s–60s, which inaugurates my own study, a time of "racial liberalism." That period is succeeded by the "liberal multiculturalism" of the 1980s–90s. Both are periods in which whiteness gets rehabilitated by its newfound capacity to include more than just white people in the category of the human—so long as those who are to be included agree, explicitly or tacitly, to accept the basic neoliberal premise that a world realized as a free market has once and for all leveled the playing field, opening a clear path to the good life for anyone willing to be hailed by that call. There are entire genres of Twitter feeds, often authored by white men working in the tech industries, that play out this logic in their allegiance to meritocracy, to color-blind hiring practices, to neutral algorithms, and to the guiding ethos of *On the internet no one knows you're a dog.*

The list of milestones that have been said to mark the end of any sort of racial deficit in America is long, beginning with slavery itself, often justified by those who benefited from the institution as a kind of humanitarian, "civilizing" mission. These alibis extend beyond the formal end of slavery where individuation was the price the newly freed had to pay for a freedom that would perpetuate the ongoing logics of the plantation. Individuality itself was the key technology here. And those plantation temporalities feed forward, into and through racial liberalism and the different promises of freedom that the personal computer, with its graphical screen, whispers to users and materializes as an empty space for self-elaboration.[26]

In Sylvia Wynter's terms, this history is structured by the logics of "dysselection." The graphical screen of the personal computer—by which we might as well mean the personal itself, given the personal computer's ubiquity—helps to set the standards for what would come to be understood as success: are you creative, a self-starter, independent, good at networking, at finding and sifting data? The graphical field thereby defined the parameters within which unsuccessful groups could be identified in terms that felt less biological, less epidermal, less cultural, and more about who is good at navigating the present tense and its labile scenes of value production.[27] Key to Wynter's formulation, though, is that the dysselected are those people who can be seen as neither successful nor unsuccessful. They are, rather, the people who are illegible precisely by those standards. Failure carries with it the potential for redemption, always given in terms defined by the successful. So while failure and success are starkly different subject positions in terms of the allotment of resources, they together form a single recursive system, a self-reproducing set of values.[28] This is how, like McKittrick's thinking about mathematics and black life, Wynter offers a full-scale reconceptualization of modernist melancholia, rendering the otherwise epochal tension between alienation and freedom, the grid and the human, as just so much intramural whiteness. As Clyde Ford's memoir about his father's time as an early computer engineer at IBM makes painfully clear, whiteness comes to understand itself in the period of the personal computer's development not as a racial formation so much as a disposition toward success and toward the present tense—that is, not racial at all from its own perspective.[29] It is a disposition that defines what counts as success, which makes success come to seem equally accessible to all, given the right attitude. In the context of the world the graphical field helped make, whiteness shifted, slightly, from being an *atmosphere* encompassing the smooth operation of a massive system of domination and violence, to being an attitude toward the present divorced from historical violence precisely by the power of one's attitude, one's disposition toward a world understood to be a "free market," a space of unrestricted movement such as was visualized and made operational, at the level of the personal, by the graphical field of the computer. As such, whiteness made allowances for people who were nonwhite to join their ranks, but only if the standards for success were strictly adhered to. This was the work to which the graphical interface was yoked, the forms of self-elaboration it was designed to accommodate.

This line of thought is important for media studies and for art history precisely because it registers what has always been nonrepresentational in race and racialization, and what is specifically nonrepresentational about the graphical field and computational technologies more generally. Even while computational and networked technologies have rekindled hopes that representational politics have finally found their most empowering medium in the internet, those same technologies work beyond representational politics at a technical level, and at social, cultural, and political levels as well. This perspective turns out to be as crucial for reckoning with computational technologies such as the graphical interface as it is for reckoning with black abstract aesthetics. While an efficient view of the history of black abstraction posits that the enjoinment to represent black life, or what Darby English calls the strictures of "black representational space," started to loosen after the Black Arts Movement, recent work on the Black Arts Movement has given us reason to think that nonrepresentational tactics teem, if quietly, in work made by black artists before and after the official discourses of abstraction.[30] The chapters on Alma Thomas, Jack Whitten, Charles Gaines, and Julie Mehretu bear out this thought. The graphical form or modality of personhood this book tracks from its coalescence in the fifties (not emergence, nor origin—those are far older and more dispersed, as I'll hope to at least suggest) to its exhaustion and ubiquity in the aughts, is importantly nonrepresentational both in its technicity and in its operation as a mode of subject formation.

I call this form of mediated personhood "graphical" after the graphic user interface, or GUI. But the GUI isn't my only or even primary case, even if it is an instigating one. While the history of the GUI plays a key role, to see the graphical in the full flight of its ambitions, we need to range across a number of cases where that mode of personhood was encoded, elaborated, and insistently racialized—where, in other words, personhood was adapted or seen to be adapted for a graphical field that was to be both its training ground and its field of elaboration. These include: the gendered and racializing politics of early twentieth-century experiments in the scientific management of labor; postwar exhibition design and its attempts to recuperate racial whiteness for new democratic modalities of citizenship; and early computer research groups working out the forms of the computer's interface.

The remainder of this chapter will be spent dwelling in those three scenes, elaborating the role each plays in the larger gathering of the graphical as a system for producing personhood. In the following chapter, as a bridge to the rest of the book's focus on art practice, I look closely at art historian Leo Steinberg's thinking about "operational processes" in relation to midcentury painting, postindustrial labor, and cybernetics. Here I draw the conceptual and technical work of the current chapter into an explicitly artistic register, showing how the graphical was always an aesthetic proposition. The following chapter, in other words, addresses the question of why artistic practices are part of this story at all.

The diffraction patterns created when the latter history of artistic practice is laid over the former history of the technological gathering of the graphical is where this book lives. The GUI is, in other words, just one of a cluster of historical cases that I think register the impacts of this mode of graphical personhood. If the GUI assumes some priority here, it's not because it was first or most important; it's because it and its technological afterlives so explicitly worked to recondition whiteness for a period where information would come to subsume so many regimes of personhood, both imposed and chosen. But if the conditions for the elaboration of whiteness have changed, one thing about whiteness remains consistent here: it is not a subjectivity or an ethnicity or even a culture. It is a vast latticed structure of violence masquerading as an attitude that both requires and generates differentiation and individuation, or what scholars in media studies sometimes refer to (usually with no reference to racialization) as *discretization*.[31]

The graphical doesn't name a medium or mode of representation so much as a scene of concatenation, accommodation, and adaptation: human to computer, human capacity to computer capacity. This involved an explicit project of changing the very nature of the human. So it couldn't not be a racializing project, insofar as the human itself has been a lively site of race work.[32] The graphical computer screen becomes the primary space where the human would be adapted to the imperatives of communicating with and through information. It was and is not the only such space. And while a kind of technological imperative motivates each of the scenes that I sketch in what follows, each scene's interest in the fate of the human after World War II also makes it a site for the rehabilitation and reform of whiteness itself, but now traveling under the new universalism of the diverse, the multicultural, and, eventually, the postracial. All of this, of course, took time to achieve, and no one site instigates, completes, or stands in for the story as a whole. The GUI, a center of gravity for my own project because of its ubiquity today, isn't the first or most important engine of graphicalization, nor the only site where its terms were elaborated and contested. It is simply, now, omnipresent, ineluctable, unavoidable. But it is also true that the GUI does encode within itself—inside all those managed windows and folders, those scenes for managing the self—the various ambitions articulated in the disparate cases that round out this chapter.

In what follows, I track the formation and logics of the graphical through three disparate scenes, scattered throughout the twentieth century, each of which gathers together some of the ways of thinking that would be necessary to entangle computers, labor, and humans in the field of the graphical: first, the work of the Gilbreths (Lillian and Kenneth) and the labor and management systems they initiate in parallel to Frederick Taylor's own systematizations of labor; second, the exhibition strategy that Fred Turner calls "surround media" and its role in the *Harlem on My Mind* exhibition at the Metropolitan Museum of Art in 1968; and third, the work of Douglas Engelbart to transform computing by conceptualizing an early graphical computer interface. This third case acts, in the geometry of history, like something of a knot, where historical threads enter into the field of Engelbart's work, get tangled, and exit in different configurations.

All these scenes mark the shifting relationship between labor and personhood that was endemic to the era that witnessed the birth, spread, and eventual dominance of the graphical computer screen. Not all mark race as part of their explicit and self-conscious discourse, but all move in and through the racial politics of the postwar period in the United States and the renewal of whiteness that was so central to the various projects of the burgeoning tech industry.

The Managed "I"

Alan Liu has, more than most, helped us pay attention to the formal significance of the graphic user interface. His book *The Laws of Cool* (2004) is worth quoting at length. Here is how he introduces the graphic user interface, or what he calls the "user-friendly interface of knowledge work," by which he means the interface to an entire socioeconomic and cultural period of history:

> Turn on a networked personal computer today, and the face of information looks quite different. Instead of a character-based monochrome screen, we see the descendant of the bitmap approach first devised in primitive form in the 1960s by researchers at The Stanford Research Institute's Human Factors Research Center and the University of Utah's Computer Science Laboratory. The approach was further developed in the 1970s by the Xerox PARC group, before being adopted in 1984 by Apple for its groundbreaking Macintosh and finally brought into the corporate mainstream in the late 1980s and 1990s in the successive revisions of Microsoft's Windows operating system.[33]

Liu continues:

> We see a graphically bitmapped main "window" whose menu bars and office-themed visual icons (file folders, trash cans, calendars, phones) construct a metaphorical "desktop," the great landscape of the cubicle. Above all, the function of such a desktop is to coordinate (and also subordinate) operations and modes. Clicking on desktop icons, for example, initiates sequences of actions or opens up individual windows that, as [Steven] Johnson points out, are what we now have instead of "modes." Or, rather, such windows obviate the awareness of modes by making mode switching as much as possible a matter of "direct manipulation." . . .
>
> Nor does the modeless coordination of computing stop there, for with the advent of tightly integrated application "suites," individual word-processing, spreadsheet, database, or e-mail programs display what amounts to whole interior desktops complete with cross-application menu bars, templates, embedded program "objects," and "wizards" designed to stitch all the suite into a single, virtual work surface.[34]

Liu's attention to the design of the GUI then turns symptomatic: "In reality, as both Johnson and the cyberpunk novelist Neal Stephenson (in his nonfiction *In the Beginning . . . Was the Command Line*) have argued, the user-friendly interface is symptomatic of a whole way of relating to culture."[35] Liu brings this line of thought to a head when he implies that there are essentially no boundaries to the graphical field as it exists in and as the very substance of today's world: "And since the desktop is now networked, there is in principle no outer horizon to that single work surface."[36]

What Liu describes, across this whole symptomatic chain, are various modes of systematization, including those that traveled under what might seem to be the ideologically opposed concepts of "decentralization" and "distributed centralization." Liu links all these forms of systematization, by way of genealogy, to Frederick Taylor. Where Taylor systematized physical labor, the personal computer and its graphical interface systematized knowledge work—the labor that, in Liu's history, best defines the contemporary period his book describes. It is through the dispersive logics of decentralization that those technologies could issue their ultimate promise: democratization. Decentralization, in Liu's account, all but requires what he calls connectedness and consistency, something achieved by the internet protocols that made personal computers as well as their graphical environments systemic and pervasive—in fact, impossible to escape.[37] So while the promises Liu historicizes are all voiced in a democratic mood, the specter Liu identifies, again and again, is of a minimally updated threat of homogenization—of everything becoming the same under the impress of systematization. And what rushes sharply into relief, in any account of homogenization, is the individual, that bastion of resistance to the forces of sameness, that fragile form of selfhood forever threatened by modernity's forces of homogenization. Who is this resistant individual? What sustains a faith in their coherence and political importance? And what if the individual isn't that which is threatened by the graphical field and its modes of systematization, but is itself the danger?

Liu is led to this account in part because of his genealogical approach, his looking back to Taylorization for the ideological roots of knowledge work and the technical forms, such as the GUI, that propagated it. The story of Taylorization is always one where individuals are lost to a system: overridden, erased, violated precisely in their individuality and autonomy. It is always a melancholic story, where the lost object is individuality. And so, histories of Taylorization have protected, even aggrandized the individual. Melissa Gregg's *Counterproductive: Time Management in the Knowledge Economy* allows us to begin to imagine a different genealogy, one with a more capacious imagination for the space between the human and the individualized subject.[38] For my purposes, Gregg's book gives a prehistory of the graphical field in relation to a far longer history of explicitly gendered and implicitly racialized work management. By shifting the history of knowledge work from Frederick Taylor and Taylorization to the husband-and-wife team of Lillian and Kenneth Gilbreth, and eventually to Lillian Gilbreth's work on her own after her husband's early death, Gregg teaches that the model for time-management studies, that which it seeks to install in the human, isn't so much the generalized system as it is, specifically, the white middle-class woman managing the home. In other words, the prototype and engine of the managed human is the augmented individual, now gendered and tacitly racialized—not, crucially, just the worker organized as a systematized mass.[39] This recognizes the key role that Lillian Gilbreth played in this history, while at the same time uncovering the way that domesticity was the scene for not just early time-management studies, but for later twentieth-century books aimed at improving time management in relation to labor, addressed now to individuals rather than to corporations. While Taylor was an obvious, if uncited influence on Engelbart's thinking about the trainable human and the analysis of tasks, the Gilbreths' work more closely models the tacit gender and racial politics of the research that generated the graphical field.

As Gregg describes, the white middle-class woman running a home performed the manual labor of housework. But under the influence of Gilbreth's efficiency studies, or what Gregg sometimes more pointedly calls her "fatigue studies," they were also to understand themselves as the managers of the home, supported either by servants or by a suite of technical and managerial resources that would stand in for the work of servants. In other words, the *I* who does the work also, and more importantly, experiences herself as the *I* who manages the work. In this individual, there is a splitting so that one can take up a certain attitude toward oneself and one's labors. All of the labor usually resides in one body, but with or without actual servants, that body, in her own self-conception, now occupies the more valued category of manager.[40] For Gilbreth, this wasn't about gender emancipation so much as it was about efficiency—but the narrative of gender emancipation would come in the wake of her work, in the later self-help literature aimed at contemporary office workers.[41] So while the role is expressly gendered (female) and more quietly racialized (white), that role's aspirational managerialism can seem to supersede those kinds of classifications, those zonings of the human and its populations. The soi-disant manager might—if only in her own self-conception, here aided by the products of Gilbreth's work studies such as the management desk that she wanted to install in every kitchen—feel as though she has overcome any collective identities that might have determined her life before. Gilbreth's management consulting and the tools that emerged from her research fostered an attitude toward gendered and racialized work that might seem to lift one out of those categorizations. So if the interfaces of Gilbreth's managerial tools weren't yet graphical, they fostered an attitude toward self and work that would become central to the graphical interface that Engelbart would famously demonstrate in 1968 (Gilbreth died in 1972).

Fast-forward to the end of the twentieth century, the historical center of Gregg's book, and this history helps explain the wild explosion of a market for time-management books and apps aimed at individuals. On the one hand, such resources emphasize what Gregg calls the strenuous "athleticism" of time management. On the other hand, they reveal the prevalence of technologies that act as servants in an age when far fewer white-collar workers had access to secretaries but still desired the cachet associated with being able to offload "nonessential" tasks to an other. An other whose very presence would then play the invaluable role of setting off the work of a delegating authority as special, essential, core, and perhaps above all—as Lillian Gilbreth asserted in contrast to the rote systematicity of Taylorism—as creative.[42]

The new ethos of knowledge work that Fred Turner would link to 1960s counterculture and the hippie movement (with all of its own well-documented gender and race problems), Gregg links to a long-standing ideology that tightens the aperture of time-management efforts ever more concertedly around the individualized worker, where what the individual was to become feels open-ended. That is, Gregg's work offers us a history of the individual not just as the liberal avatar of freedom, decision, and will but as the manager of one's self. The individual who, in internalizing a certain managerial function, also incorporates structural elements of white masculine paternalism.

But most importantly, the individual who incorporates those elements into an encompassing attitude toward the self was incentivized to become indifferent to their own historical conditions as the platform for successful individuation. In this fantasy, the individual was never autonomous; they were always augmented by an imaginary scene of servitude. The creative self who would find a home, eventually, in the graphical fields of the personal computer thus arrogates a historical prerogative of whiteness—the power and right to be served by another—as an element of their own self-possession, even while getting to embrace inclusion and diversity, life beyond identity, as part of their self-conception. Here, the individual, modeled on the white middle-class woman, is a driving force of modernity just as much as the masses who have been more often feared, and whose threat of homogeneity lingers like an eerie fog around Liu's own Taylorist account of the GUI.

In Gregg's account, twentieth-century industrialization begins with a scene of the white woman in the home, efficiently managing a household of real or internalized servants who were racialized less as any particular identity and more as what Sylvia Wynter calls the dysselected. This periodization culminates sometime near the present, with the lure of a widespread personal regimen that might appeal to any gender willing to take on the increasingly strenuous work of managing one's own time ever more productively (what Leo Steinberg, in the next chapter, will call a "he-man" attitude toward the self and one's life).[43] Gregg's research, in other words, narrows the spotlight for the American history of knowledge work, locating its center not with information itself, cybernetics, information theory, or computers, but with the historical construction of the individual and an expansive infrastructure of individuation. This was an individual supplemented by time-management technologies (a renewal of a past relationship to servants, secretaries, and further back, slaves, now instantiated as an attitude toward self); by a new bifurcation of labor, where the management function externalized in Taylor becomes internalized, possessed as the engine of self-possession, generating a self-directed and ever more fulfilling form of work where one is one's own boss. This would be true, or feel true, as much in a large corporation as in a peripatetic freelance setting. Such an individual thereby retained their privileged relationship to a far longer history of white patriarchy, by way of a white matriarchy, by way of its relationship to proxy-servants. This figure was compelled to stand out by inventing new modes and models of productivity through ever more athletic feats of self-composure, self-possession, and self-discipline. All these new modes and models would find a home in the graphical field of the personal computer.

The Whiteness Surround

Fred Turner argues, in his book *The Democratic Surround*, that after World War II, in the American context at least, this figure of the individual was more an open question than a definite statement, still in formation.[44] The question, as Turner articulates it, was this: what form of the human would be most resistant to fascist modes of address? This question was pursued across a range of fields, from military-funded computer research to exhibition design. The specter of fascism is the crucible for Turner. More to the point, and in line with Liu's account and Taylor's ambitions, the specter is of the lone, vulnerable, racially unmarked member of a mass, made susceptible to fascism's comforts by the blanketing address of mass media. Exhibition design, and museums broadly, addressed this vulnerable member of the mass and in doing so felt that they could inoculate them. What Turner describes as an exhibition ethos, Engelbart, at around the same time, implemented as the new approachable face of the computer. Both were engines of subjectivization, and so both were addressed to the human, to a stripped-down American subject, now divested of their postwar subjectivities, and set free within a renewed American ideal of liberal democracy where the discursive claims of content delivered as information might serve to inoculate its users from strong forms of authoritarian address. A question driving all this research was: What environments could be constructed to form this new human, who would be shaped into a subject inside a political context looking to distance itself from the genocidal whiteness of fascism in Germany? Here, whiteness was to be not an identity or national formation but a kind of managerial ethos or attitude (which in part explains both how and why the subsequent communist threat in the United States would so often be racialized as black[45]). "The democratic surround" is Turner's name for what would become the answer to this question, and he looks to exhibitions like the *Family of Man* to describe the formal features of the surround. The democratic surround amplifies and augments the project started by Lillian Gilbreth and taken up later by Douglas Engelbart.

The Metropolitan Museum of Art's infamous *Harlem on My Mind* was an exhibition built explicitly in this mold, as Susan Cahan insinuates when she links the curator, Allon Schoener, to Charles and Ray Eames and their midcentury multimedia displays.[46] The lineage Turner draws is longer: from El Lissitzky through László Moholy-Nagy and the Bauhaus to Herbert Bayer at the Museum of Modern Art in New York City. The quiet race work of the idealism that drove postwar ideas about exhibition design becomes unavoidable in 1968 with *Harlem on My Mind*. In prior exhibitions, the universalizing logics—of the subject inoculated against all forms of monolithic address by being encouraged to think for themselves—could issue inside an echo chamber of whiteness and count on the fact of the museum's propriety and mostly white audience for this to never cause much friction. But with *Harlem on my Mind*, the subject matter of the exhibition would not submit to this renewed liberal address. Susan Cahan details the ensuing controversy in forensic detail.[47] In her account, the Met management comes off looking tin-eared and inept, unwilling to respond to advice, which was abundantly available, bringing on themselves the disaster that the exhibition would become. But the reason for Schoener's arrogance wasn't just that this attitude toward criticism is a timeless prerogative of whiteness, although it was that too. The reason Schoener could feel self-righteous, even when faced with multiple warnings by the Harlem community, was that the liberal ethos of the exhibition tradition in which he was working felt itself to be regenerating personhood as precisely postracial, beyond any and all homogenizing categories. Black criticism, in the eyes of that ambition, would have been seen as a backslide into a crude racialism. The specific exhibition design choices described by

Turner, in fact, operationalized that attitude, making it available to anyone who would accept it or who was willing to be trained by it.

As Turner describes, the exhibition design relied on clusters of photographs, none attributed to any author, combined with sound, the whole paradoxically both overwhelming the viewer and aiming to set them free inside the bounds of "the whole personality" that it was the exhibition's ambition to reanimate. This required producing an environment or surround that was not determined in its meanings or outcomes so much as managed in its design. In Herbert Bayer's famous exhibitions as well as Schoener's, rooms were filled with photographs, mostly black and white, addressing viewers in a kind of scatter logic. The photos did not conform to the architectural environment, as when images are hung neatly on walls; they formed environments. One navigated photographs as much as one navigated rooms. Movement through more photographs than any one person could process or assimilate, now understood as so much information, was designed to be tolerably overwhelming. As such, it was a distant reflection of a prior stage in the amassing and selection of the images. That stage, for the *Family of Man* exhibition, involved Edward Steichen and Wayne Miller reviewing, as Turner documents, two million images. These they winnowed down to ten thousand. And from there to the final 503. A heroic effort to be sure, and one that was quite explicitly meant to be replicated, in miniature, by visitors to the exhibition. In this, the managerial ethos of curatorial work could itself be understood less as guiding others than as modeling a behavior. This process of information sorting and retrieval was a key element of all the exhibitions designed in this democratic mold. With *Harlem on My Mind*, it was, in a sense, blackness itself that was transcoded from biography, history, and experience into information. The individual encouraged to move through information—to inhabit an informational environment, to make their own categories of relevance and noise—was, in this logic, thought to be crucially different from the individual who was subject to the authoritarian address of mass media or fascism or, for that matter, the Black Power movement and its various threatening forms of collective life. However managed the final selection of photographs, and it was of course highly managed, the exhibited scatter of images, their profusion and assembly, was to be a kind of inoculation against losing one's individuality to such strong forms of address.

But it was more than that too. Here's Turner: "[*The Family of Man*] grew as much if not more from the promotion of diversity as the basis of national unity in the early 1940s and from the museum's wartime efforts to train its visitors in the ways of the democratic personality."[48] Turner continues: "With images literally all around them, visitors to *The Family of Man* had to make choices about where to look and how to integrate what they saw into their own worldviews. This process, in turn, exercised the psychological muscles on which democracy and perhaps even the future of the world depended."[49] Inside this democratic purview, importantly, the management of information was understood as the management of diversity, of difference itself. Information processing was the core activity of this Cold War strategy for rebuilding the individualized American subject. The citizen who could process information was the citizen who could exercise a kind of energy, both creative and social, where self-enhancement becomes synonymous with democratization, and eventually, with incorporating difference in order to facilitate an attitude that race no long mattered.

This same logic is hard at work in Vannevar Bush's famous 1945 essay "As We May Think"—an essay that Engelbert named as the direct precursor to his own work on the graphical interface.[50] The key conceptual leap of that essay was something Bush referred to as "associative indexing." This was a nascently graphical dynamic that Bush spoke of less as a technological feature or affordance and more as the unique feature of human creative labor that needed to be freed from the kinds of "repetitive" work that characterized the prewar period. Here we find an echo of Lillian Gilbreth's own work in this area, which she understood as management and modeled on the white housewife.[51] Bush's interest in his hypothetical memex was to create a machine that worked with, and even facilitated, the human capacity for associative indexing. The memex arranged photographs in a kind of semivirtual spatiality that fostered what was to be understood as the user's *own* associative indexing. The memex, in other words, created an information surround in which the labor of information management could become a form of self-elaboration. Bush's enthusiasm for this project, like Engelbart's after him, and Gilbreth's before him, gathered around the reconstruction of the human on a new basis. As Bush ruminates, "Presumably man's spirit should be elevated if he can better review his shady past and analyze more completely and objectively his present problems."[52]

If the rooms of such information displays looked like a proto-windowed interface, we can begin to see why this is not an accident of visual likeness. *Harlem on My Mind* was informed by the same logics and involved in the same long project of renovating the human as those pursued by Gilbreth and Bush, as well as Engelbart and the computer's later interface designers. Schoener's and Bayer's photographs constituted an information space. Movement through that space was understood as lightly managed but nonetheless personal research, the pursuit of individualized interests and insights. Creative labor was here reconceived not as the creative expression of exhibition design, which, as Turner says, could easily turn coercive, but as action within a field of "aesthetic indeterminacy." What Turner describes as the overriding intellectual project of Steichen's exhibition and what Cahan's book allows us to extend to *Harlem on My Mind*, might as well be a description of Engelbart's work on early computing interfaces. And it certainly describes Apple's later approach to both the implementation and the marketing of their GUI. This, one last time, is Turner: "In other words, while Steichen's show would have a message in the general sense, it would not seek to *impose* its views on the audience. Rather, it would attempt to build a framework of principles, draw visitors into that framework, and there allow them to see themselves as free individuals among a world of others."[53]

We learn something about whiteness in the swirl of these events: something about how whiteness would seek to renovate itself after mid-century, at least in its own bastions of culture like the Met. One lesson is spatial: the geometry of whiteness would now not be sequestration but the surround—a spatiality that Julie Mehretu's work will later take up in its infrastructural expanses (see chapter 5). In fact, as Cahan documents, so many of the ambitions of *Harlem on My Mind* were bound up with a desire to be seen as integrating themselves, and Harlem most prominently, into the wider surround of New York City. Even if Cahan reveals these overreaches of liberalism to be a bad-faith ploy to annex more land, they nevertheless reveal that the public strategy of that bad-faith effort was to be a pretense of integration, of breaking down geographic and urban barriers between the races. Meanwhile, inside the exhibition: blackness documented, blackness refracted, blackness displayed, blackness sequestered by the new apparatus of its democratic surround. A tactic is being added here to a repertoire that would still, of course, whenever needed, have recourse to sequestration, to barricade and raw violence. We find those old brutal tactics, in fact, used to quell protest just outside the doors of the Met, at the very moment this new tactic was being exhibited inside. But inside those barricades, far from those hardwood batons, a softer face emerges: a documentary impulse, an impulse to include, a willingness to integrate, to surround, and to thereby set free inside the sharply delineated boundaries of the individuated self. The black faces postered on the facade of the museum were accompanied by an eagerness to relegate whiteness to what Turner, in an echo of Lillian Gilbreth's work, calls a "managerial" background. It's a nearly perfect figure for the relationship of whiteness to the new technocultures of its own creation: no longer the face of the proceedings, now they can seem to merely (and magnanimously) share the limelight—but only because whiteness retains a managerial relation to the technologies of that display and circulation. Schoener and the Met did what they could to advance this tactic with the resources at their disposal, inside the limits of the art world's idealism. The computer industry, with the invention of the personal computer, would massively expand and advance the tactic.

Engelbart and the Augmented Human

It is now possible to see how Engelbart's research, along with all the research strands that made the personalized, graphical computer interface possible, played an integral role in this longer history of the particular individual person-form that Gregg and Turner help establish. Engelbart's graphical interface was to be a training and testing ground for just such an individual, while also being quite literally where they were to be integrated with a computational environment designed as an information surround. Gregg's work also helps us track the ways that a longer history of whiteness pursued a subterranean channel into the so-called meritocratic, race-blind cultures of the twentieth century's newest privileged form of technologized labor: namely, personal computing. Here, exclusion and marginalization are still weapons, but like a mutation of Saidiya Hartman's "burdened individuality," this exclusion is encouraged not only to be almost entirely oblivious to its racial dimensions, but also to think that it sits in the service of getting beyond race. The engine here was the universalizing rhetoric of self-improvement performed in an open field (no obstacles in a graphical field save the self itself), galvanized by the ideal of a meritocracy in which such performances of self could be recognized for their inherent quality, without interference from history, from context, from the messiness of the social. All such interferences the graphical field very consciously bracketed in favor of a new infrastructure for life, a terrain that integrated work and play as communication. The graphical

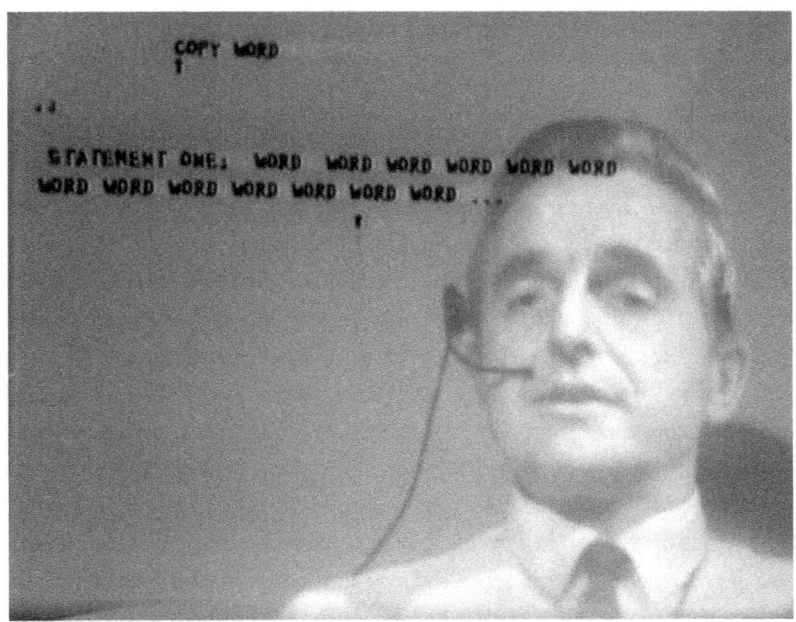

I.1 Still image from Douglas Engelbart's demonstration of the oN-Line System (NLS) at the 1968 Fall Joint Computer Conference, San Francisco, December 9–11, 1968. Courtesy of the Department of Special Collections, Stanford University Libraries, and Christina Engelbart.

interface was an uncommonly dense infrastructure for the construction and eventual work of this individual: at once effective metaphor, training site, and theater of performance.

In the 1968 demonstration that would announce the graphical interface to technologists, and thereby to the world, and that has come to stand in too much for the announcement of the graphical project in its entirety, Douglas Engelbart and his team employed a trick right out of the long history of what Tom Gunning calls the "cinema of attraction."[54] As a way to display the kind of space this computer interface promised, the team superimposed a live video of Engelbart's face over a live feed of the computer screen itself. The presenter thereby appears to be presenting from inside the mostly blank interface that he is there to present and whose content he himself becomes. This is, in fact, precisely the affordance that became most important to the subsequent history of the graphical field, even if it wasn't exactly on the agenda that afternoon. Engelbart inhabits the graphical field. That is, above all else, what makes that field graphical.

It is a visual trick, in some ways merely a metaphor. But it more than suggests the larger ambitions of the project, where the graphical field was to become a kind of home or habitat.

In that demonstration, to an audience of approximately one thousand computer professionals assembled for the Fall Joint Computer Conference at the Convention Center in San Francisco, Engelbart and his team demonstrated what they called the "oN-Line System" (NLS). They did so through a closed-circuit televisual feed. The feed cut between close-up facial shots of Engelbart himself working the interface and feeds from the computer terminal thirty miles away in Menlo Park. Engelbart himself was on site in the convention center, as presenter. But his ghostly image, beamed through a high-powered TV projector onto a 22 × 18 ft. screen, was the presenter most present. The closed-circuit broadcast was simultaneously recorded on film and is now archived in full as part of the Engelbart Collection in the Special Collections archive of Stanford University. Six people, connected by headsets, some in San Francisco and others back in Menlo Park, orchestrated the event behind the scenes, controlling the video mix and sound. The total effect was of an expansive networked system at work, but all seemingly controlled by the person sitting at the terminal, facing the screen and inhabiting the screen, doing nothing more technical than manipulating that screen's graphics. This figure, the user, was not a node in that network because part of what Engelbart was demonstrating was how the user of the graphical interface could be heedless of the network of support that made his presentation and his presence there possible—free to make creative, associative leaps. Like Lillian Gilbreth's homemaker, they command the network while living inside of it. Engelbart is framed from the chest up, wearing a white shirt and dark tie. His banter is easy, relaxed. He's not particularly in a hurry to sell anything. He refers to his wife and to family dinners. He uses the capacities of the graphical screen to categorize a grocery list. In this, the graphical screen subsumes not just the face of its user but home life as well. Its uses were to be extensive—as extensive as life itself.

The graphic user interface so demonstrated, the GUI or "gooey," is a thing and not a thing. An infrastructure and a superstructure. A space through which other things are screened, transmitted, executed, done. A platform. If we know it—and I arrogate the "we" here to index the GUI's ubiquity—it's because the graphical interface is a thing that enrolls people. It was designed precisely for this. As a real estate proposition, or simply understood as an image, it is mostly empty space—space in which to move. In his demonstration, Engelbart organizes and reorganizes lists, he draws lines between items in those lists, and he toggles between otherwise discrete tasks. In this, he establishes connections between those tasks. But always the blank screen is the default, the space of reset—just the screen and the image of the user superimposed onto and so into that space.

Today, that space is outfitted in metaphor and figuration: the desktop, files, trashcan, windows, mouse. It is a space navigated haptically—this being what opened the computer up initially to the human in a new way, almost literally inviting the hand of the user into the space of the computer via the proxemics of the mouse. This hand, and it is significant that it was the hand, was a dense site for the accumulation of skill and expressive potential. Engelbart had played with the knees as a source of input—like Taylor and Gilbreth, he was interested in the most efficient forms of input and action—but the mouse that he invented makes use of the hand's historical connection to expressivity, to interiority directed outward through gesture. Chapter 3 addresses the significance of the hand in this story through Jack Whitten's digital experiments in paint, which were also manual experiments in making the self appear without individuality or the vaunted expressivity of the hand.[55] For the human using a mouse, metonymized by the hand, the graphical was not a calculator. Nor was it something that foregrounded the experience of being rendered a service. It was a creative workspace, a work surface in which the human could be augmented by access to information and the tools to manipulate information. On this basis, and in line with the experiments in exhibition design that Turner calls the "democratic surround," the inhabitant of the graphical would be freed from the kinds of labor that characterized the prewar world. But that human would also be inoculated from the kinds of mass address so feared by a liberal modality of whiteness that had just witnessed the latest explosion of its own genocidal fantasies.[56] In the longer history, pre-Apple, pre-Xerox, when the graphical screen was merely part of an intense ideological debate in the computer world over what the computer could be, who it would serve and how it would serve them, the idea behind the graphical screen was that it made the computer more human. Engelbart understood it this way, although with the acknowledgment this his project was about transforming the human as well. In other words, this anthropomorphism was just Engelbart's way of beginning the longer process of occupying the human to transform it from the inside.[57]

As perhaps this begins to hint, the graphical interface of the computer screen is not exactly a space, just as the work of the artists I discuss in later chapters is less interested in inventing spaces than in reconceiving the coordinates through which the human can be understood. But the graphical does draw on spatial conventions when convenient, such as its use of Euclidean geometries and the proprioception needed to navigate those geometries with a mouse. Before the graphical field, one didn't inhabit a computer, didn't move within in. One issued "commands." The command-line interface flattered the sovereignty of the human issuing the commands, couldn't but make humans feel as though they controlled computers, even inside a frustrating debugging process that, precisely in taunting the sovereignty of the user, became an arena in which to exercise an esoteric, increasingly occult mastery.[58] With the graphical screen, as was Engelbart's and other's intent, one no longer had to know how to speak a computer's language. And so these sites for the exercise of mastery were lost and had to be replaced by new opportunities for self-possession and self-elaboration. In the graphical field, one could gesture, move, click, rearrange objects, toggle between screens and windows that were all conceived as tasks in a workflow—a flow that felt like one's own (one's own grocery list), not something prescribed by technical protocols. These gestural proxemics were modeled on familiar paradigms of movement: dragging, reaching, pulling, connecting, expanding, collapsing.

Engelbart, an engineer who was one of the key proselytizers of the graphical screen as a more human interface for the computer, was explicit about his ambition to have the graphical interface train his users. Apple, in their later popularization of the graphic interface, would eschew this idea in favor of "user friendliness"—a promise that no training would be required to achieve mastery. But even here, of course, a retraining was occurring, if only a retraining in how to imagine oneself folded into the fields of a computational interface that was so naturalized that it required no training.

Though first imagined in a variety of forms in the sixties and seventies at computer graphics labs around the United States, the graphical form of the computer screen—manifest in the raster of the cathode-ray tube (CRT) monitor, and now the encompassing environment for basically all facets of life accommodated and actively solicited by the computer—took shape in the years immediately following World War II. Nearly imagined by Vannevar Bush in 1948, importantly conceptualized by J. C. R. Licklider throughout his work in the military-funded development of computing after World War II, nascently realized by Douglas Engelbart and his team through the early and middle sixties, first demonstrated by Engelbart in 1968, taken up and then abandoned by Xerox PARC in the early seventies, streamlined and mass-marketed by Apple Computers in the eighties, ubiquitous and unavoidable by the early years of the twenty-first century—with Microsoft Windows and Apple dominating the market for personal computers—the graphic user interface has so realized its universalizing ambitions that its precise technical name, GUI, can only underdescribe its impacts, while setting the misleading expectation that the discussion to come will henceforth reside in the realm of appropriate specialists: computer historians and design historians and critics, the people to date who have cared to write about the GUI.

Today, the GUI ships with every personal computer and is arguably native to every smartphone. At its simplest (and it has been designed to appear simple so its user can appear autonomous and fully manifest in the space left open by the supportive unobtrusiveness of graphical space), the GUI consists in an overall desktop metaphor, with icons representing units of work (software or apps), all organized within a space one can navigate through the prosthesis of mouse and cursor, inside a landscape of icons, pull-down menus, and windows.[59]

That is, the graphical interface did not and still does not offer much in the way of structure. But it was navigable haptically and visually. A field then. Always contained to a predefined rectilinear area, even if that area was forever expanding, it thereby, and from that precise containment, aspired to encompass more or less everything (chapter 5, on Julie Mehretu's work, elaborates on this idea of containment and expansion). It did so while achieving massive dissemination into almost every office, school, and home, transgressing various containers of life: public and private, professional and personal, institutional and informal, personal and computational. The spatial idiom is convenient (sometimes unavoidable) because this space, graphical space, hosted life—that is its most essential definition. Life needs spaces of existence, even if those spaces are just the vocabularies and technologies that exist for the impoverishment, appropriation, and destruction of certain lives. To speak of the graphical then is to speak of an almost blank field, of the work that nothingness can do when its inhabitants are induced to read it as openness, a space for their own self-elaboration. Whiteness, in such a field, could understand itself not as a racial formation but as an opening, a praxis, an open field that was in theory available to anyone—precisely postracial. That was the modality of its whiteness. More than just unmarked then, whiteness in its new graphical home implied openness, availability, possibility.[60]

This research was gathering from the fifties to the eighties, on both coasts of the United States, at Stanford with Douglas Engelbart, at MIT with J. C. R. Licklider, as well as in the middle of the country at the University of Utah with Ivan Sutherland and Alan Kay (who would go on to work at Xerox PARC). It amounted to a revolution in a long history of thought about what the computer could be and do, with the revolutionaries advocating for a computer that, in feeling manageable and knowable, in feeling natural and even bodily, in feeling human, would encompass and transform the human, becoming a place for the human's augmentation. As such, it would propagate itself far beyond any redlining of race. In the postwar decades that saw the development of the graphical interface, questions of nationalism, knowledge, and personhood were at the center of a massive multidisciplinary effort, spanning public and private realms, to imagine, bring into being, and then parade globally a form of distinctively American subjectivity that would be resistant to authoritarianism of the sort that so concerned governments, corporations, and critical theorists alike.[61] There is a line that can be drawn within this scattered field, not a straight one for sure, between Licklider's dreams of "man-machine symbiosis," Douglas Engelbart's research at the Stanford Research Institute on the "augmented human," and Apple Computers' eventual codification, mass marketing, and attempted patenting of the graphic user interface, at which point graphical space becomes both entirely ubiquitous and entirely backgrounded, merely a field for other activities. No one person's research was isolated or singular, but Engelbart and Licklider play a central role here because they, of all the others working on computer displays across the country, perhaps most clearly articulated the stakes of this research, which Engelbart called, tellingly, the Augmented Human Intellect project. Their vision was also, it is widely acknowledged among the actors in this progress narrative, massively influential on the way that computers and computation would develop in labs and universities and eventually private corporations all over America.[62]

Engelbart believed that digital computers would eventually circulate scientific information through a global network that would repair the postwar world by converting war machines into new and powerful human-machine hybrids designed to produce not death but knowledge.[63] His was an idealist project in the extreme. The labor performed by these new human-computer dyads, joined in by the graphical interface, Engelbart called "knowledge work."[64] As first demonstrated to a scientific public in 1968, the graphic interface was an open expanse whose finite dimensions could be infinitely expanded with windows, each containing discrete but connectable types of work. In his words, Engelbart aimed to grant the user "considerable freedom as to the positions and circumstances under which he can operate."[65] "We want to develop new communication means that allow a human to control or make use of machines (especially information-handling machines) with minimal interference in other physical activities associated with his primary tasks."[66] A particular organization of the computer screen, an open field accessed proxemically, would become the means to this end. "Considerable freedom" was to be a primary objective of that screen form. Although for Engelbart, freedom was as much a mode of work and productivity as it was something felt by the user *as* freedom. With Apple, the story becomes more about feeling, about how it feels to use the graphical screen.[67]

The graphical screen—for Engelbart, a minor implementation of his larger and more ambitious research efforts—was to be the answer to this question of how to retrain the human worker for the coming age of computers. "The system we want to improve can thus be visualized as a trained human being together with his artifacts, language, and methodology."[68] That ensemble is what Engelbart called the "system." Labor, newly organized in the graphical field of the computer screen that Engelbart prototyped and there reimagined as knowledge work, was to be the crucible of this new subject's formation, its proving ground. The graphical screen itself made this labor and this form of subjectivity possible.

Although Engelbart had bigger dreams, his work on the graphical screen formed the acknowledged basis of Xerox PARC's creation of the graphic user interface. And Xerox PARC's work made Apple Computers' own work possible, even if the exact details of inheritance and debt might never be known definitively. But however unclear the details of propriety and ownership, these histories are well documented. For my purposes, the most significant contribution that Xerox and later Apple would make to this history was to inflect Engelbart's somewhat ambivalent conceptualization of the individual—free, yes, but also highly malleable, trainable—toward the kind of idealized creative type that Apple dreamed into being with slogans like "Think Different," and "The Power to Be Your Best." At the most obvious level, Engelbart and later Apple Computers proffer freedom from the command-line interface, from having to interact with a computer on a computer's own terms. Beyond this, and especially in Apple's later technical and marketing schemes, freedom would come to mean creative freedom generated by a graphical field that wasn't just an interface to a computer, but was, in effect, the computer tout court. And the computer, in a closely related sense, was nothing more and nothing less than the user itself. The graphical operationalized this syllogism: computer/human. The graphical field aimed to dissolve any copulas remaining to separate human from computer, dissolve them in the acid bath of a progressivist humanism that would reuniversalize humans—so recently revealed in their violently racialized differences in World War II—as something better, something augmented, something more suited to the coming era where work would become synonymous with information exchange. An era, as well, in which whiteness needed new dematerializing enclaves, away from the bright lights of racial warfare (at home and abroad) and a coordinated set of decolonizing global movements (evident in theaters of war as well as in an anxious, violent relationship with movements closer to home such as the Black Panthers, Black Power, and civil rights).

Subsuming the computer, and in this sense erasing it, the contemporary graphical screen allows a user a far more "considerable freedom," although never more than an extension and amplification of the kinds of freedoms dreamed into being by Engelbart and his team: freedom to manipulate everything, to place oneself anywhere in the field of the screen, to physically move objects rather than issue commands in language not one's own, to be afforded random access to whatever one might dream up as a form of self-elaboration through information space. This was to be a "natural" language, intuitive, user-friendly, creative.[69]

The Human in Bits

In Dawn L. Martin's account of black poetics, creativity starts not from freedom but from the space of impossibility that is black selfhood. Martin's thinking here illuminates, by way of contrast, how utterly reliant the graphical field was on a model where creativity is predicated on and made possible by a human conceived of, from the start, as limitless. Engelbart, Licklider, and others could aim to accommodate and amplify this human as though it were a blank slate, without history, without identity, immanently trainable and amenable to what the graphical space was making of the computer (this interplay between possible and impossible selfhood, the self in and outside of history, elaborated in its relationship to creativity, is where chapter 2, on Alma Thomas, begins).[70]

The graphical field didn't emerge on its own to single-handedly launch an entire industry of personal computers and computing—though it did make the computer personal even as it dissolved itself into a million de-sign improvements and new haptic interfaces (from mouse to track pad to touch screen). The ubiquity of the graphical today saps perspicuity. What *is* the object of such a study? It can't be the graphic user interface as such, neither as Engelbart at Stanford imagined it nor as Apple mar-keted and refined it.

But the object also can't be whatever it is that is screened on or in the graphical field—as implied by studies like David Joselit's on image popu-lations or Pasi Väliaho's on biopolitical screens.[71] Design and computer discourses rarely theorize the human they are designing for; or rather, they do, but tendentiously.[72] Their universalism, of course, hides this tenden-tiousness, which is precisely what made the graphical field so amenable to a postracial discourse.

The object, then, will have to be the graphical field as such, but where, inside the syllogism human/computer, "as such" refers to nothing other than the spidering out of the graphical field through rhythms of habitua-tion, training, individuation, and informatization—where the graphical field refers precisely, in other words, to the human reborn along with and within that field. In this way, the GUI's minor status in the larger scope of computing history might turn out to be a way to combat what many more materialist histories of computing disdain as the fetishization of "the vi-brant colors and sleek displays of the interface."[73]

Which is to say, computer historians might see my focus as too nar-rowly trained on a particular form of the computer screen—the GUI. And while I don't dispute that characterization, it belies the fact that the history of that particular set of technologies is itself far more expansive than has been acknowledged, and will take us sometimes far away from a consideration of any aspect of the screen in itself, given that the express goal of that space was to inaugurate a renewed form of the human. My in-tention is less to illuminate these histories each in themselves (and so to work across something like analogy or even comparison) than to illumi-nate the space where they blur, way out at their edges, into indistinction, a space that belongs to no particular history, hinting at the limits of seeing any history as organized and isolated inside a discipline, medium, racial categorization, or technology.

In Fred Turner's periodizing terms, the particular modality of freedom touted by Engelbart and later Apple partook of the larger postwar interest in a form of democratic personhood that was free to make choices within a gently constrained field of options, to feel as though the choices are one's own so that those very choices come to define one's individuality, even or especially in interactions with new technologies. In this version of modernity, crowd, mass, and audience are thereby defused as threats to individual autonomy because they come, in the period of graphicalization, to exist most strongly within the ambit of this individuality, in service to it, setting it off, marking its distinction. In the period influenced by Gilbreth and Schoener and Engelbart, masses no longer subsume the individual, they highlight everything that stands out about the individual. This is what is so suggestive about Wendy Hui Kyong Chun's argument that this history of computing operates inside a toggle between freedom and control. The individual, so reconceived, operated as a form of control on collective forms of life.[74]

But if collectivity was a choice for the white population (something that could be considered optional, and so defended against by technologies like the graphical interface), for a black population it was always also a yoke, a lifelong sentence, while also being, precisely as such, the source of its reinventions of life. Claudia Rankine says, "We suffer from the condition of being addressable," meaning that every address to black life (including this one) enforces a mode of collective life that is imposed from without and so becomes part of both the enabling and disabling conditions of black collective life as lived impossibly from within.[75]

Related problems being worked out in other fields of activity, ones that were indelibly marked by racialization, asked their questions about the graphical in other idioms and with other urgencies, so much so that they can seem to be entirely distinct fields—what, after all, does the computer screen have to do with abstract art by black artists? But this is just an effect of the way that whiteness sequesters all conversations that are burdened by the necessity of taking race, and specifically blackness, into account. The graphical field was not an artwork to be sure, nor was it primarily visual, and certainly did not feel it had anything to learn from experiments in the field of art practice. But the graphical interface was a field that became the stage for the performance of new forms of the self as that self became entangled with information and computing. Howardena Pindell, Alma Thomas, Jack Whitten, Charles Gaines, and Julie Mehretu were all, in their ways, concerned with this very problem—the problem of the human in bits.

Human/computer, or, personhood/technology: this was the interface that early experiments in computing and, as we'll see, certain practices of black abstraction were all working at so manically. Sometimes these two histories, of personal computing and black abstraction, evince conscious awareness of one another, although mostly they did not. More often, that awareness is partial or part-conscious or oblique. But the commerce between these histories is real nevertheless. Both sides experimented with forms of the human and human labor that were non-representational and—in that strict sense rather than in relation to figuration—abstract. One can see this commerce, for instance, in the context of civil rights debates that revolved around ideals of freedom. Often these ideals were focalized around the person-form of the individual as a potential site of freedom, of dignity, of respect—be that in the form of the exemplary individual, the talented tenth, or those who, precisely in failing at the politics of respectability, have been punished for failing to uphold those values. These debates become even more resonant when we notice that, during these same decades, the various technologies of the digital computer were beginning to actively transform the sites and valences of personal freedom, of individuality as a mode of subjectivization.

To follow the decades of this long-form development, this book focuses on art practices that span the sixties to the present. Each artist has spent their career insistently, iteratively, repetitively working out the possibilities and constraints of what we can, for now, call gridded space—although we can already glimpse how this conventional artistic idiom will give way to a language of bit and field, raster and screen, all the implements of the graphical. While the literature on the modernist grid is vast and influential, none of it reckons with blackness or black personhood, despite black artists' frequent use of the grid. And none of it deals with the graphical computer screen. Both of these forces have fundamentally transformed the history of the grid. This project asks why each of these artists turned to gridded or, as I'll want to say, graphical space as a way to transform the labor of art and to thereby experiment with possibilities for black life.

Together, their work offers persistent, incisive, restlessly exploratory accounts of this history of the graphical—a history that is, precisely in its ordinariness, now more or less coextensive with life. Put the other way, my thought is that the work of Thomas, Whitten, Gaines, and Mehretu operates in adjacency to, if not inside, the larger field of this history of the graphical and graphical personhood—that something important about their aesthetic experiments finds purchase in and offers a kind of explanatory framework to this larger history. The whiteness of the long graphical project shows up, fluoresces, in and through their projects not because all the artists are black and so naturally or essentially oppose that logic, but because the particular blackness of their practice reveals the racializing ambitions of the graphical project.

Which is to say, this is not a book about black resistance, opposition, or subversion. The aesthetic experiments this book describes are attuned to other modes of aesthetic and social labor.[76] More than just "quiet" in Kevin Everod Quashie's sense or "reparative" in Eve Kosofsky Sedgwick's, the artistic practices and procedures I study in what follows simply don't inherit, and so refuse to propagate, the presumption that something in the human is fundamentally at odds with the computer. Their history, as they knew—and as Katherine McKittrick and Louis Onuorah Chude-Sokei (and W. E. B. Du Bois; see chapter 3) give us ways to understand—cautioned them against simply choosing the "right" side of the human/technology or human/mathematics divide. Thomas, Whitten, Gaines, and Mehretu are, in their works and working procedures, wary of the computational, the mathematical. But their practices and the restlessness of those practices are better explained when we see that their wariness didn't gather around a single pole of this antinomy—human-number; person-machine—but around that antinomy as a whole. And so they all experimented with various combinations of human and computer, working with the graphical as a scene whose volatility might point to ways out of that defining American antimony altogether. Or not. They wanted to find out. The point, for them and for this book, isn't that they found answers—although they did, provisionally—but that their experiments, in their capaciousness, their willingness to play with all the variables mobilized in the graphical embrace of human and computer, show this history in a far more expansive and lively light.

The problem their art inhabited wasn't, in other words, the vortex of exclusion/inclusion. It didn't lie within the possibilities offered by representational politics. Theirs were practices keyed to the wider ambit of dysselection, that longer and larger problem. The graphical, whose icon and theater of operation was the personal computer, was a site where all the artists whose work I discuss, in their different ways, saw that problem playing out in the latter half of the twentieth century. The procedures they invented to experiment in that space were sometimes quiet, oblique, orthogonal, ambivalent, and all the more elusive when assessed in terms of visual likeness (to the computer, the computer screen, or to the GUI). Unfortunately, but necessarily, there will be very little visual likeness in what follows—of the sort that might say, for example, that mark looks like a pixel, that painting is organized like a computer screen. Again, the visual, insofar as it is a logic of representation (and that, of course, is not all that it is), gets subsumed as so much content *for* the nonrepresentational. Thomas, Whitten, Gaines, and Mehretu were always restless with how resistance and subversion tied their projects to logics they might want to reject more entirely.[77] It was from this footing, then, that their work addressed questions of personhood as it transitions into and comes to inhabit the computational circuits of the graphical screen.

But who needs to hear that the contemporary world of information, data management, and the associated modes of labor and subjectivity—all of which would come to find a home in the graphical screen—were made for and by whiteness? This seems obvious enough . . . maybe. But such is the status of claims about whiteness in the United States, which, for white people, might sound like news when in fact their aim, here as elsewhere, is not to make the bearers of whiteness more self-aware but to make the sensorium of whiteness less habitable.[78] By and large, the graphic user interface of the personal computer, that graphical field, that space made to harbor life and labor, that place where human and bit mingle in an unmarked, open field, has made whiteness more habitable, if also more expansively and fugitively destructive. The four artists whose practices I try to learn from saw another set of possibilities in the graphical—if nothing else, the possibility for a confrontation with the human-computer interface that wasn't internally geared to provide sanctuary to whiteness. And so, together, they track the promises of the graphical, but also its elasticities. To follow their work, to see it for all of its dense enmeshment with the graphical, the raster, the computer, and with spaces where information and the human would come to re-form one another, is to follow the silverfish movements of an elusive hope. That hope flickered in a graphical environment that scrambled older technologies of self-possession, and in which it might have been possible, therefore, to reimagine the relationship between the human and their work, between the encryptions of personhood and the decryptions of racialization. For me, this story begins in Alma Thomas's stripe paintings, with a first stirring of interest in a kind of technological imaginary, moves through Whitten's and Gaines's wary uptake of digital systems—Whitten's ever restless, Gaines's steely and resolved—and ends in aporia with Mehretu's almost furious attempts to force the graphical to live up to its promise of including everyone and everything, even, impossibly, the studio assistant. From wary potential to conflagrational hypertrophy. Seen together, these chapters tell the story of the graphical as a space where black artists experimented with an abstractionist politics of personhood and collectivity while—and because—an incipient politics of white informational personhood was prototyped and eventually consolidated in the graphical field of the personal computer.

The art historian Leo Steinberg, in his famous 1972 essay "Other Criteria," started to feel out the terms of this proximity, the points of extension between technological research and art practices that were each interested in the implications of the graphical field for racialization and the engineering project of the human. So Steinberg's "Other Criteria" is the subject of the next chapter. It forms a bridge to subsequent chapters that describe various logics and implementations of the graphical as they took shape through artistic practices that took the human in bits to be their subject and their problem.

Operational Processes: Leo Steinberg

1

Art critic Leo Steinberg's 1972 essay "Other Criteria" is justly famous for what it most obviously is: an intervention into art criticism specific to a particular part of the New York art world at a particular time.[1] But not as much attention has been paid to what motivates that intervention. It's clear that Steinberg is attempting to test out some vocabulary for describing something that he thinks is happening in, and therefore to, the field of contemporary abstract painting. He refers to this phenomena, both its nebula of causes and its effects as painting, as "the flatbed picture plane." That particular vocabulary harks to the horizontality of printing, while many of his other experimental idioms come from information theory and cybernetics. "Data" is one way he finds to refer to the varieties of matter that get arranged and rearranged in the picture planes that concern him. It's hard to say, in the end, if his prior awareness of these technical discourses induced Steinberg to see contemporary painting in a particular way, or if the paintings he was seeing led him to seek out vocabularies in far-flung fields. What he was noticing, I believe, are the gathering strains of thought that I've been calling the *graphical*. For Steinberg, it mattered most that such graphical logics had appeared in the realm of the painted picture plane. But he knew, or intuited, that he needed to reach for vocabularies that exceeded modernism's reach, and that even broke the grip of modernism's descriptive power, in order to adequately address these newly configured picture planes.

In this, Steinberg helps us see a particularly important and vexing feature of the graphical field: the fact that, despite its penchant for images, for being read as an image, for being populated by images, and for being grasped through visual metaphor, the graphical is a nonrepresentational space or logic. And this swing to the nonrepresentational, in turn, significantly alters the ways we can think about the transforming relationship between personhood and racialization in a computational context. The positive formulation Steinberg gives to the nonrepresentational is "operational processes."

For fields outside art history, for whom a consideration of Leo Steinberg won't be self-justifying, there are a few reasons for this return to an essay from almost fifty years ago. Each reason addresses a particular discipline, and thus disciplinarity itself, at a slightly different angle. For art history, the persistent, and I believe reductive, belief that in "Other Criteria" Steinberg is really talking about Michael Fried and Clement Greenberg and thus participating in a parochial debate about the New York art world, perpetuating art history's baffling insistence that Fried and Greenberg's own thinking is more or less coincident with modernist art practice, if not with modernism itself. My account of "Other Criteria" sees the address to what Steinberg calls "the dominant formalist critics" as a minor part of the essay's work. This clears space to perceive in Steinberg's thinking the nascent apprehension of a set of economic, social, and cultural forces that were very much in formation during Steinberg's lifetime, forces that begin to significantly change the landscape for aesthetic and political intervention. Media studies has recognized this shift better than art history has, although it often tends to understand the role aesthetics plays as merely illustrative. Black studies, the third field in play here, has recognized these shifts persistently and expansively, although it is not often enough recognized for its broad and historical thinking on media technologies, or for its work at the intersection of media and aesthetics. My shorthand for this shift is to refer to a move from representational to nonrepresentational politics. Steinberg, for his part, refers to a shift from experience to operational processes. The vocabulary Steinberg derives speaks to the changing conditions for the formation and inhabitation of personhood, or, drawing from the work of Sylvia Wynter (but also Steinberg seen through Wynter), the conditions for attempting to understand the human as praxis (rather than as being or ontology).[2]

Steinberg's essay is famous among artists and art historians for its attempt to oxygenate a modernist painting tradition that Steinberg felt had stultified under the forceful but extremely partial account given to it by the people he calls "the dominant formalist critics."[3] In this sense, the essay's title names what the essay performs. But I am interested not in the otherness of Steinberg's criteria, nor in the opposition Steinberg offers to "dominant" art criticism, but in what makes that "other criteria" so necessary. And while my interests revolve around what gets opened up by the specific way Steinberg phrases those other criteria, these interests are not all that dependent on whether Steinberg himself would have articulated those openings in the language I intend to give them here. I don't think Steinberg's essay was prescient so much as perceptive, precise, and forthrightly speculative about what he was seeing or sensing—he was willing to wager and lose a great deal, setting himself significantly at odds with most cultural critics and almost all published art critics, in order to produce a vocabulary adequate to a set of forces that he felt were coming to bear on labor and personhood by way of painting. His particular point of entry to those questions was the picture plane, where labor and personhood can't but inform one another. This was a set of forces that Steinberg feared were going dangerously unnoticed by art critics who were myopically focused on the history of art seen as prophylactically cordoned off from other histories that were even then gathering strength—histories Steinberg references through his explicit interest in manufacturing processes, new technologies, and (only slightly more obliquely) cybernetics. Steinberg's essay was always the start of something and not its end. He knew this: "There is a proposition here. It is unclear," he says, near the conclusion of the essay.

This is the key passage for my purposes:

> The flatbed picture plane makes its symbolic allusion to hard surfaces such as tabletops, studio floors, charts, bulletin boards— any receptor surface on which objects are scattered, on which data is entered, on which information may be received, printed, impressed—whether coherently or in confusion. The pictures of the last fifteen to twenty years insist on a radically new orientation, in which the painted surface is no longer the analogue of a visual experience of nature but of operational processes.[4]

"Flatbed picture plane" is Steinberg's way of naming something that was happening to the canvas, and that was simultaneously playing out on the canvas, as though paintings had started to generate themselves. What Steinberg is talking about, he tells us (twice, to make no mistake), is not the physical orientation of the art object once it's hung for display (as he says, rugs can be hung on walls; for that matter, so can televisions and computer screens). He's talking instead about what he calls the "psychic address" of the work, its "special mode of imaginative confrontation."[5] If "visual experience" and "operational processes," or "nature" and "culture" as he later phrases the distinction, are both terms subsumed within the larger category of "psychic address," then what Steinberg seems to be getting at is not a distinction that turns on some spurious or idealistic opposition between the earth (nature) and its human inhabitants (culture), but rather a distinction that resides inside a notion of the human, or just in excess of it. The radical reorientation of the picture plane, from vertical to horizontal, expresses, or rather, simply is a shift from an unquestioned, universalized notion of the human to a notion of the human that would have to be left unspecified, for now—a placeholder (in life no less than in Steinberg's essay) because it vectors through culture, and thus through the volatile industrial and technological transformations Steinberg references so frequently in the essay. This is a notion of the human radically reorganized at the pace of industrial change: away from the human who walks upright, eyes forward, acquiring the world as so many possessions by way of eyesight and the ways of knowing that visual perception has supported. So the shift Steinberg is trying to get us to see is from a reified notion of the human as a kind of surveyor—a particularly colonial inflection, which Steinberg hardly needs to say would have to be presumptively male and presumptively white—to one where the human, its capacities, its histories, becomes a product of the new technologies with which Steinberg seems so centrally concerned. The ones he names are the printing press, the projection screen, the dashboard. But this process isn't as causal or deterministic as it seems, as an elaboration on his idea of operational processes will make clear.

The flatbed picture plane is a place where data is entered, and as such, it is a place issuing its own strange form of psychic address. In such an address, some confrontation necessarily occurs between a familiar concept of the human and the world now arrayed as data for . . . whom? It's not yet clear. As Steinberg asks earlier of the kind of human imagined by Kenneth Noland's "one-shot" paintings of the late sixties: "Is he a man in a hurry?

Is he at rest or in motion? Is he one who construes or one who reacts? Is he a man alone—or a crowd? Is he a human being at all—or a function, a specialized function or instrumentality, such as the one to which Rauschenberg's *Chairs* (1968) reduced the human agent."[6]

The questions Steinberg asks of the addressee of Noland's "one-shots" predict the kinds of machines, the kinds of industrial processes, the kinds of technological mediation that, coming in the immediate wake of the essay's publication, disturb every picture plane, every surface on which data is entered and in which people operate—operate as agents but also get generated as products. Every surface in which people become "a specialized function." These processes were very much in formation, and visibly so, during Steinberg's lifetime—for instance in cybernetics, information theory, or the development of the personal computer and the electronic networks that that form of the computer always presaged.[7]

But the phrase "operational processes" also invokes labor. This is why Steinberg later refers to the reconfigured picture plane as a "work surface" —and also why "operational processes" doesn't describe every painting ever made. Steinberg was after a particular form of labor, then nascent. Flatness in this description, so important to the "dominant formalist critics," and differently important to Steinberg's own account, is therefore no longer a pictorial category. It was an affordance of work: the receptive surface of the desktop.[8] Like any labor process, "operational processes" aren't just performed by humans; they also go to work precisely on the human as a unit of capacity, the capacity to work.[9] The human becomes one of the products of operational processes, and maybe, as things have gone, the most important product, meaning not just most historically significant but most economically valuable.[10]

With "flatbed picture plane," Steinberg of course had in mind an older work technology: the printing press, with its scatter of objects and implements. Steinberg, however, was not drawing on the common association of the printing press with mass reproduction, but on the kinds of work that could be performed on that surface—a kind of work that, in the ascendance of the tech industries and the personal computer, would undo the massifications of mass reproduction, without ever giving up on its ambitions to work at massive scale.[11] In this sense, the modern white-collar office desk might be seen as successor to the printing press, especially in the age of the personal computer and desktop publishing. It too receives and produces, its scatter of objects an index of a process that is always in motion, always ongoing—a rebus of work done, as well as of aspirations for work to come; a site of production but also a site of display (making more recent phenomena like hot desking especially telling, historically[12]). Steinberg's description of this shift centers on labor and the implements of labor. To get there, Steinberg correlates several histories: American industry, advanced technologies of the day, and painterly surfaces. This correlation of histories does not, however, track along the standard art-historical axis of an artist's biography and what it might have been possible for a particular artist to think given what they can be proven to have known. The artist who works in the medium or genre or, better, labor modality of "operational processes"—Robert Rauschenberg, Jean Dubuffet, and Andy Warhol are three Steinberg singles out—need not themselves be psychically oriented toward such a project.

In fact, the human possessed of psyche, self-conscious as a mode of self-possession, is precisely what "Other Criteria" calls into question so devastatingly. The potential absence of a psyche at the site of imagined address seems to be part of what haunts Steinberg's essay—if not a human with a psyche, a human addressor to human addressee, then what? What form could such an address take, delivered to or from the site of the human deracinated from the painterly expressivity of the hand or the imagining mind (for more on the hand, see chapter 3 on Jack Whitten)? While Rauschenberg is Steinberg's privileged case, Rauschenberg's biography conspicuously plays no role in the argument.[13] The self that is a back-formation of operational processes cannot be presumed to be a biographical self, a self whose own history accretes into something autonomous, unique, enduring, a possession of the self who becomes thereby self-possessed. That is not how operational processes accrete meaning or value at the site of the self; it is not how those selves inhabit (or are erased from) history. One doesn't *author* receptor surfaces where data is entered; one programs them and becomes subject to them insofar as what is being programmed is a potentiality more than it is an actual thing in itself—a capacity for action more than an action or its consequence.[14] This will turn out to be key to how Steinberg prepares us to talk about art, personhood, and labor in what I and others propose we think about as a broadly nonrepresentational milieu.[15]

So while the flatbed picture plane itself may issue what Steinberg calls a "psychic address," that address need not be directed at, or issue from, anything with a psyche, a hidden interiority that finds expression in and as representation. This is one reason why, despite some superficial similarities, the artist of "operational processes" is not the same thing as Harold Rosenberg's "action painter," described in an equally famous essay published a decade prior.[16] The common conception of the action painter (Jackson Pollock is the archetype, which probably tells us more about white masculinity than about action painting per se) is more or less mimetic of the painting seen as a site for action—both are active, masculine, vigorous, reproductive. They imbue each other with those qualities. To name those qualities themselves, but also to name this vigorous reciprocity, Steinberg associates Rosenberg's action painter with "he-man talk," and specifically with the special brand of workmanlike heroism attributed, at that time especially, to military captains and the soldiers they command. Steinberg quotes a captain in the Vietnam War as though it were something Rosenberg's action painter might say and expect to be admired for: "It was definitely a good night's work. I don't know how many gooks we got really but we got plenty." Here, Steinberg marks, and in dramatic fashion, what's at stake if we don't recognize the distinction between Steinberg's questioning of the human form and Rosenberg's racializing presumptions about it.[17]

No such mimesis operates across the barrier of the flatbed picture plane, artist to artistic product. Operational processes suspend the commutation of properties across that barrier—suspend them because they are always in the process of altering them, but also because they force us to suspend the assumption that humans make things as analogues to their own experience. That is part of what operational processes are, because it is part of what they do. So while action paintings are lingeringly representational (even indexicality, if that's the relationship between the action painter and the action painting, is a form of representation, just not one governed by visual likeness), operational processes are nonrepresentational.[18] Here we approach the heart of why Steinberg's essay has the potential to reorient us toward the products of culture once that culture's formative matrix is a broadly computational and specifically graphical milieu.

To approach this idea of the nonrepresentational and what it entails as a periodizing concept, not least for art historians, take what John Cheney-Lippold calls a "data subject," or Simone Browne, after Frantz Fanon, calls "digital epidermalization."[19] While not synonymous, both terms refer to the psychic address of the data-gathering industries, which include everything from the National Security Agency (NSA) to Facebook to border patrols to ancestry kits to robot vacuum cleaners. These industries are nothing other than (but also nothing less than) the entirely predictable commodification of the very world that Steinberg had started to glimpse:

the world arrayed as data.[20] Far from First World subjects situated on the happy side of the digital divide, "data subjects" range from the devastatingly poor to the apocalyptically rich. Biography in a nonrepresentational milieu matters not less but differently as a determinant of life (even if wealth still, of course, provides life with a fallout shelter).[21] As subjects whose lives are determined, in significant part, by numbers and calculations (for instance, in algorithms for data acquisition or search engine personalization), "data subjects"—or what Michelle Murphy, referring to the various processes that produce such subjects, more encompassingly calls populations—are deeply related to race and racialization. As McKittrick argues, "The seeming neutrality of mathematics—the governmental trust in the technologies that calculate the textures of skin, eyes, hair—is trusted as innocuously objective, thus providing an alibi for racism."[22] McKittrick's call to understand the history of data as deeply rooted in, if not in many ways synonymous with, a long history of slavery and its afterlives doesn't mean that all people are now equally racialized; it means that racializing logics are a historical precursor of the data industries.[23] As always in this longer history, whiteness is defined in part by its capacity to elude or exceed or find buffers from such mathematical logics while also claiming to manage them on behalf of others (or, as in some speculative fiction, to idealize those logics because, for white subjects, the stakes are so low[24]). As Murphy says, borrowing from Frank Wilderson by way of Jared Sexton, "Race is the grammar and ghost of population."[25] And populations are built when bodies are rendered as data. Katherine McKittrick, Simone Browne, Safiya Noble, Jonathan Beller, and Aria Dean have all made this point in different and forceful ways.[26]

If we casually assume that a representation is more or less a picture generated through whatever means, then we would probably have to acquiesce and say, yes, even a Tinder or LinkedIn profile is a representation. And yet nothing that falls into the vast and powerful resources of representational politics could ever change a thing about the conditions that have made such a form of address possible, except maybe how we feel about them (which is not nothing, but feelings in a nonrepresentational milieu are far less connected to the structures of those feelings than, say, older print ads were). Maybe what most earns a representation its status as such is the temporality of the process that produces the representation. "Re-" tells us that representations must exist in some relation, defined first and foremost temporally, with a source image that might exist in the material world, or in our mental impressions of it, or somewhere else. The point isn't the form; it's the "priorness." This image is then usually thought to be originary, or if not an origin per se, then at least generative.[27] This temporality also works in reverse, as in theories of the simulacrum, where the representation now precedes and constructs so-called reality.[28] In any case, the representation exists always tethered to a source by a relation of priorness. And while those sources might come into different sorts of valuations (original, copy . . .), and assume a wild variety of forms (pictorial, mental . . .), the tether is what defines a re-presentation. A representation repeats; it plays something again, forward or in reverse, introducing a difference, or not enough of one.

In other words, representations (and counterrepresentations) bring into being another world, a world that operates at some remove from the world of presentation or the real or materiality, separated by the length (short or long) of the tether. There have been many names for what exists on the other end of this tether, conceived as another world into which we might be fast collapsing: simulacrum, spectacle, image worlds, even sometimes postmodernism. And the political movements these terms have spawned have found it important to fight their battles precisely on the grounds of representation, which such movements have, with differing degrees of totalization, taken to be the grounds of postmodern life itself. Thus, the epochal importance of representational politics. The Guerrilla Girls, ACT UP, the Black Arts Movement: all have understood that some significant portion of life, life as it is lived, is lived in and through representations. And so that is where the politics that would confront such problems must live too.

Gregg Bordowitz gives us with the life-and-death stakes of such a politics in the first line of his essay "Picture a Coalition": "As a twenty-three-year-old faggot, I get no affirmation from my culture. I see issues that affect my life—the issues raised by AIDS—being considered in ways that will probably end my life."[29] What devastates about this sentence is the contraction at the heart of it: the collapse of a space between "being considered" and "end my life." Such consideration—reflective, genteel, rational, deliberative, and seen from without, as on television—exists in the world of representation. The AIDS crisis was only one of a long series of deadly events to demonstrate, always on the bodies of the structurally vulnerable, that the genteel act of representing a problem through careful consideration could be weaponized to take life.

But there's little more to be gained from trying to rigidly define a concept as energetic and restless as "representation." Nor am I trying to signal a definitive shift away from representation as a form of life or politics, as though some representational era had ceased. That obviously hasn't happened. What I'm after is more like what Steinberg was after: a reorientation, spurred by recent developments that I think seriously compromise the capacity for the resources of representational politics to continue to address the conditions of life today.

Jared Sexton and Steve Martinot show us one danger of ignoring this exhaustion of representational politics. Describing the utter gratuitousness, the utter banality of violence directed against blackness, the absolute exposure of black life to threat, Sexton and Martinot suggest at least two ways in which representation fails to take the measure of this violence, to provide any analytical purchase at all: "The gratuitousness of its repetition bestows upon white supremacy an inherent discontinuity. It stops and starts self-referentially, at whim. To theorize some political, economic, or psychological necessity for its repetition, its unending return to violence, its need to kill is to lose a grasp on that gratuitousness by thinking its performance is representable. And therein it hides."[30] Sexton and Martinot don't just mean that the violence is unrepresentable because it is ineffably terrible, although they mean that too. They point instead to a different problem: that to bring particular acts of violence enacted on black bodies into representation by way of video or photography or writing (and there has never been a shortage of such representations) is to rely on a logic of exemplarity that can't but suggest that the act of violence stands out in some way, if only against the faded promise of some forever-withheld justice (examples need a background of ordinariness against which to stand out as exemplary). Sexton's point is that the logic of exemplarity, a representational logic, utterly fails to account for the absolute pervasiveness and structural ubiquity of violence in and around black life. The absolute fungibility of black life in American culture can only be disguised and softened by strategies of representation.

Bordowitz and Sexton and Martinot show us, each in different ways, how representational politics transcode violence into a different medium (thought, pictures, words, discourse) in order to establish another world or register of existence, removing life to that register, often precisely so that life can be exterminated or allowed to die there.[31] With this, we begin to see how computers and computation culture are not the cause or cultural dominant of the spreading logic of operational processes so much as they are a recent, now-omnipresent automation of logics that have long coursed beneath and around the politics of representation.[32] Steinberg in no way apprehends this fact directly. But in his insistence on opening up the question of the human who is both addressor and addressee of operational processes, he produces an opening through which this longer history—one which, at the very least, displaces a certain primacy accorded to white humanity—can be glimpsed.

While representational politics continues to course and course violently through the present tense, still both a problem and that problem's grounds for redress, culture generated by computation, operational culture say, doesn't generate images only in this way. "The flatbed picture plane lends itself to any content that does not refer to a prior optical event."[33] As data subjects, we are not even the generative source of our own images. The temporality doesn't work that way (source first, then representation), and neither does the spacing or tether, even if the data industries sometimes want to convince us that its products are nothing but representations, which can thus be judged accurate or not, improved consciously or opted out of—even if it has wanted to convince us, in short, that its products exist in a realm where individual will still matters, where we can at least aspire to control something about our images and how they are generated or transformed.

"Representation" names an image thought to be generated by will, someone's will, secured in a decision or refused by the same. It operates, in this sense, well within the bounds of a liberal tradition in which personhood constellates around individual decision-making that can be either arrogated to the self or alienated from the self. But when a search engine personalizes our search results, it does so by extracting data from the activities of search engine users, amalgamating that data with a vast set of other users by way of measures like likeness and preference, and then reintegrating data, in the form of recommendations and other personalizations, back into the lives from which it has been extracted. This process is ongoing, operational; it never ceases, and so the profiles that result can never sit still long enough to function as re-presentations. There is no remove, because there is no delay, no priorness, and in any case, the profiles that are the ultimate products of these processes get delivered directly back into the lives that we might otherwise say were the "source" of the profile, thereby at the very least marking those lives, but often transforming or significantly inflecting them so that no prior source could ever be isolated. This leaves only a ceaseless operational process that, in its flux and constancy, is easily mistaken for life itself.[34]

Late in the essay, Steinberg says that the flatbed picture plane, the workspace arrayed for and as data, "admits the artist in the fullness of his human interests."[35] This doesn't mean that the flatbed picture plane is re-surgently humanist. It means that operational processes admit all human interests as new material for remaking the human, for operationalizing humanity itself—just as the graphical field was designed to potentially accommodate all human interests as so much information. Better, therefore, to call these "operational processes" than "representational" ones, even if, as with the computer screen, we seem to be dealing with a predominantly visual medium. As Steinberg might have put it, we must now be concerned with processes—art-world ones of course, but far more urgently, cultural ones, industrial ones, technological ones—that exist far outside of modernism's familiar oppositions: between representation and formalism, subject matter and material support, illusionism and modernism, the human and technology. These are oppositions, Steinberg says, whose persistence has hindered the capacity of cultural critics and others to confront a present tense where the artwork has become a scene for self-elaboration and the picture plane has become a space for data management.

"Operational" gets more nearly correct the temporality of the labor involved in a Rauschenberg (or, for that matter, a Thomas, a Whitten, a Gaines, or a Mehretu)—any surface where data accumulates, where the question of the human is not presumed but suspended. It also implies an ongoing function, something activated, always on.[36] And unlike the "process" of process art, it does not segment creative labor into discrete stages, with process coming first and product and encounter coming later. In fact, as Steinberg implies, the artist—that reliable, if evasive, source of meaning—is more than a little occulted in the operational process. We don't learn much about their intentions, their making processes, their informing biography. Rauschenberg himself, in Steinberg's account, is little more than an operation, or part of the broader operational process that gets set in motion by his work. The surface of the operational image is a workspace, and never ceases to be that, even when the active work of assembly has ended.

"'Somewhere in the image there is a proposition. It is unclear.'" This is Steinberg quoting David Antin writing about Warhol, another artist of the flatbed picture plane, the data image, the informatic image that no longer issues an address to a presumable human. From this, Steinberg concludes that the flatbed picture plane is "the picture conceived as the image of an image. It's a conception which guarantees that the presentation will not be directly that of a worldspace, and that it will nevertheless admit any experience as the matter of representation. And it readmits the artist in the fullness of his human interests, as well as the artist-technician."[37] "Image of an image" previews a coming postmodern vocabulary, and Steinberg ends with reference to what he calls "post-Modernist painting." In the conceptualization of postmodernism that was to come, the idea of an "image of an image" tends to refer to a waning of the referent, a deepening, dizzying descent into simulation or spectacle. Antin's quote, admiringly reproduced by Steinberg, bears out this anxiety of the departing image, the loss of something once possessed.

But "operational process" holds another potential, distinct from the postmodernist trajectory with its anxiety about the fraying tether of representation to reference. If we think about a graphic user interface as an "image of an image"—a recursivity that might express the distance and abstraction of that form of the screen—then the spiral of departure isn't back toward a lost referent, but forward into the ongoing voracious accumulation of data that feeds the circulation of information. As long as people keep living lives in graphical spaces, now online or in proximity to networked processes (such as border patrol or facial recognition technologies or shopping at Target[38]), they will keep generating "images of images" that we might as well just start to call a life rather than a representation of a life, given their dependence on and inextricability from the lives that generate such images. Here is how Ramon Amaro puts this point: "Structuring perception through machine architectures is problematic when considering the racialized object. To bring forth a visually coherent future in computer vision, or an incoherent and speculative one for that matter (using [the artist Joy] Buolamwini's example), one must first reduce the hall of possibilities to a set of pre-existing conditions."[39] In other words, one must express the nonrepresentational as a representational process, belying the unclear proposition, the speculative and incoherent form of the racialized object. For Steinberg, the unclear proposition is the human itself and those who persist in the folly or privilege of thinking that's where they live. To admit artists in the "fullness" of their interests is to say that any part of the human who we call an artist can be made to perform labor, can be made over into a going concern, an interest, a product. An artist then comes, at best, to manage this dissolution of the artistic self as part of the ongoing labor of an operational milieu.[40]

What haunts Steinberg's essay is that the "other criteria" he calls into being are not just a set of criteria replacing a prior set (although obviously when the essay is read as a rebuke to the dominant formalist critics, this is precisely the work that "other criteria" is meant to do). In a periodizing sense, "other criteria" doesn't initiate a toggle through discrete states—where we would expect that Steinberg's own set of criteria would have since been replaced many times over—but names an ongoing, ceaseless production: the operationalization of other criteria as an ongoing process. In the world of operational processes that Steinberg feels out, "other criteria" are always being generated, every time a new image of a data subject is produced.[41] "Other criteria" is no longer a point of passage between one plane of ordinariness and another—understood as crisis or transition—but is the ordinary itself, uninhabitable though it may be.

"But something happened in painting around 1950. . . ."[42] Given his diverse interests, if something happened in painting, then why not in and across a number of other sites? In films?[43] Music?[44] Or even in the far more readily apparent art-historical examples of conceptual and minimalist art practices (this story picks up in chapter 5)?[45] Not to mention the cases I've discussed that we might once, in spurious opposition to the fine arts, have called popular culture: the GUI, Google, Facebook, likes and preferences, facial recognition, etc. Steinberg hints at the strange logic of exemplification at work in operational processes. He concludes:

> What I have called the flatbed is more than a surface distinction if it is understood as a change within painting that changed the relationship between artist and image, image and viewer. Yet this internal change is no more than a symptom of changes which go far beyond questions of picture planes, or of painting as such. It is part of a shakeup that contaminates all purified categories.[46]

How far beyond picture planes? If we know that the change internal to painting is no more than a symptom, that doesn't mean we know what else could count or come to exist in the full set of symptoms. In fact, it means we precisely do not know what else counts, that we don't know what criteria would justify inclusion. And this confusion itself is a mark of the age that I think Steinberg's essay so surprisingly and so incisively describes. Life is operationalized when a machinery is put in place to accommodate information to life, life to information, as those lives are being lived. In such a milieu, all points of contact become sites for the accumulation and manipulation of data. This can describe border controls just as much as it describes social media or hook-up apps or, more simply, the graphical field in which such forms of sociality are often lived.[47]

We enter the world of the nonrepresentational here because one can't discern what would even count as a re-presentation. Because no counterrepresentation does anything to affect the machinery of operational processes, but also because life often proceeds through other circuits now, managed and even generated by other criteria. Operational processes inflect life no less than picture planes—in fact, the spread of operational processes throughout the social makes this very sentence and its separation of life from pictures planes tautological, even if the grammar of surviving such a spread requires that we continue to insist on the distinction between life and the surfaces where it is imprinted and lived. The shake-up that contaminates all purified categories starts with the category of the human itself, thus, life itself. There is a proposition here. It is unclear. Its lack of clarity is not what undercuts the power of this proposition—it is what empowers it to operationalize life. The graphical field was the theater of that operation. What was done there? What else could be done there? What was the human becoming? What could it become? These are the questions taken up skeptically and searchingly by the artists at the center of the four chapters that follow.

The following chapters each work to show how a particular artist and their practice took up the problem of the human in bits, operating inside the same exigencies, although often mobilizing different grammars and histories. There is no claim here that these four artists—Thomas, Whitten, Gaines, Mehretu—should be seen as harbingers of a distinct era or period of art production, say, graphical aesthetics or anything of the sort. At the same time, the parallels between the user of the graphical interface and an artist working out the terms of their appearance and existence inside the delimited fields of a canvas are far more than just an analogy.

In, Around, Above, Behind, and Other Forms of Space Flight: Alma Thomas

2

Gil Scott-Heron's 1970 song "Whitey on the Moon" is easy to understand as a protest, in a moral and a political register, about financial priorities.[1] Namely, the priorities that would make it more important for a nation to land a white man on the moon than to address the ongoing immiseration and incarceration of that faction of American society who were welcomed into the public for the US space program so long as they didn't think their blackness entitled them to any special treatment. And of course, "Whitey on the Moon" does do that work. But it is also a song about the role that technology would play in the movements to create worlds for black life. In 1967, Martin Luther King Jr. had broached the same issues. King's invocation of the space program was in the context of his call for a guaranteed annual income for all Americans, which John Kenneth Galbraith (cited by King) had estimated would cost approximately as much as the moon landing that had been so recently achieved. "John Kenneth Galbraith said that a guaranteed annual income could be done for about twenty billion dollars a year. And I say to you today, that if our nation can spend thirty-five billion dollars a year to fight an unjust, evil war in Vietnam, and twenty billion dollars to put a man on the moon, it can spend billions of dollars to put God's children on their own two feet right here on earth."[2]

The math exposed here is brutally simple: the value of black life on Earth versus the value of white life on the moon. But Scott-Heron also invokes a more complex accounting by way of a menagerie of prepositions. His sister gets bitten by a rat *while* whitey is on the moon. But his sister is also bitten by a rat *because* whitey is on the moon, and *with* whitey on the moon. In the later verses, the preposition drops out entirely and the relationship between the events of black life rub up rawly against the sheer, ridiculous, extravagant fact of whitey on the moon. Scott-Heron, like King, points to the US space program as an example of investment without bounds, understanding that the progress thereby sponsored would support a white future, but one now proceeding in the guise of an event televised for "everyone," a victory for American democracy. In doing so, both Scott-Heron and King place black life into complex dialogue with technological investment and infrastructure: technology is the cause of black misery insofar as universalist values make infrastructural investment a zero-sum game (black life vs. white flight). But it is never just the cause, and never a direct cause in any case. "Whitey on the moon," in this sense, stands as a name for technology as such. NASA, that ultimate symbol of democratic aspiration, launches a white man as far away from sister Nell as it is possible to go, and both King and Scott-Heron see in that astronomical distance a perverse proximity, itself figuring the existential proximity between black and white. Sister Nell grows ill from living *with* whitey on the moon, and her life is given its shape *by* whitey on the moon. That is more than a poetic figuration, acting at an allegorical distance. As King and Scott-Heron both state, yes, this is a question of financial priorities and what counts as a value in the official public of the United States. King states that fact as a question of shiftable priorities; Scott-Heron ironizes it, presenting it not as a problem that might be solved but as a question of the multiple imbrications of black life and technological research, where the latter has become, in the space age, synonymous with white life. "Whitey on the moon" thus names the atmospheric status of whiteness when progress and humanism were being driven by the technology industries that first found their homes in the warrens of government buildings that housed NASA and that eventually migrated, often with that same federal backing, to the more chic wall-less work spaces of the private tech industry. A status so diffuse that almost any preposition would link black life to it.

King's and Scott-Heron's work here is important because it has been difficult to document the interface between race and technology, as that interface is so often stuck between two forces that each in their own way make race and racialization recede: One, the banality and deep violence of obvious exclusion. A film like *Hidden Figures* (2016, dir. Melfi) makes the point, both in its own narrative of inclusion and exceptionality and in the extradiegetic fact of its existence, the very need for it to be made. Two, the way that all white spaces, such as those that witnessed the research and development that led to the personal computer, have a way of coming to look not white but raceless, even postracial, such that the mention of race in those contexts can be heard as an insult to their own higher ideals.[3] So the grounds for what is to follow can't be the shifting sands of inclusion and exclusion. That means that they also can't be based in a politics of representation. Representation's terms (inclusion/exclusion; visibility/invisibility; public/private) will not get us very far when the analysis needs to move through sites where race and technology inform each other, sites where the technologies in questions are forging new realms of personhood that are not based in representation but that are still so importantly informed by racialization and racial politics.

This book tries to understand how the line between violence and resistance shifts when the graphical field becomes the environment for so much life; to understand what those terms come to look like in a period when creativity gets harnessed by the graphical field as a source of labor; when capture and surveillance are emanations of ordinary life, even ordinary life lived among one's own chosen community; when the very terms of the human are being reorganized by the graphical field and its ways of enrolling people as users in an open field seemingly limited only by one's own personal limitations; when all sorts of new claims of neutrality break out, from the neutrality of the knowledge worker to the neutrality of technology and the graphical field itself; when so much gets delaminated from personhood in the wake of World War II precisely to rehabilitate the human as newly productive in an information era, which could only be, given the conditions under which these changes were to occur, a project to rehabilitate whiteness on the newly technologized grounds of neutrality and universality; when the individual becomes a bastion of selfhood positioned not only against the anonymity of the mass but also against the fungibility of anything that produces knowledge as data, the favored commodity of the late twentieth and early twenty-first centuries.

The painter Alma Thomas worked at this interface between blackness and technology not through the striations of in and out, included and excluded, but through Scott-Heron's prepositional intimacies. Among the artists whose work helps tell the story of the graphical field and its ambitions to remake the human by becoming a primary infrastructure for life,

Thomas's questions are the most basic, the most fundamental: What possibilities open up when one accepts that the human isn't separable from technology, isn't a pure category and never was? What forms of vision, of flight become possible in that embrace of both the human and technology, not as limitations to be overcome, but as a set of constraints to be inhabited? What happens to race and the history of racialization when one asks questions of the human in this register, when one situates the human in relation to technology such that neither can be ontologically discrete? These are also the most fundamental kinds of questions asked by Engelbart, and by anyone invested in creating a computational space that would allow the human to merge and mingle with technology in a new way—a field of questions that, seen in relation to the history of the personal computer and the logics that made it possible, I've been calling the *graphical*. Thomas's and Engelbart's investigations led them to very different places and very different answers. What gets opened up here happens not by seeing their projects as aligned, or by any sort of claim that Thomas was self-consciously investigating screen space, but by seeing their projects as working out from the same starting questions. With Thomas's painting, this will involve paying close attention to how she situates her labor and her self in relation to the bits that constitute the fields of her late paintings, her loose but always rhythmically ordered grids or rasters.

In 1972, when she was ninety-one years old and still inspired by space and the space program that had made space visually and imaginatively available to her, Alma Thomas (1881–1978) painted *Mars Dust* (plate 3). Like almost every painting she had made since 1966, when she turned to painting full-time, and every painting she would make until her death in 1978 at the age of ninety-seven, *Mars Dust* is composed exclusively, even astringently of small rectilinear blocks of paint arrayed in loosely gridded space. Which is to say, the blocks of paint exist within a loose but unequivocal homogeneity, a field. The field is composed of irradiated hashes, small units arrayed in loose but enduring columns. The units—hashes, tiles, bits—are variegated when compared one to one, but form a field when seen together. Their alignment in a coordinate grid makes them exist in a provisional unity. The columns are surrounded and set off by a blue that ranges from a muted indigo to a fluorescing royal. This blue pulses in a way that confuses *between* and *behind* by sometimes forcing an "infrontness." The prepositions won't stand still. They pulse too. Bits and field thus animate each other. Within the overall field, there is the regularity of the brush touching down in the field, a kind of methodical allowance of spontaneity. But there is also deliberation in the blue ligatures that have been overpainted, edits made later, to emphasize a particular difference or distance, a spacing—to confuse the prepositions.

Looking at any one Thomas painting, or looking across her body of work, one could feel that variation was being sacrificed to sameness, or that individuality was being sacrificed to some sort of system, that her units of paint exist only or mainly to be subsumed into a larger pictorial field. And while this move, seemingly away from expressive individuality, was not unusual in American art of the postwar period, it delineates certain boundaries of the human that I think are evaded, if not actively challenged, in Thomas's work. This, along with a host of what art history tends to reduce to "contextual" factors, will force us to think again about the way that this dynamic between sameness and system, expressive individuality and minimalist flatness bears (hard) on the relationship between blackness and the things made *by* a person who inhabits blackness—which is to say, to think again about the question of labor in Thomas's paintings.

The question of labor turns on the relationship between bit and field, as that is almost all there is in what are often called Alma Thomas's Earth Paintings. This could sound to some like an allegory for questions of part and whole, individual and group, self and other. And this is not untrue, although in a scene of graphicalization, the relationship between bit, field, and the humans who would represent bits and fields through the prophylaxis of allegory will turn out to be uncomfortably closer than analogical— only just less than an equivalency. This wasn't Thomas's doing; it was, rather, an existent problem she explored relentlessly and restlessly in her paintings.

Given her status as a black woman artist who succeeded in a starkly segregated art world at a time when so many forces aligned to make that success impossible, even unthinkable, Thomas's story is frequently rehearsed. As Thomas herself feared, her biography too often stands in for discussion of her work. Like many marked subjects whose need for institutions was quite different from their need for her, Thomas, we could say, has been burdened with biography. A high school art teacher her whole life, but also a lifelong painter, her success in the New York art market in the later decades of her life, coinciding more or less with her retirement from teaching, creates a ready narrative in which her early MFA training in art at Howard University seems to finally have matured into a profession or career, allowing her to exit the obscurity of her teaching service. In being recognized by the art world, Thomas seems to finally emerge, as she deserved all along, from (feminized) service work to become the particular kind of independent, autonomous genius that the New York art establishment so craved, and to which their imagination of successful personhood was strongly yoked.

Thomas was grateful, if not persistently bemused, by her success in those spheres, but I doubt she would have had much time for the racist and classist denigration of service work that has become the concomitant of this success narrative. In any case, succeed she did, on terms both her own and not. For the last two decades of her life, she painted, and those paintings garnered audiences in DC, New York, and eventually world-wide. She was the first African American woman to have a solo show at the Whitney Museum of American Art, a fact that is simultaneously an in-dictment (of the art world) and an accolade, well deserved and hard won.

During this period, Thomas was dedicated to the kind of paintings I discuss here: large paintings (some larger and some smaller than five feet on a side), acrylic on canvas, composed entirely of lozenges of paint arrayed in a grid. Thomas herself called these her "Alma stripes." Some stripes were oriented vertically, others horizontally, others in circles. Some were tightly gridded. Others, especially near the end of her life, were loose, as though something were breaking or drifting the grid apart. It is, all told, a stunning body of work, not least for the fact of its invariance, or its belief in minor variation and the forms of attention such small scales might in-vite. In this late period of her life, when she was asked so often about her race and her gender, Thomas had little use for gender or race as categories of identity, experience, or belonging. If forced to choose a category, she chose painter—which is not a rejection of race and gender so much as a rejection of the raced and gendered positions offered to her by such ques-tions. So the discussion of her work in relation to race will need to proceed along lines not governed by identity or representation. If there has been very little writing on Thomas's work in relation to race, to blackness or to black femininity, this says less about the work itself, and more about the ways that blackness in art history and the art world is either made to do work for whiteness, or else it doesn't show up at all.

Given the look of Thomas's late paintings—their austerity, I want to say, their commitment to abstraction, the persistence of a repeated unit or compositional element, along with Thomas's own desire to have her work understood in a modernist tradition—a history of painting might refer in this place to "dabs" of paint, as art historian Richard Shiff does when describing the work of Paul Cézanne, an artist who was a conscious influence on Thomas.[4] Or, similarly harking to painting at the start of the twentieth century, we might refer to Maria Gough's "schistose" fields of the Russian avant-garde: colored stones sliced as though with a sharp sword.[5] And these dabs or schists would, in a modernist trajectory connecting Cézanne and Thomas, become untethered from perception, from the sovereignty of the perceiving, categorizing eye (given as, say, representation or figuration), so they can then take up their place within that peculiar category of emergent thing: abstraction. But even as the figure of a perceiving subject of experience recedes from the public side of modernist painting, a newly organized human subject emerges on the side of a painting's production. Painterliness, action, abstraction . . . these are some of the terms around which that painting subject, the modernist painter, would come to be organized.

And Thomas's paintings do not lack for *painterliness*, for a delicacy of touch, an inventiveness of approach and process. But I'm interested less in what that means for the look of the painting and its place in modernism, and more in what a claim to painterliness says or means to say about the person of the painter, about the human who is no less resident—implied, invoked, even addressed—in the physical painting than is the receiver or viewer. Modernist painting, in other words, is also a history of personhood, or a record of the small fissures made every now and then between, as Fred Moten puts it, subjectivity and personhood, or between "Man" and the human as Sylvia Wynter might put it.[6] For Thomas's surfaces are greatly varied within the homogeneity or systematicity that I've emphasized. One could even sense, in this variance, a human hand—a signature touch, something a connoisseur could identify, the warmth of quiddity over system. The problem will turn out not to be that the irregularity of her brushstrokes seems to contradict anything I will want to say about systematicity, technology, or the graphical screen. The problem will be—and this I take to be Thomas's central concern—that whatever the human becomes in Thomas's paintings, it doesn't emerge in distinction from, or even antagonism with, the systematicity of Thomas's gridded space. Technology or technicity, to the extent that it plays a role, will not play the role of the dehumanizing or alienating force. And so Thomas's quiddities will not play the countervailing role of the humanizing force. Her painterliness will not, in other words, be what gets Thomas free.

It is here that Thomas's work most insistently encounters the nascent history of the graphical screen, which similarly worked to de-antagonize human and system, although to very different ends. And it is finally in the relation between human and system, the transit between those terms, their derangement in the graphical field, where we'll find the graphical screen's claim to participate in the conceptualization of a postracial form of whiteness, although this is mainly a story for later chapters. So, as a formal concern, while it will be important to pay attention to Thomas's brushwork, the quavering, the inconsistency, the delicacy, the light touch, the errancy of Thomas's brushstrokes, those terms will not recuperate something human from something machinic. And more vexing still, this fact will not imply an abdication of Thomas's critical responsibility as a modernist artist—this is where Thomas's story diverges from the modernist culture-industry story, in which art either resists capitalism and commoditization, so often allegorized as technology, or else fails in those responsibilities (and fail it always does, eventually).[7]

Thomas works these problems from a different standing, asking what it means to invent forms of the human inside systems, as systems, as ways to deracinate both system and the human figure that has so often received its coherence, in the modernist story, from its resistance to systems, or otherwise from its constant besiegement.[8] And from this standing, Thomas makes it possible to see the ways that the graphical screen was participating in a shift in the very terrain of critical engagement with capitalism and its regularizing systems.[9] The story of the graphical screen *is* the story of the overcoming of that antinomy between art and commodity, between human and various forms of its systematization (subject, person, user)—overcoming it for labor broadly, but overcoming it for whiteness in particular. This was the technical side of what would be a longer and larger process of postracialization, in which whiteness came to be subsumed into the diversity pools that it created for its own benefit. As such, the graphical field plays a role in a postracial recuperation of whiteness precisely on the basis of a new collaboration between machine and human to be staged and performed inside the graphicalized screen, that gridded field of bits where grid becomes an infrastructure for the human so that humans can feel their humanity to be both augmented, unbothered, and served by the various systems at work (computer, raster field, pixels, memory). The particular ways that Thomas inhabits her own fields, playing with the ligatures between human and system, help us see these larger dynamics.

Inside her fields, Thomas's brush strokes are sometimes controlled, but at other times they are quick, almost casual. In *Gray Night* (1972, plate 4), some of the most obvious, casual marks appear in the interstices of the gray blocks of paint. Thomas appears to have laid down a grid of gray blocks, leaving the white intervals between as negative space. These intervals occur almost exclusively between blocks in a column, never between the different columns. Columns are differentiated entirely by the hairbreadth of space left between blocks of gray paint. Or, where the blocks immediately rub up against one another across the horizontal axis—and this is frequent—they are differentiated only by the act of laying down the blocks in individual moments of contact with the canvas, one at a time. Picking up the brush and putting it down within the confines of a delineated column of space. This act seems to have been organized by Thomas's commitment to columns as a spatial unit, or artistic constraint.

But in what appears to have been a later stage of the painting, probably done in response to viewing the painting from a distance (as much as was afforded by the Washington, DC, kitchen where she worked), Thomas painted over some of the interstices in white, effectively reshaping them. The effect moves toward a kind of uniformity in these interstitial spaces. Not uniform or perfect or regular, but Thomas has nudged those interstices, those shapes, to each curve and bend at their edges. This lends the gray bits a rounded shape while the white interstices tend to look concave or hollowed out. This is the vocabulary of a nesting, gray in white, shape on shape. Overall, this causes the painting, in some passages, to appear to fall or drip or sag, top to bottom. But again, if this is a pattern, it is one interrupted all over by deviations from that pattern: deviations that look, or were made to look, less like preplanned variations in a pattern and more like casualness or speed, as if some overall effect was more important that the proceduralism of getting the blocks of paint down exactly right.

This toggle between negative space and overpainting, where Thomas sometimes adjusts, after the act of painting, what would otherwise just be the space left behind by a set of marks, is responsible for the way that foreground and background never achieve a stable relationship with each other in Thomas's canvases. Often, in *Gray Night*, the white shapes that set off the gray lozenges seems to cohere, somewhere beneath or under, into a contiguous background. At other times, Thomas overpaints the ligatures or prepositions between blocks, giving them a certain shape, underscoring their presence precisely as interval. Dabs are sometimes thick and multilayered. Sometimes they are thin, barely there. The canvas shows through always, all over. In *Gray Night*, Thomas seems mostly to have used the same width of brush to make the light gray blocks. But there are two exceptions in this painting—an exceptionality that recurs in many of

Thomas's Earth Paintings. There are two stripes or vertical bands, extending from top to bottom, composed of columns of gray painting executed with a thinner brush, or else, with the side of a wide brush. In the overall field, these bands give a sense of compression. One effect is to amplify a sense of casualness, a sense that regularity wasn't the most important effect sought; that proceduralism wasn't what was important to Thomas (in the way it would be for Charles Gaines, the subject of chapter 4). But another effect is to create a kind of gentle, inconsistent but striking spatial illusion, the narrowing of the columns now indicating a recession in space, as though the canvas had buckled in that place.

There is then in all of Thomas's work, as Shiff has put it in a different context, the question of touch, of gesture. So Thomas, at the most basic level, forces us to think touch and system together in the same thought, to hold them together even as the graphical field was holding them together. That, in fact, was the graphic field's precise invention. But if the history of modernist art since Cézanne has, as Shiff recounts, often been told as a story about the dissolution of the picture plane, its scatter into autonomous marks, each carrying with it, precisely in its flight and scatter from representation, some quotient of the artist's own autonomy, then the artists in my story, Thomas first among them, seemed to want their touches to block autonomy, individuality, the isolated unit augmented by the field. For a variety of reasons, their prepositions were oriented toward a different horizon.[10]

Mars Dust, whose title offers a referent as indelible as it is mysterious, helps us begin to understand the prepositions that scatter the relationship between Thomas's labor and her existence within technological systems. Like many of her paintings, Mars Dust was in part a product of Thomas's interest in technologically mediated modes of sight. It is an oft-rehearsed fact of her biography that Thomas was fascinated by the space program. She sometimes explained her paintings—that is, the persistent use of blocks of paint arrayed in columns and rows—as a product of seeing the earth "as if" from high altitude. This is the origin of the name "earth paintings." The title of one of her earliest Earth Paintings, 1966's Air View of Spring Nursery, makes this explicit. There is an invitation here, if we want it, to think about Mars Dust's relationship to its referent in phenomenological terms, which is to say, realist terms when the particularities of embodied sight are taken into account. In other words, they're "just" what a planet looks like, seen from above. Her paintings are, in this framing— a framing that might be true but that always underdescribes Thomas's work—resurgently representational.

In *Arboretum Presents White Dogwood* (1972, plate 5), Thomas again gives us a world composed of blocks, blocks differentiated by the variables of spacing, shading, and the hues that peak out in the cuts between tiles. To attune ourselves to a particular way of seeing these paintings, let's again take the title's referent at its word and say that there are dogwoods present. If so, the reference must be to their white blossoms, their patterns, the negative spaces themselves limning leaves. But if there are dogwoods present in the form of their blossoms, it's not their difference from the rest of the picture that makes them stand out so much as their likeness. If so, then we can be struck by how much they share with whatever isn't dogwood: their basic building blocks, their overall color and shading, their verticality, their existence in and projection of a basic gridded structure of composition. We're led into strange syntax wherein we accept a basic representational structure for the image while appearing also to affirm its aggressive abstraction.

One way forward is to try not to resolve but to inhabit this strange syntax. And one way to do that would be to say that Thomas was inventing not a style of abstraction in flight from (or back to) representation so much as a machine for remaking syntax in an age of *bodily* abstraction. Bodily abstraction would be what happens when one sees Earth as photographed from space. Or when one drags the mouse through an open field of the computer screen to pull one's cursor, a prosthesis, through information space. In this view of abstraction, human-machine interactions of various sorts allow bodies to visualize Earth from so far above that the view opened onto a sense of the planetary, or to move through information as though it were a space. Here, representation itself is abstract, beginning in a matrix of abstraction. In other words, the locus of abstraction lies not in Thomas's work or in modernism, but in the world that they would inhabit—and precisely a part of the world where technology and the human meet in tense, disorienting encounters, and which fascinated Thomas. In this sense, Thomas's painting are about the ligatures and prepositions of relation—primarily, in my view, the relation between human and machine, but therefore also about how Thomas's labor of composition becomes a recomposition of the human on other terms. In creating a painting made from her kitchen table, painted as though seen from above, Thomas is inventing a position for herself that doesn't exist, that can't exist in her world. Thomas, in other words, invents prepositions for living; she thereby makes of the canvas not an abstract image but a procedure, what the previous chapter called an *operational process* wherein her sight is reinvented at the very same time, and in the same process, as the world outside her window.

Sometimes Thomas lets us see things, referents, worlds as though in reflection on the surface of her tiles or bits. In *Pond—Spring Awakening* (1972), we might imagine we see something like reflections of spring-touched leaves on the surface of water. Sometimes she creates things, referents, worlds out of her tiles, using the tiles themselves and the space in between to insinuate not reflected light but dimensionality, as in *Arboretum Presents White Dogwood* (1972). Sometimes we seem invited to see behind her surfaces, tiles turned scrim, as in *Evening Glow* (1972). Sometimes we seem only offered a view of the tiles themselves, with nothing mediating those tiles that would require the spatial-grammatical work of a preposition, as in *Antares* (1972, plate 9). Sometimes Thomas's paintings teeter on the border of several of these modes, as in *Late Night Reflections* (1972, plate 6), where the relationship of blue to yellow is hard to pin down, seems always on the move.

The confusion of prepositions that we find in any one Thomas canvas, and across all of her Earth Paintings, wrenches us out of a phenomenological frame—at least one that assumes it knows something about the human and its capacities. Couldn't we then say that with her semiregular matrix of ligatured tiles, Thomas disassembles, decomposes as much as she assembles or composes? That she disrupts the world, and the human within that world, in the act of remaking it? I think this better accounts, affectively, for the experience of seeing these paintings. Something feels blocked, not given, screened, even as Thomas's gestures of making are so seemingly composed and laid bare, set down in regular columns and rows, adhering to a programmatic dimensionality like a rhythm, stressing variations but only in folds of likeness. Some of the usual comportments toward painting, indicated by the prepositions that would put us in stable relation with an image, won't work here. Something has been scrambled. Thomas's canvases are scrims, obstructing our vision, that in turn become what there is to look at. They become an encompassing environment that encodes not the world in its phenomenal availability, but a disposition toward the world, a view from above, less sight than a reimagination of what sight can be and do and how it sits within and across the boundaries of a body. Like the graphical screens whose history they run alongside, even if they never reference them directly, Thomas's paintings procedurally transform aspects of the world that have themselves informed their making and their being.

These two areas of experimentation, the graphical field and Thomas's paintings, revolve together if in distinctive orbits around a question that was raised explicitly in early research into the graphical field of the computer screen: of the human and human capacity. In an age shaped by the needs of information, the need for it to move and flow, for it to become labile for the human who would become its inhabitant and laborer, the human would be imagined as a set of limitations to be overcome. This, in fact, was the express charge of the graphical field, as Engelbart and his team imagined and executed it. Could the human think fast enough to work amid such an overwhelming number of resources—the world's knowledge amassed, or as Vannevar Bush referred to this new realm of computability, "the detailed affairs of millions of people doing complicated things."[11] Here is how Bush articulates the problem that would find a solution in Engelbart's graphical field: "The difficulty seems to be, not so much that we publish unduly in view of the extent and variety of present day interests, but rather that publication has been extended far beyond our present ability to make real use of the record." The human, in other words, would need to become more like this world of information: vast, mathematical, flexible, fast. Would need, in other words, to be procedurally transformed by the very graphical field within which they would understand themselves to be working. That part of the story is well known, the stuff of dreams and nightmares.

But Sylvia Wynter teaches us that any such positing of the human divides the world into those who are selected and those who are dysselected from the category, not only not included but pushed outside the realm of possible inclusion. In other words, there are those who can be seen to have succeeded by some measure (the selected), as well as those whose existence and eventual inclusion are implied by the successful: that is, all of those who might become willing to accept those standards of success sometime in the future. And then there are the dysselected, those whose collective narrative is, by force or self-exemption, neither successful nor unsuccessful in a way that could ever be included or corrected through good education or proper self-discipline.[12] The dysselected, as Hortense Spillers intones, never had a chance.[13] Through a stunning act of historical compression, the graphical field comes, from the sixties forward, to bear the burden of maintaining this boundary (rather than the older standard of dysselection that relied on the antagonism between the alienated self and the democratic self, or the individual seen against the mass). Not by walling off its inhabitants and their capacities, but in more cybernetic fashion, by sending those inhabitants on a developmental trajectory that Engelbart would come to refer to as "augmentation" and Apple simply as "user friendliness." In this schema, there are those who have the means to become augmented, and those who do not (yet). As both Wynter and Frank Wilderson would argue, black subjects—seen in their blackness and not as part of a reformable group willing to accept the conditions for inclusion offered them—are part of neither category: their "grammar of suffering" registering not as exclusion so much as dysselection. That is, not even registering, hardly mattering. The black subject's vulnerability to gratuitous violence, natal alienation, and fungibility (see chapter 5) are both the evidence of this status and its effect, both its grammar and its ghost.[14]

Gil Scott-Heron's poem "Whitey on the Moon" expresses both the structure and the feeling of this process of dysselection, the distance across which it operates for black subjects:

A rat done bit my sister Nell
(with Whitey on the Moon).
Her face and arms began to swell
(and Whitey's on the moon).[15]

Directly, violently impacted, yet categorically expunged. So what do we make then of Alma Thomas's professed fascination with the space program, the moon landing, and all of the possibilities each might have seemed, from that kitchen table sitting at that easel, to open onto? Thomas's turn toward outer space seems to place her not in the position of Nell, for whom the space program can only be a violent extravagance. It seems to locate her, instead, with the population of people invited to imagine themselves as astronauts, projecting self and fantasy into space. Sun Ra (musician, prophet, and resident space alien) shows us another possibility. He identifies with space, and with Saturn in particular, because he sees it as an out mode of dwelling on Earth. Sun Ra turns this formulation on its head, indicating that there is not just one way to direct one's fascination toward space.[16] As Ra, emissary from space, says to a rec room of young black men in the 1974 film Space is the Place: "You don't exist in this society. If you did, your people wouldn't be seeking equal rights."[17]

In paintings like Mars Dust, Thomas projects herself into space precisely to then see or resee Earth, looking back on those she now joins in a new fashion. In this, she signals an allegiance neither to Earth nor to space, but to the space of suspension that marks them not as two parts of a whole (e.g., the haves and those who do not have . . . yet). This is an operation of and for the dysselected, the uninvited, for whom there can be no inclusion. The title, after all, directs us to turn our attention to the dust of Mars. Dust is not detritus, cast off, dirt to be discarded; it is the necessary artifact of all existing. It is both living and dead. From this grounding of dust, Thomas launches an investigation into the capacities of the human who exists within a space defined by bit and field, as though she is both a NASA scientist and an invested onlooker, but also, someone who already exists on Mars. The work of that investigation is to test what kinds of capacities and what kinds of constraint operate in such a field, to test where constraint begins to merge with capacity in the space of the dysselected.

Thomas's gesture, far from critique or intervention or anything so direct, is an imagination of the conditions under which another form of being might emerge *out of* the concepts and constraints that were being tested, in tests guided by different values, in the computer's graphical interface.[18] Conditions and constraints that Thomas's work illuminates in its parallel trajectory, in its haunting proximity and adamant distance.[19] The project to invent a human interface for computational machines simply *was* a project to invent new forms of labor and new modalities of personhood, which is why I think the word "interface" can sometimes undertheorize its object. This was true even in the sixties, when Engelbart's face was appearing in overlay on his own new protographical computer display. In that field, what was being demonstrated wasn't just a new toggle point of communication, a mediating screen, but an entire system for seating the human inside a graphical field, a field comprised of bits, designed to facilitate a kind of informational touch as well as a rehabilitation of the human on terms better suited to an informational field.[20] From the nascent computer industry's point of view, this was understood as graphics research as well as human-computer interaction (HCI)—a telling synonymy, bespeaking the collapse of graphics into human, and human into graphics, that I think was one of Thomas's more insistent, if more recondite, subjects.

Like the graphical screen configured for the cathode-ray tube (CRT) monitor, Thomas's paintings were materialized on a raster of repeated units or what, in that context, we would call pixels. This basic likeness is important, although also misleading insofar as it makes the graphical computer screen seem like an image-based medium, with Thomas's paintings appearing also as an image, a representation of the screen's pixels—or invoking them by analogy. But while the graphical screen comfortably hosts images, it is not an image-based medium. Neither, I think, are Thomas's paintings.

As recounted in chapter 1, in the seventies Leo Steinberg sensed a fundamental reorientation of the picture plane, which was also a reorientation of the kind of human thought to operate in that picture plane. In the service of this reorientation, Steinberg described a new form of what he called "psychic address," exemplified by the work of, among others, Rauschenberg and Dubuffet. He called that mode of address (note: an address not a medium) "the flatbed picture plane." Steinberg's sense was that, with the flatbed picture plane, artists were starting to experiment less with a medium and more with new forms of the human itself in relation to new technologies and new modes of labor. By the mid-1960s, the period about which Steinberg was thinking, Alma Thomas had begun to paint a collection of works that she would experiment with until her death in 1978.[21] I don't think they are a receptor surface in the sense Steinberg describes; I think they are more elemental than that, something more like the constitutive, if invisible or nonperceptual matrix of that receptor surface. They are, in other words, precisely what makes that surface so receptive. They ask questions about what happens when a person, and their labor, come to inhabit a field of bits such that that field forms the conditions in and constraints under which that labor operates. They are products of vision while transforming and reseating vision. Their representational aspects take their place within the operational processes of that transformational fold.

There are many other ways, of course, to explain the patterning of Thomas's surfaces. Formalist criticism would be one. As Steinberg characterizes formalist criticism: "the criterion for significant progress remains a kind of design technology subject to one compulsive direction: the treatment of 'the whole surface as a single undifferentiated field of interest.'" If one is committed to it, then one might easily accommodate Thomas's paintings to this description, and in doing so, offer Thomas entrée to the inner sanctum of modernist art. One might speak also in terms of mosaic, as does a major section of the 2016 Studio Museum retrospective of Thomas's work.[22] This approach emphasizes the act of assembly, of putting together pieces to create an image that subsumes and transcends its constituent parts. Others have appealed to phenomenology in order to describe these paintings: e.g., what it would *look like* to see flowers from an airplane, or to see the surface of Mars through radio transmission or (more recently) photographs.[23] These approaches find meaning in abstraction through an appeal to a universalized mode of vision and visual experience.

One could also of course speak of grids, and so doing, place Thomas within a long modernist lineage of artists who, as Rosalind Krauss claims, "committed their careers" to the grid. It is here that commentators, and at times Thomas herself, are able to appeal to that opposition between aesthetics and politics that was so dear to Steinberg's dominant formalist critics and curators. In this view, Thomas's work eschews "political content" in favor of "aesthetic form." In the literature on Thomas's work, this is often read as a black artist throwing off the shackles of a racist dictum that confined artists like herself to an essentializing representational politics so that she could then take her place within a canonical modernism—the happy side effect being that such inclusions never much disturbed the regulatory tenets of the modernist canon, including its criteria for exclusion. The grid, in this account, becomes yet another useful concept for anyone who wants or feels compelled to bracket Thomas's blackness in favor of a more humanist, unmarked notion of the artist.[24]

But if we pursue the ways that Thomas seems to be playing with machine vision, with views beyond the human, in spite or in disassembly of the human, then these works can also be understood as existing in parallel to and in some tension with the history of the graphical screen, itself seen as a particular site for the dis- and then reassembly of human-machine relationships. "Thomas' blue strokes [says Bridget Cooks, speaking of *Evening Glow*] are thick and painted closely enough together to create an interlocking screen."[25] Cooks, the author here, is probably appealing to a historically unspecific form of screen. Computer historian and media theorist Jacob Gaboury, discussed at length in the next chapter, gives us more precise language about the kind of thing a screen is, or was becoming in the late twentieth century:

> The computer screen is [also] a cathode ray tube phosphorescing in response to an electron beam, modified by a grid of randomly accessible memory that stores, maps, and transforms thousands of bits in real time. This is to say that the screen is not simply an enduring technique or evocative metaphor; it is a hardware object whose transformations have shaped the material conditions for our visual culture.[26]

Gaboury insists on this point because screens in their current, reified iteration as graphical are so easily overlooked in favor of their content, the image itself, as though screens were technologies of representation. Gaboury argues that screens are not ultimately representational, that they are not that kind of picture plane. This is precisely the argument Steinberg makes about the flatbed picture plane. They do not, that is, store and then present an image. The graphical screen isn't a picture technology, just as, I think, Thomas's paintings are not. Rather, "ordinary random-access computer memory (RAM) stores everything in discrete pieces—bits at the lowest level. But pictures do not fit well in one-dimensional lists, so a frame buffer stores the picture divided up into rows and columns of what we now call pixels—a 2D array of memory locations."[27] Gaboury elaborates: "Thus the frame buffer allows for random access to the procedural image, mapping the control structure of the grid onto the linear flow of the television screen through memory. This is the image made digital, the random access image."[28] Gaboury is explaining, precisely and nonmetaphorically, a key conceptual element of the graphical screen and all the forms of labor it was designed to host. In the visual culture of the graphical screen, the world is broken down into bits, organized as lists, which then must be reconfigured when something like an image or working surface is needed. The frame buffer aggregates an image world from quanta of information, but it is now an image world that begins to bend toward the needs of accommodating a particular kind of user. This is an operational image because the procedure of assembling the image *in* a graphical field, *as* the graphical field, is effectively the working image space, the graphical space, and not its precondition. This is the case because the mapping has to happen in what feels like real time. The user's actions in that field need to feel like they have direct, unmediated consequences on, and *in*, and *as*, the screen.[29] The graphical screen is, in other words, fundamentally interactive. This feeling was key for Apple and their vaunted user friendliness. Apple made a kind of culture out of the graphical field. This had the potential to make a user feel amplified or augmented, but also recognized as though for who they were; the computer deferred to the individuality of the user by way of the graphical space of the screen, a space in which one could move and think freely, a friendly space, a space that overcomes constraint—secondarily the constraint of using a computer, but primarily the constraint of difficult human labor itself.[30]

Try one final time to sense the slight but determinate interval between Thomas's experiments in paint and this history of the graphical—the tense proximity between those two bodies of research. In *Late Night Reflections* (1972), Thomas animates a canvas almost entirely with blues and yellows. One can easily imagine the visual referent that must have launched this painting: the reflection of artificial light in darkness—say, a dark wet street. But Thomas hasn't played the image out across the canvas in any way that recognizably tracks from that referent. The pieces aren't assembled that way. The mode seems neither phenomenological nor realist, expressionist nor abstract, if by abstract we mean nonreferential. It's more like Thomas took a single quantum of visual experience—artificial light reflected off wet pavement, maybe spied fleetingly—and played with it, worried it, ramifying it over and over again, starting again and again, spreading it out until it didn't end so much as become coterminous with the canvas itself—not a picture so much as a succession of visual phenomena, a kind of listing procedure. The picture seems less like a record of some translated experience than it does an attempt to reconstruct a new world from parts of a previous world, but in a way that also destroys our familiar, often bodily ways of reckoning with that other world. The role of the hand here is not to express what the eyes once saw, nor to sacrifice such expressivity to a cold, logical system. It is to take apart the elements of the experienced world while finding new ways to see, inhabit, and maybe even love those elements once they are discomposed. The tension here between assembly and disassembly, making something and destroying something, is key to understanding the way that Thomas's blackness persists as a determinant of her work, imagining a world out of the wreckage and pieces of an older world. And so it's part of my attempt to see her blackness as one of the multiply-imbricated sites of her labor, but operating beyond the tethers of essentialism, representational politics, or identity.

Still, one could notice how Thomas's Earth Paintings have all of the loosening and improvisational structure one might expect from an image that employs a traditional modernist grid as ballast. In this sense, one could even trace out a progressive loosening of structure around the grid over the course of the last years of Thomas's life, from, say, *Breeze Rustling Through Fall Flowers* of 1968 (plate 7) to *Garden of Blue Flowers—Rhapsody* from 1976. In this account, the grid exists as one pole of a polarity—it even, in a sense, instantiates this polarity as an engine of history: with the grid, on one side, and productive historical flux, perhaps even progress, on the other. "Once the grid appears," Rosalind Krauss says, speaking to this polarity, "it seems quite resistant to change."[31] For all of its novelty at the time, this discourse of the grid was also a renewal of a commitment to a basic model of modern, liberal personhood, where variety, difference, variance, independence, and *individuality* all struggled to win out over homogeneity, rigidity, commonality, and the so-called authoritarian personality. Debates about the grid, in other words, have often been debates over how to return the human to a particular form of individuality.

But by the eighties, when the graphical screen had established what kind of labor-space and what form of the human was going to be best accommodated by a coming computational culture, the grid was a different sort of technology altogether—better called a raster both because that is more accurate and because the connotational range of "raster" doesn't insinuate a structure so much as a field in movement, an environment in which to perform, to labor. It could no longer, for instance, be slotted into such simple oppositions as that between system and human. We could even say that the grid of the graphical screen, the picture plane as real-time configuration of the image as workspace, was one of the forces that helped shove aside this mode of oppositionality as a historical determinant. The grid or raster of the graphical screen was precisely a technology for opening up a new kind of historical flux, of creativity and novelty, one in which an imagined computer user could join with the computer in order to float free, unimpeded, and productive within the open field of the graphical screen.

The historical work of the grid in computational culture is, in other words, not to impose rigidity, tamping down the creative potential of the individual. In the scene of the graphical, the individual emerges, rather, from an encounter with the control structure of a grid now designed to allow "random access," which is to say, creative license, within the graphical field of the screen. In other words, individuality in a graphical milieu is a *product* of systematization, not its enemy or foil.

This shift in the constitution of the individualized subject is registered, although never endorsed, in the plural prepositionality of Thomas's rasters. The raster in Thomas's paintings is *what* one sees as well as what one sees *between* and sees *through*. Here again, a certain indecision about prepositions tips us off to the intensity of Thomas's experiments at the edges of both the human and the machine. For Thomas, as a black woman, the world was never arrayed as a set of resources to be mined. It was, rather, a set of limitations to be confronted, in her case, through acts of projective vision where the human gets discomposed by its encounters with technology. What is most striking to me, and does most to establish the sometimes-small gap across which Thomas's parallel aesthetics can operate, is that Thomas chooses to materialize these acts of projective vision—of experimental, procedural world-building—not within an ideology of freedom from constraint, but from what appears instead to be a rejection of the very idea that constraint or violence or exclusion is the defining polarity of freedom.

Thomas imparts this reconfigured form of human capacity to her viewers. We can sense this in how hard it is to adapt prepositions to her paintings. This is why in *Evening Glow* (1972) the blue tiles block our vision while being our vision; they become the matrix in which vision becomes possible as something else. And it is why, in *Grey Night Phenomenon* (1972, plate 8), unlike the famous grid that so grievously defined Rosalind Krauss's ambivalent modernism, the role of the grid is precisely to establish (and not by way of opposition) a real-time structure of adaptation that experiments with configurations of human and machine, with seeing as though from above or elsewhere. And, finally, it is why the question of the hand for Thomas—so vexing a question for so many postexpressionist painters and for so many black artists, and a central theme in the following chapter on Jack Whitten—was never a question of expressivity *in opposition* to the constraints of a system, be that a system of representation or of racism. In more ways than one, Thomas's was never a free hand. Later in her life, when creating the works I've been discussing, hers was a hand stiffened by age and severe arthritis and slowed in its coordination by damaged eyesight. But rather than strive to overcome disability, age, or her blackness, Thomas's hand refuses the *polarity* of expression and system, human and constraint, to practice possibilities of constrained personhood. Blackness, disability, and age are part of the enabling conditions for the work as well as the self in question. Thomas's Earth Paintings are a product of the negotiations that follow from this acceptance, but they are also the space where those negotiations are screened.

The project of the graphical screen as pursued at Stanford in the sixties, and Apple in the eighties, and by all of us ever since, was, on the other hand, explicitly about overcoming constraint. Specifically, it was about overcoming the limitations of the human body and the human intellect when faced with a postwar world that was more and more being imagined as a vast information space. Douglas Engelbart's graphical screen, and even more so, the Apple GUI that was to follow, were the arena in which humans might be trained to exceed the limits of their own intellectual capacity to organize and make meaning in a world now understood as an information network. "Augmentation" was the term that guided this process for Douglas Engelbart, and that best reveals his assumptions about the human subject he wanted to create. This provides one final understanding of Gaboury's notion of the "procedural image." The graphics of the computer screen were procedural in the sense that they caught the human up in an ongoing and cyclical process of training, such that human and computer would, over time, come to augment each other. We could say, to put it a little overschematically, that Thomas's procedure was no less about a certain kind of training, but that hers was a kind of training *in* and not *against* constraint.

To articulate one last time how I think Thomas's work exists in parallel to this larger history, in which personhood was rethought in relation to a particular form of the screen, I want to look at a quote that appears many times in the literature on Thomas. It appears in an article by the art critic Holland Cotter, writing in the *New York Times*. Cotter says, "When asked if she thought of herself as a black artist, she said: 'No, I do not. I'm a painter. I'm an American.'"[32] This statement is always read to mean that Thomas's humanity exceeded any exigency of her skin. It asserts that in a properly humanist view of the subject who can shed identities at will (with will, though the marshaling of will), we have to acknowledge that Thomas transcended her racialization. And of course she did. But if we locate Thomas's works in a scene where white personhood—which is to say, recalling Melamed and echoing Engelbart, that particular attitude toward success—isn't the default subject position, and see them, instead, in a scene where notions of the human were being explored, broken down, and reconfigured, then we have to qualify the relationship between Thomas's "Americanness," her labor as a painter, and her blackness. Her labor, in other words, does not transcend her blackness, even if it must exceed the strictures of her racialization.[33] We might even say that the locus of abstraction in Thomas's work wasn't in or against figuration, in or against modernism, but in and against the human itself. Thomas worked inside the graphical field, within the ligatures of its bits and the openness of its fields, not to augment the human or overcome any particular limitation, but in order to expand the prepositions of its possible inhabitation.

Nonrelational Blackness: Jack Whitten

3

For Richard Shiff

Alma Thomas was a grammatist. She invented prepositions for inhabiting her grids as a way to see whether the material and imaginative translations involved in moving between outer space, her garden, and her loose arrays afforded her any purchase on what it meant to live as black but not as a black painter, as a modernist but not a black woman modernist. Her hand, her gesture, the body in pain working with and inside constraint—these were critical parts of her practice. But her hand and her hand's gesture never stood apart from the technology of the grid, which meant it never simply stood against it, as some human residual against the incursion of the technical. Her brushwork is fragile, vulnerable, both energetic and relaxed, but I don't think it's made to operate as a bulwark against whatever is predatory about technology. Her blackness afforded no such fantasy of the human, no such refuge, as the constant biographical questions about being a black artist so aggressively reminded her. Her approach to technology was to test how it could be inhabited in order to see what distortions would be entailed, what possibilities might open up, which close down. So hand and screen technologies dance, refusing to embrace each other, refusing to reject each other, animated by a flowing, agile set of prepositions manifest in the ligatures of her painting, in the flux of surface, in the topology (never the background/foreground) of canvas. In this work, Thomas showed that the grid was a technology of personhood even as it abstracted personhood, a technology that played with the boundaries and constraints of the human, an operational process not a representational one.

If Alma Thomas was a grammatist of technologized life, Jack Whitten was a technologist. He made machines that generated images. Where Thomas began with her hand and worked through negotiations with arthritis, age, canvas, paint, grid, screen, outer space . . . Whitten began his technological experiments with gesture but without the hand. Gesture for Whitten dissolved the hand's relationship to the artistic self, to the self. In building machines for generating his images—fast machines with his developers, slow systems of accretion with his later tessellated works, all undergirded and fueled by his work on African sculpture pursued during summers in Crete—Whitten searched for other ways the self could be manifest in the world, other mechanisms. By "self" I mean—because I think Whitten meant—blackness, but not as an American identity (the usual machineries of blackness's conscription) so much as a form of gathering that emerged from and always in excess of history, and specifically in excess of slavery. "It's my culture that I am putting back together. Due to Slavery, it was fractured and its' [*sic*] my job as an artist to put it back together."[1]

Thomas worked on problems also confronted by early work on the graphical computer screen; her work exists somewhat at a distance, but squarely inside the logics of the graphical—in fact, we could say she was an early explorer of those logics, before they had been codified, before their generative relationship to individuated selfhood had been encoded by the GUI. Whitten understood his practice as engaged directly in the history and logics of screens: specifically, their pixelation; the nonrepresentational part/whole logics of what Leo Steinberg intuits as operational processes and Jacob Gaboury describes as procedural images; their processes and metaphysics of image generation and flux. And, maybe most concertedly, Whitten understood his work to be an exploration—restless, often frustrated—of the various ways that the human can dissolve into an imaging technology to then reappear on the other side, which is on the inside too. In such a process of transmutation, Whitten would try to rewrite the relationships between human and work, hand and canvas that he felt had dominated modernist art history, which is to say, had emanated from and been entailed by the whiteness of that institution. Whitten saw in digital technologies and the screen, in their nascent operations, a way to interrupt modernist painting and its cults of selfhood, its hardwiring of hand to individuation, to style, to expression. But also a way to interrupt all that stood opposed to, and so not all that far from, style and expression: concept, Idea, system. He sometimes referred to his work as nonrelational.

Whitten will help us see, by way of the restlessness of his example, and his commitment to the nonrelational and its own collective modalities, what it has meant for the tech industries to pursue research into the graphical field of the computer screen without this collectivist commitment, to pursue that research in the race-neutral or color-blind logics of early Silicon Valley cultures and the computational logics they have propagated into the present. Art historian Richard Shiff calls Whitten's relationship to technology an "inversion:" "This was his inversion: to discover through paint what the new sciences and technological modes may have concealed within them, a concealment demanding exposure."[2] And this, in turn, was Whitten's lifelong strategy for addressing the intractability of anti-blackness in the United States. He would look to technology, but a technology with an inverted relationship to the human. Addressing himself—his body, his senses, his energies, his historical formation—to the materiality of paint was the means by which Whitten experimented with techno-logics as well as with specific technologies. The graphical screen was at the center of this project.

In many ways, Jack Whitten's *Apps for Obama* (2011, plate 10), completed just seven years before Whitten's death in January of 2018 (he was seventy-eight), is the most overt, even literal case I will discuss in this book. Part of his Black Monolith series, *Apps for Obama* is the one artwork that actually, visually figures a screen, establishing a representational relationship with what I've so far described as a fundamentally, even ontologically nonrepresentational field (a reminder: nonrepresentational fields are not incompatible with representational—they nest just fine once the nonrepresentational takes priority). In this case, we see the screen of a pocket-sized computer, magnified to massive proportions (84 × 91 in.): an iPhone with its adapted and stylized but fundamentally consistent graphical interface. With the smartphone, the sort depicted here— although we see only the screen, not the hardware of the phone itself—the graphical environment becomes what it seems to have always wanted to be: part playground, part gerbil wheel for the hand itself, requiring only the slightest flicker of will to operate, to activate.[3] This is why Jim Hodge refers to Lauren Berlant's concept of "lateral agency" to describe the gestures associated with smartphone use: with barely more than a flicker or twitch of the will, people scroll, drift, get absorbed, and move but with no particular intention except the intention to have no intention if only for a single moment of self-abeyance.[4] The more one sees people operating touch screen phones, the less the concept of will seems relevant to a discussion of labor or even life once it inhabits graphical fields. Liberal values concerning will and choice and the freedom to exercise either may envelop Silicon Valley like an atmosphere, like a history. But as a technical matter, the products turned out by that industry have never not been in the business of circumventing will as the software of personhood, even while supplying people with various ways to feel that their lives and livelihoods depend on choice, self-discipline, and creative gumption now more than ever before.

With the touch screens invoked by Whitten's painting (presaged by but not equivalent to the mouse), hand and personhood come into a newly pressurized relation. *Apps for Obama* evokes the hand in a way that almost no other Whitten painting did—it seems almost to supplant the eye as the human organ most insistently addressed by painting. But if it evokes the hand, it also references its circumvention by and in the graphical: the way that in a graphical environment, the hand becomes less the instrument of an interiority seeking expression (although this will be how it is marketed), and more the platform for a suite of gestures that, in manipulating data, generate data and thus regenerate personhood from a new, proleptic basis.[5] It took the data industries to operationalize this process; but the graphical field made it possible, had always envisioned it.[6] Whitten here evokes the hand and the hand's fate in a graphical field, but he doesn't tell anyone, least of all Barack Obama, how to use the apps Whitten has arrayed for their benefit.

Whitten spent a great deal of time trying to excise his hand from the act of making a painting. This effort was an integral part of Whitten's lifelong work to discover various resonances of what he called "nonrelational and nonreferential" abstraction. In a sense, Whitten wanted to digitize touch, abstract it, precisely in order to refound the self on some other basis, untethered from gesture, from touch, from the manual. But most of all, untethered from all of the expressive entailments that seemed so inevitable for a painter working during the sixties and seventies, where a conjunction in the histories of painting, blackness, and the civil rights movement placed a great deal of pressure on the relationship between selfhood and expression.[7]

All of Whitten's work emerges from an effort—protracted, iterative, never all that linear—to learn how to connect his experiences as a black man, born in what he called the apartheid of the US South, to the procedures and outputs of his abstractive practice.[8] He has declared that "abstraction is the only possibility for this type of situation [where his art, as he said, must be 'part of the total structure of things'], with figuration we are forever depicting something other than the rock-bottom meaning of universality. For this technological age abstraction is the language."[9] He has generalized his approach to these problems as "digital abstraction," and refers frequently in interviews and his studio journal to digital technologies.[10] But most of this thinking, this painting, this experimentation, has taken the computer screen, the graphical screen, to be one of its primary loci—to be that which is figured, meaning abstracted. Across Whitten's work, and not just in *Apps for Obama*, Whitten seems to have taken the graphical computer screen, in both its visual affordances and its nonrepresentational, conceptual underpinnings and entailments, as the place to work out these questions. Not just his subject but the very scene and means of his experimentation.

But, given his commitments to abstraction as "the only possibility," what does it tell us about Whitten's abstraction, and about abstraction in digital environments, that Whitten wanted to reference the screen of the iPhone, right down to the detail of the operating system's virtual platform, the tilted plane above which the suspended apps hover? At a deeper or more microscopic level of referentiality, one might even cite, as many have, the affinity of Whitten's tesserae here with the pixels of a computer screen. In this painting, the figurative impulse appears to be layers deep: at the level of depiction (Whitten made an image or a prototype of the thing he appears to be thinking about), of appearance and phenomenon (it looks like what it references), and at the level of construction or materiality (it is seemingly made of the same stuff as the thing it pictures, it is built in the same way, that is, from pixels or bits). Whitten, in other words, not only figures the screen but builds it up from bits.

It will turn out that Whitten had alighted on a mode of abstraction that isn't at odds with figuration or referentiality, but that constructs a new environment *for* figuration, becoming its condition of repurposed possibility. If he was never before or again quite as direct as he was in this painting, many of his paintings flirt with a kind of referentiality built on, built out of, abstraction—digital abstraction. His Black Monoliths, each dedicated to key figures in black life, reveal this relationship maybe most clearly, with their outlines, their tessellated forms that are both silhouette and massing working across a fragile border. In this, they can't but invoke a body, even a particular body, a black life seen in service of other black life—not an individual so much as a kind of social preposition, working across a fragile border. This form of abstraction was possible because Whitten never treated his practice or himself as opposed to or in any way outside of technology or forms of representation that were reorganized in the graphical field. Instead, he purpose-built scenes of digital abstraction into which he could disappear—as a black artist, as a modern subject of violence, as a product of the apartheid South, as a human always emerging from and exceeding the various ways the world had categorized him somewhere just outside of the human—only to reappear as though inside the graphical environment in different conjunctions of labor, technology, and blackness. In this, Whitten's work parallels, while inverting, the valences of relation and selfhood in the longer and more expansive history of the graphical screen—working those experiences in another direction, where the self is not enveloped, aggrandized, and renewed by the graphical environment, but dissolved.

On the screen of *Apps for Obama*, enlarged to the scale of three doors hung as a triptych, there are fourteen squares, rounded at the edges, hung at the top of the painting—these, in their geometry, most closely follow Apple's own app iconography. Below these sit seven shapes that also must be read, in this context, as applications, apps, but whose geometry starts to bend and warp. It's as if Apple's infamously tight control over the graphic design of their environments has started to waver and gives way to something else, although only just. Below these are several different kinds of shapes, looking less and less like apps, but evoking apps in their proximity and gridded regularity: slabs of quartz, of crystal, of matter shaped by geological force; rectilinear but angular forms with what appears to be a fold in their upper left corners, making these shapes look both flat and pliable, as though they were paper; and in the bottommost row, four perfect circles, varied in color, spaced evenly, and centered on the complete expanse of the triptych. All of these hang neatly in space, adhering, despite their variance, to the invisible but structuring grid of the graphical screen. The virtual platform on which the apps sit is constructed of white tesserae outlined in red. Referencing Apple's iOS 4 and 5 from 2010 and 2011, the platform is a rectilinear shape made to appear as though it recedes into a background, giving it and the space in which it sits a rough but distinct dimensionality. This is the only aspect of the painting that does this kind of work, and one perverse effect of its dimensionality is that it highlights how dimensionless the rest of the painting is. What we must then read as the background of the screen is largely blue, lighter shades at the bottom, darker at the top. If this is a screen, it's activated, turned on, ready for use. All of the preceding is, of course, rendered in the language of representation—one of the painting's idioms for sure.

The whole emerges from the procedure Whitten first began to develop in the nineties: breaking up dried acrylic sheets, which he continued to call his "slabs," into small frozen chips of paint, and constructing the painting by laying down those tesserae like mosaic tiles. Such a procedure makes sense of a crucial verb shift for Whitten: he often said he didn't *paint* but rather *made* paintings. The difference is subtle but important. To start to make sense of it, we could say that Whitten didn't apply paint to brush and brush to canvas; he made paintings appear. Sometimes this happened instantaneously, almost photographically, as in his earlier Slab paintings. Sometimes it happened with painstaking slowness, bit by bit, as in *Apps for Obama* or any of his Black Monolith series.

When Whitten made the painting, Obama was in the third year of his first presidency. According to Gallup polls, his approval ratings were significantly lower than his disapproval ratings.[11] As Whitten says, "he was in trouble." Whitten later recounts in the same interview with the Museum of Contemporary Art San Diego how he set out to create a device, meaning this painting, to "help the brother."[12] Here we move through the representational and toward the animistic: toward the idea that this isn't primarily a representation but a device to be used. Perhaps that makes it less figurative, perhaps more, uniting figure and figuration, as any graphical field aspires to do.[13] Nevertheless, the work seems to stand in some concrete relation to a thing in the world—a graphical screen, that device—call it representational, figurative, or animist. But what kind of referential or figurative field *is* a graphical screen? That question hangs over this book. Given the graphical field's availability as a site for self-investment, for the making and remaking of the self by way of what Gaboury calls the "random access image," given the way that the graphical screen produces a feeling that it is not blank or empty so much as a manifestation or extension of the user's will—a theater, as Brenda Laurel has conceptualized it, for the elaboration of the self—it would seem that the graphical screen is neither an object nor a referent in the world so much as it is a space of production, a site for the labor of self-investment and creative expression. This is one way to begin accounting for the utter stillness of *Apps for Obama*: Whitten renders the space available, but without the investment in any particular mode of use, or the forms of personhood built up as the product of those modes.

"Digital abstraction" hints at this shifting relationship between abstraction and representation.[14] The ostensible reasons are maybe too evident: composed of discrete parts, countable, quantified, discretized, pixelated, Whitten's paintings are synthetic things, acts of translation or conversion, converting the manual, the African, the African American, particular black figures, a history of blackness, even digital screens themselves into another realm, which we may call digital or abstract, conveying these things as so much information, measured in bits. In fact, in this sense, all the artists in this book—Thomas, Gaines, and Mehretu too—are digital artists. All are committed to building up from bits, and all work through and with and within what Bernard Stiegler, following Jacques Derrida, calls *discretization*: organizing the flux of "chance" into a sometimes fragile, sometimes robust grammar. "Chance" is Du Bois's term for that which strains against knowing, against capture by a grammar (for him, a sociological grammar), for that which edges knowledge, teaching us about the limits of our capacity to know, to organize, to capture, precisely to grammatize in Derrida and Stiegler's sense.[15] R. A. Judy describes how Du Bois had to learn how to see his black subjects not as the problem to be solved by sociological concepts with their universalizing ambitions, but as the figures who, precisely in their unfitness for those concepts, open up other ways of knowing altogether.[16] In this, they scatter sociology, making it something new, something better. Du Bois here offers us the means to rethink the digital. In the black life that Du Bois studied, the discrete black individual isn't that which, in being collected into a field or population, adds up to a society and thus to sociological knowledge. The black individual is precisely that which turns knowing toward the unknowable, "cutting a bias across the field" as Judy puts it—unruly, improvising the laws that would govern that life, and so making that life less governable.[17] Insofar as the digital maps a relation, say between chance and system, black life occasions that relation's inversion or involution.

I think it's right to say that Whitten's "digital abstraction" works this involution of the analog and the digital because Whitten saw possibilities in it for inhabiting and reworking blackness in the present tense. He, like Du Bois, was forced to rethink his own particularity in relation to the social broadly, and the history of art more specifically. Du Bois's method: let the blackness of the individual undo method to trace the limits of knowledge. Per Whitten's method, "allow the paint as material to take care of the black thing" (studio log, October 8, 1998).[18]

Whitten's early abstract expressionist phase coincided with his arrival at Cooper Union in New York City in 1960 and was inextricable from a search—following his departure from Alabama and the violence directed at the civil rights movement—for his own identity as a black artist. After this phase and self-consciously working against it, Whitten's work moves through a series of procedures that lend themselves neatly to art-historical categorization within a oeuvre secured by an artist's proper name: his gauzy Ghost paintings starting in 1964 (often called *Heads* now), immediately after having graduated from Cooper Union, which were shelved and didn't get exhibited for several decades; his colored slabs of the 1970s (first exhibited in 1974); his monotone slabs, one-liners, and toner paintings of the late 1970s, also known as his Greek Alphabet series, which emerged out of his work with the Xerox Corporation in Rochester, New York, in 1974 and which Whitten sometime called his "geometric spectral" works; his return to vertical or easel painting in the 1980s; his mosaic or tesserae paintings and Black Monoliths of the 1990s; his paintings of e-stamps and technologies like the phone screen and digital compact discs from the aughts. And all along, as the world discovered with the Baltimore Museum of Art exhibition *Odyssey*, curated by Katy Siegel, Whitten made sculpture (mostly in Crete, at what was to be his summer home starting in 1969). Whitten's avowal of sculpture as the primary motivator of his painting, and his interest especially in African sculptural traditions, finally undercut any narrative of sequential progress just as the *Heads* had done, proleptically, in the early 1960s.[19] This has all been well rehearsed. Although Whitten didn't get the kind of attention that would make a neatly chaptered description of his career possible until the latter part of his life. And much of this kind of attention to his career as such has come after his death in 2018.[20] America has always preferred to encounter blackness in the past tense.

In an interview with Courtney J. Martin, Whitten has this to say about the pivotal transition in his painting, from early neoexpressionist paintings to the digital abstraction of the slab and later the tesserae: "My use of tesserae, for example: it's a bit of information, no different from the information we use in our computers and so forth, it sits right alongside of it. To get to that, the sculpture led me to what I call the Slab, a sheet of acrylic I made in 1970. The minute you have that Slab, paint becomes three-dimensional."[21] So the slab preceded and included the tesserae that would define a later phase of his work; but the tesserae included and enfolded—in a sense remembered—the slab. And his sculptural practice energized his painting all along, allowing him to establish a connection to Africa and African practices all across his work.[22] So the art-historical language of progression through phases, punctuated by "breakthroughs," of the artist working progressively through modernism's problems, as though Whitten has always been welcome in that world, is not going to be enough here. There is movement and thought and an eye always on the art world that at first seemed so close and yet so far from his studio doors, a restless searching and a voracious scrambling for resources. By his own account, Whitten's work and movement through varied procedures was motivated less by modernism's problems (including those of history, oeuvre, and seriality) than by experimentation with blackness and the blurry outer boundaries of the self. All of which was located inside a set of sociopolitical problems defined and emblematized by contemporary digital technologies, the graphical screen central among them, acting as both metonymy for technology more generally, but also as its own singular problem set within the aftermath of sixties' civil rights politics. Whitten was, in other words, working precisely and consciously between blackness, the graphical screen, and that screen's recuperation of white selfhood.

As with Alma Thomas's paintings, Whitten's tesserae and slabs force us to ask what vocabularies we have for conceptualizing bits that form a field—a question that conjoins questions of collectivity with questions of digitality, as does the graphical field itself. Consumer/mass, part/whole, citizen/nation, individual/community, work/series, nation/world, person/ race—all can seem to partake of a part/whole logic, with the smaller element comprising component parts of the larger, adding up to it in order to then be subsumed by it. Even within an expanded logic of *the whole is greater than the sum of its parts*, the parts still add up, but just not to enough. But this logic isn't Whitten's (neither in his artwork, my primary point of reference here, nor, I suspect, in his response to civil rights politics— although this latter point can't be more than speculative given how little Whitten has said about that time in his life).

In the 1905 essay introduced above, "Sociology Hesitant," Du Bois confronted these problems in the context of the nascent discipline of sociology and his own attempts to make sense of the data about black life he had gathered in Atlanta and Philadelphia.[23] The bit in that work, what Du Bois calls "that singular unit of highest human interest," is what he calls "Individual Man."[24] The field is sociology and its abstractions, to which populations must conform or become illegible, and into which the life worlds of individuals must disappear in order to generate sociological understanding. Du Bois finds two paradoxical, and explosive, forces nested inside "Individual Man": "the evident rhythm of human action," but also "the evident incalculability in human action." Frustrating as this fact was for Du Bois, his essay "Sociology Hesitant" announces the importance of being brought up short by the individual, of being reminded of the limits of what it's possible to know. Data must gather around this individual, but it can never fully subsume it: something remains. Far from being defined by autonomy or choice, Du Bois's Individual Man was defined by its indefinability, by the maddening and productive obstacle that figure posed to all attempts to gather people up into populations, as subjects of knowledge, thereby subject to that knowledge. This incalculability was Individual Man's mode of collectivity. R. A. Judy beautifully announces the fact and the paradox of this mode of gathering: "The celebrated 'doubleness' of the Negro is about being in a situation of ceaseless movement and ruses. Being a problem, being the Negro problem, that is, involves style. It is about cutting a bias across the field without there being a determinate reference by which to judge the opponent's strength—at times, one's opponent seems infinite in power, and at other times frail and seemingly without any autonomy."[25]

Whitten seems to be thinking along the lines laid down by Du Bois. Each tessera becomes its own slab, carrying in itself the weight of the acrylic sheet, remembering that sheet. So when we imagine Whitten arranging tesserae to create a work like *Black Monolith III for Barbara Jordan* (1998, plate 11), we miss something if we see an artist building up a picture from component parts, as in a mosaic, even if the effects are easily confused. In one kind of mosaic logic, which is also a socio-logic of the sort Du Bois was trying to dissolve, parts are incomplete, fragmentary; their presence in the final picture renders them fragmentary after the fact, whatever their status prior to composition. Each tile in this logic is the equivalent of a painterly gesture; expressive in its way, adding up to something, if slowly and mediated by other parts of the body than just hand and wrist united in gesture. One could then attribute something like style (the accretion of particularity in accumulated gesture) to the cant of any individual tile, their spacing. And this attribution would grant individual tiles the kind of autonomy enjoyed by the brushstroke. One could imagine a replay of modernism, this time in the medium of the tile: the picture comes apart, individual marks stand out while they still vestigially add up, marks get invested with authorial agency so that when they split from representation to take up their place finally in abstraction, there the author is, an autonomous remainder. This was likewise not Whitten's path. It was the path he set out to undo.

We could say that Whitten's sense of collectivity is situated otherwise, as is his sense of the particularity of black life. Both are the product of hard reckoning with what it meant to be a black artist who worked the way he did, and to be black in a world whose logics were increasingly dominated by screen technologies, by the graphical. We could also say, relatedly, that his sense of personhood is situated otherwise, pulling ever away from subjectivity and toward a more experimental selfhood, expanding the space, the breathing room that others have also discovered between subjectivity and personhood, which spacing Fred Moten understands precisely as the insurgency of blackness, its very work and being. Whitten sought out other ways of assembling collectivities—not identities accumulated in a commonality, and certainly not the universalist blankness of an unmarked collective humanism. Something more like bits in a graphical field, which he put in the service of and saw as an extension of the ways that blackness could be understood as making space between subjectivity and personhood—space, precisely, for life. "Allow the paint as material to take care of the black thing" (studio log, October 8, 1998).[26]

While it's closer to right to say that each tessera is a whole, a whole canvas, a complete sheet, a photograph of Whitten's thoughts; they are not wholes in themselves. In *Black Monolith III for Barbara Jordan*, the tesserae are, for instance, taken together and individually, galvanized by and to Barbara Jordan, although not to any particular trait of her biography (1936–96, lawyer, teacher, civil rights leader, first southern African American woman elected to the US House of Representatives, child of Houston's Fifth Ward, twenty-year partner to Nancy Earl and 2012 inductee into the Legacy Walk, an LGBT monument in Chicago). Whitten liked to say that the painting contained Jordan, that she was in the paint that he poured to lay down the slab that would, in turn, through division, sometimes with a hammer, sometimes with a knife, become tesserae. The painting is 69 × 65½ in., or more than five feet on each side and not quite square—in fact a pentagon with a very gently peaked top edge. Though flat in general orientation, though arrayed on a wall in a posture of outward visual display, the surface is anything but smooth. Tiles are variously raised, uneven, a topography—although maybe not even that unified. Tiles cant away from others at angles that are not repeated or echoed by neighboring tiles. The result is a nearly patternless surfacescape, chaotic, which only means patterned but not discernibly, which only means scattered, the whole containing both Jordan and the scattering that is remembered by each tessera. Patternless, then, or anyway, not patterned for humans—"'there is a proposition here, it is unclear.'"[27] Whitten explains this chaos as a way to direct the light, each tile a kind of reflector, each tile creating its own space, its own room or vestibule—complete, but not in itself.

But it's also clear that the tesserae are semiregularized in shape and size: roughly rectilinear, roughly arrayed in a continuous grid without interruption except the interruption of color, laid along rough but unerring X and Y coordinates (this latter is not the case for all the Black Monoliths). Diagonality, sinuous turns, curves that feel analog, washes—all of the soft vocabulary of painting comes by way of color more than tile. Colors wash across tile, softening their isolation; but then, tiles cut against colors, insisting on their discreteness. Clusters of black tiles; punctuations of a single yellow tile incrementally bigger than its immediate neighbors; fleet arrays of green tiles, all framed but also internally rent by planes of white that are only white from a distance and in blunt contrast, but up close are actually mottled black and white, averaging out at something like gray. Spacing shows through the tiles as a uniform black, even a void, but also as a filamentary network of lines as containing net. These filaments pulse forward, escape back, backgrounded and lost amid the more than seven thousand tiles, laid down individually. The greater expanse, the field, contains those tiles, holding them even while separating them.[28] Whitten says that the Monoliths "memorialize" their subjects.

Remembering the logic of pixel and raster from chapter 2 and the discussion of Leo Steinberg and Jacob Gaboury, we might say that each tessera remembers Barbara Jordan, memorializes her—rendering her as memory. Not a part of Jordan, nothing that would pretend to add up to Jordan or even attempt to produce her equivalent, but remembering rather their own place in the overall field. This requires remembering also the coordinates by which a tile is set within and set loose from the surrounding tesserae. Remember, from Gaboury, that pixels are instructions, not parts of whole images: procedural not representational.[29] Each tessera is a world, Barbara Jordan herself, in this precise sense: taking their place as reflected, directed light, remembering a coordinate location that in turn remembers every other location. Tesserae remember each other. There is a model of personhood here which is at the same time a model of collective being. In being for Barbara Jordan, the work is toward her. In being toward her, it carries a memory of its generating engine, Whitten himself, but less Whitten as artist than Whitten as himself a product and memory of Jordan—someone whose life and work were made possible by hers. This reciprocally renders Barbara Jordan as herself a coordinate map of all who remember her, everyone touched by her. A monolith stands alone precisely to be seen by all around; by definition a monolith never stands apart. An authoritarian monolith is one that forgets these connections, erases them. "Barbara Jordan" in this portrait is the name for and body of everyone whose work and life remembers her. An improper name. A monolith is a set of instructions for how to remember what forever and already dissolved its autonomy.

In the previous chapters, Jacob Gaboury guided us to a vocabulary that reworked the part-whole conception of the ways that pixels exist within the field of the graphical. In the graphical field's different logic of collectivity, the pixel remembers its place in a coordinate raster field. When it is issued instructions from the computer, it stores those instructions as memory. Those instructions themselves form a kind of ghostly memory of the entire field precisely in being coordinated. Coordinates imply the field, and are never just *of* it or *in* it. So while pixels are a part of the field, their primary logic isn't that of the portion or part. The pixels are not, to put this another way, put there by hand; there was never a conscious apportionment or composition.

In some ways, the graphical screen reduces the body to little more than a hand: acting by way of the intermediary of key, mouse, and cursor. In other ways, the hand itself, so discretized by the mouse, is precisely the protocol that allows a body to enter into the vast informatic imaginaries of the graphical field. And the hand's ongoing lamination to agency by way of expression supports the sense that, with the personal computer, an "augmented" form of the human might come into being. In 1987, Susan Kare's "clicker" icon first appeared in Apple's HyperCard software, later to be replaced by the famous darted glove of Apple's operating system and the world's most well-known graphical screen. As Stephanie Boluk and Patrick LeMieux discuss in *Metagaming*, the white glove cursor of Apple's early graphical screens can be connected via a straight historical line, a simple iconographic link, to the white glove of Mickey Mouse.[30] It was in 1928, with *Steamboat Willie*, that Mickey Mouse first donned the three-darted white glove and assumed the voice of Al Jolson's *Jazz Singer* (1927). Apple's gloved hand, while amputated from the blackface of Mickey Mouse, retains its whiteness and its three darts. That white glove would become the prothesis for the user of Apple's graphical interface, and a direct descendant of Engelbart's own mouse and cursor. In a way, Apple simply granted an iconic visualization, on screen, for what had already been implied by Engelbart's own system, where the hand manipulates the mouse in order to manipulate the cursor. Just in case users had missed the implication that the graphical screen was to accommodate their body, Apple literalized this icon in the form of the white glove, a blackface prosthesis. As Boluk and LeMieux argue, "GUI elements like the Master Hand not only point to the discourses of twentieth century racism but, once embedded within the technical circuits of electronic forms of entertainment, they also gesture towards the largely invisible circuits of production dependent on blood and labor from the Global South."[31]

What's not hidden, and what was so apparent to Whitten as he was working out the relationship between blackness and his paintings, is the way the hand, in user-centered design, gaming discourse, and painting alike, is tethered to the active body, the expressive and able body, the body that enacts its will on the world through its dexterity, intention unspooling into action propagating effect. The graphical field of the computer screen and Apple's early cursor icon literalize this chain of transmission from and through the hand. Two capacities of whiteness are mobilized here: to take whatever histories and agencies one wants and call them one's own while erasing any racial histories embedded in the borrowing (it's just a white glove after all); and the audacity to assume such an uncomplicated link between interiority, intention, action, and effect. The graphical field was designed to extend that enchained action, an expression of whiteness itself, into the networked world of information.

To pursue this line of thought about the capacities of the hand, imagine a slide comparison. On the left, the painting *April's Shark* (1974, plate 12). On the right, *Mee I*, a painting from three years later (1977, plate 13). The historical record tells us that the techniques that produced both paintings were similar: a pool of paint resting in a perfectly balanced frame on the floor; what Whitten called a "developer" with its edge implements raking across and through that pool of paint; objects inserted beneath the canvas to register their interruptions of the movement of the developer, imprinting themselves upward through horizontal movement. The language of "developer" comes from a photographic idiom that Whitten consciously mobilized throughout his life. The wooden structure that Whitten calls his developer made images appear in paint. Here is Shiff describing the implement and procedure: "He raked the surface from a standing position in a single broad gesture (hands at a distance), using an improvised tool he called a 'developer' or 'processor' (for a small painting he could use a hair comb or afro pick). The raking removed approximately half of the slip or surface overlay, line by line, leaving an image to appear as if instantaneously, with the traces of the objects underneath being exposed in the corrugations."[32] Sometimes Whitten would attach implements to the edge of his developer, altering the effects of the pull. This pull was strenuous, requiring a burst of physical energy. What Whitten wanted out of it was speed, the painting to appear all at once so that the self of the maker, particularly the hand's relationship to expression, would disappear or radically recede. All of this, the precise carpentry, the speed, the photographic idiom, was part of a lifelong project to play out the implications of a thought that occurred to Whitten around 1964. He recorded this thought on the wall of his studio so he could work out its implications slowly: "The image is photographic. Therefore, I must photograph my thoughts."[33]

1974, the date recorded for one version of *April's Shark* (Whitten made at least three), was the year Whitten was invited to work with Xerox, where he experimented with the gathering and dispersing properties of toner. That biographical fact is one way to motivate the shift one finds between 1974 and 1977, *April's Shark* and *Mee I*: the move from color to black-and-white tonalities and the evident, if difficult to pinpoint, transformations in his process for making or "developing" the image. In 1977, Whitten was still working through the implications of what he had learned at Xerox: the registration of shape and form in black and white; the quick drying toner and its impact on the possible temporalities of Whitten's procedures. The fact that the toner can be set with heat meant that, as Whitten says in his studio log from that year, "no fixative necessary + no change in color."[34]

But in 1974 he is still working with speed, motion, and the immediate registration of the image. There is still volatility in *April's Shark*, something fast, something pulled through acceleration and resistance, sheering, flaying, force meeting interruption. Nothing in the painting stops the strong wave of rightward movement, but much resists it. One of those resistances produces a supreme moment of equipoise, a vestige or reminder of another dimension of work: a rail-straight diagonal line extending top left to bottom right, intersecting the edges of the canvas millimeters above the right-angled corners. The same line appears in *Pink Psyche Queen* of the previous year (1973), although this time leaning in the other direction and more nearly vertical. These plumb lines appear as if from another order of motion and being altogether. They bifurcate the painting, not dividing it in two spatially so much as separating out orders of being. Things come to exist in different ways, through different means, but stemming from the same single pull of the developer. If the singular pull aims to excise the intentional self, the expressive self, the self made autonomous through an understanding of gesture as exteriorized interiority, it doesn't thereby render the product of that labor singular, unified around an Idea or concept. The developer's pull fractures the world (of the painting). Whitten forces gesture not to close ranks on itself. In this, he nudges painting to stay procedural, to resist representational logics.

Three years later and Whitten has made all of this violent motion stand still. With *Mee I*, in stark black and white, the image appears frozen. Something has appeared all at once and was immediately made to stand still—or, something has been transmitted in whole, *as* a still. The scanning process of the developer is a still a memory of this image, remembered by it, but now a distant memory. Process here goes underground, splits off from product as phenomenological residue, and so there seems to be the choice to ignore process if we want, just as we might ignore the size of brush Willem de Kooning preferred, or the technology of the computer monitor itself in favor of whatever works gets done in the graphical field. The stark tonalities are part of what stills the movement that otherwise pools and vectors in the wake of resistance to pull. The interruptions from below are here more regular, more vertical. They seem to succeed this time in stopping the horizontal forces that we know, nevertheless, have made this painting. The white lines are gently sinusoidal, but forever smoothed by the overall flattening effect of straining in those lines. Not just stillness then, as though it had always been that way, but speed stilled. Made static, held, as though in acknowledgment that it is being viewed in just this moment but no other. This is why there is a temptation, with this series of images, the Greek Alphabet series, to call them screens.

But the six-sided figure suspended in but also imposed on the lower left is something else. That is a creature of impress, not scan, not contact, not signal transmission. Whitten never allows a single descriptive idiom to generalize his paintings, just as he doesn't allow the compressed temporality of the developer and its operations reciprocally performed on the human laborer to thereby reduce that labor to a function or algorithm. All around this six-sided figure, there is a drama of information, of informatics, something struggling to emerge from what always threatens to be nothing, all noise no pattern, a drama of resolution. But in this rectilinear impress (a rectangle with a square notch cut from its bottom-right corner), we find a departure from this drama: a plane leaving its mark on another plane through wet contact. Removal: direct consequence of implied action. Topography, not planography.

In a sense that is both biographical and made more than biographical by Whitten's own interests in using technology to unseat the self (e.g., the self as authored by one's *own* biography), Whitten was channeling the procedure of the Xerox printers, trying to imitate them and inviting all remainders of that attempt to enter the field too: trying to imitate, in particular, their bent toward the freeze frame, the photograph, the still record, the copy, the inanimate, the scan leaning in the direction of the administrative, where copies are always needed to authenticate, to communicate, to coordinate across multiple bodies, projects, institutions. In this field, the stars whose circular unity punctuates the frozen scan lines are something of a mystery, and it's hard to know how they matter. At the very least, they are an interruption in the field of my descriptive idiom, and as such, as both cause and effect, they interrupt any smooth transmission of labor to and through the painting, as given in any description of it. But even IBM— infamous for a corporate rigidity so extreme, so blue-shirted and buttoned-up, that it inspired by its negative example the countercultural ethos of Silicon Valley—reformed its ways eventually, inviting something like personality, individuality, and creativity into its previously rigid protocols. So we shouldn't make too much of this apparent eruption of mystery out of what Du Bois called the rhythmic. We shouldn't, that is, rush to apportion the human to one side of this equation.[35]

For Du Bois, writing in 1905, trying to understand what the black data point does to sociology and its methods, the individual embodied two forces Du Bois could relate only through paradox: rhythm (regularity) and chance (singularity, contingency). The black individual was not to be defined as human against the machineries of rhythm (the universalizing machinery of sociology as Du Bois learned it). Blackness was always both, could never, in other words, exist simply in opposition to technology, machinery, pattern, rhythm. Justice for the people Du Bois loved was not to be found in recourse to the humanistic subject as some sort of shelter from the ways violence besieged blackness. So while Du Bois accused Auguste Comte's sociology of hesitating before the fact of the individual and the ways any individual exceeds sociology's ways of knowing, he ended up advocating for his own kind of "hesitant sociology": a sociology that hesitates before the subject of knowledge, and thus before the site and source of its own limitations. This is why the human, unburdened of the rhythmic machineries of race or blackness or technology, bit and field, was never a recourse for Whitten or for Alma Thomas. Such a figure was always a specter, deathly, an imprint or offset of whiteness itself.

Pursuing the slide comparison, and at the risk of bifurcating two procedures we know to be more intimately, complexly related, we might invoke Whitten's own language of skins or keloids, seemingly so descriptive of *April's Shark*, and so starkly, even conspicuously unfit for *Mee I*. Whitten thought of his slabs as skins, but less as a question of being (their ontological or object status) and more as a response to process: they act like skins when the developer rakes over the painting's surface, responsive like skin to impression, scratch, and bruise; keloidal not representationally but materially, paint coagulating into ridges under the developer's passage. The developer, whether afro-comb or squeegee, left scars on the skin of the slab. But *Mee I* was also a work that Whitten referred to, categorically, or within the categories that organized his experimentation over time, as a slab. The developer here scrapes black, exposing the titanium-white ground. Remember that Whitten sometimes called his developer a "processor." If this, too, is skin, it is skin simulated, transmitted from one medium to another through some informatic process. A digital process insofar as the results in *Mee I*, that *are Mee I*, feel coded, as though the marks that articulate the painting have been sent through a signal processor, appearing here under instruction and sequence rather than speed and facture. Except for that patch (with every Whitten painting, there is a phrase that begins with "except . . . ") which reads very much like skin, skin pressed into and then removed slowly from a wet medium—a puckering, as though a patch of a David Hammons Body Print had been surgically removed and grafted here (works that Hammons was making nearby in New York City at the same time).

Here is Whitten: "I made a vow that I'm [going to] stop doing these gestural paintings altogether. . . . My solution was to expand the gesture while taking my hand out of it."[36] Richard Shiff extends this thought to *Mee I*: "Works of this type look like video screens with horizontal interference; but they are dimensional, not flat."[37] How does gesture have to expand to become or to produce a video screen? What is the gesture that would produce horizontal interference? When Shiff says that these paintings, the ones Whitten was making in the mid-1970s, look like screens, the key, with both the screen and the painting, is not "look like," not an image logic attuned only to outcome, output. The key is to ask about the labor implied by, even engendered in that statement. We know enough to know that Whitten didn't set out to make a painting that would look like a screen. If such an exertion of will toward a goal is relevant at all, it would be more appropriate to say that Whitten set out to design a process for producing a painting that generated a screen—but mainly to see what was entailed in that procedure, entailed for the human laborer. In fact, this is not unlike the way the screen itself embodies a procedure for generating a live environment in which a computer user sees oneself projected into a screen, learning to play and labor there. It's a distended, stuttering agency, deliberate, careful, and meticulous but only so that, at the right moment, an image or image environment would appear as though with no hand at all.

This is what Whitten calls nonrelational painting. He means that the relations that obtain in and as the painting aren't themselves a product of anyone meticulously planning those relationships, composing them, relating to them in a nameable way. Nonrelational is therefore a partial synonym for noncompositional. The individual marks that comprise the overall field of the painting of course have relations to each other, but they don't come to occupy that field by first relating one to another, as human design or as human imagination—however those relations might be motivated. Maybe one begins to hear here the strains of a post-Cagean aesthetic strategy. Nonrelational wasn't John Cage's language, nor that of any of the artists who pursued tactics that extend out of Cage's own practice (Tony Conrad, Robert Rauschenberg, Howardena Pindell, a few Minimalists). But the impulse to loosen the ties of intentionality to the act of making as a way of thinking about the self of the maker, to undo something in the coherence of the expressive self—this was a goal shared by many.

And while it's important to notice such convergences, it's equally important to notice, now, where those practices diverge. Branden Joseph, in his work on post-Cagean aesthetics, does refer to these strategies as "nonrepresentational." For Rauschenberg, in Joseph's account, the aim of creating a painting or combine or sculpture or theater performance was always to create little fissures in the edifice of the creative self, places that reveal its incoherence, and that thereby let difference in. Let difference *back* in, for the problem Rauschenberg identified, under the influence of theorists such an Antonin Artaud and Guy Debord, was a progressive sameness of experience driven by a supertechnologized capitalism. Working in neither a Minimalist phenomenological vein that might universalize the bodies that come to exist in the atmosphere of the artwork, nor toward a Greenbergian transcendentalist ideal where even the universalized body defers to the presentness of the artwork, Rauschenberg tried always to demarcate experience as split, self-differing, and singular precisely as such.[38] To the extent that Rauschenberg was concerned in his practice with the cathode-ray tube of the television, and Joseph makes a strong case that he was, it was to discover possibilities foreclosed by the monolithic field of the television screen and its homogenization of the conditions of reception. In Rauschenberg's frequent doubling of the transferred image, or in works like *Factum I* and *Factum II* (1957), paintings made at the same time to look as nearly alike as possible, the goal was to reveal the shadowy stubborn remainder of any attempt at homogenization, a kind of freedom impulse to be found in small differences, in the impossibility of sameness, and to do so by producing a scene of reception in which difference mattered, even came to be all there was to see.[39]

But as I argue throughout, the political problem posed by what Whitten sometimes calls "electronic scanning devices" was not only homogeneity.[40] If homogeneity (of experience, of personhood, of citizenship, of ideology) is the problem, then the implied (all but necessary) solution has to be singularization, individuation, and difference, as Joseph argues was the case in Rauschenberg's and Cage's work. But as research by Saidiya Hartman, Melissa Gregg, and many others has shown—in a parallel history whose imaginary is not dominated by the white fear of becoming the same— individuality has long been a machine for inscribing law onto and into the bodies of human subjects: laws of self-reliance, self-sufficiency, autonomy.[41] If autonomy was a goal pursued by modernist aesthetics, it was, at the same time, also a goal pursued by a constantly self-regenerating liberalism, from whose promises blackness has always been not just excluded but remaindered, so that even the beleaguered privilege of exclusion could accrue only to bodies who would eventually accept individuation as the price of admission into a tenuous safety or citizenship. And it was from that position, as remainder, as force to be tamed by some other means than legal enslavement, that black Americans were invited to share in the burdens of individuality.

The long history of this particular threat becomes explicit in Charles Gaines's work, the subject of the next chapter. In Whitten's work, his attempt to get his hand out of the painting, to work nonrelationally, wasn't part of an effort to clear space for the viewer, where the scene of reception begets an atmosphere of autonomy, and autonomy counteracts lingering threats of homogenization. It was instead part of a lifelong effort to dissolve the self into the field of his works to see what might come of such a dissolution, to see what might be built on its other side, but also to see what becomes of labor once nonaccumulation and nonpossession are included among its aims. Whitten's Monoliths were, in this framing, an attempt to discover forms of incorporative personhood or, as I have learned to call this from Gaines's work, contiguity. So Whitten circuited the relationships discoverable in his canvases through developer and slab, which is to say, through some externalized program that itself comes to inhere in individual mark and incident, not as unifying force but as giver of coordinates. The slab was not a discovery for Whitten because of its unity but because of its graphical possibilities, the ways that it opened up the field of the canvas to a variety of incident and movement. The developer was Whitten's first major strategy for working out the possibilities of the canvas conceived as field, and constructed as a slab. His tesserae were a later strategy employing a radically different temporality.

The computer screen has its own argot for this manifestation of labor, both as the predicate and distillate of the screen. The screen is not an image medium, is how Gaboury puts it. This is his shorthand for an argument that the specific technicity of the cathode-ray tube screen, as the interface to a computer, doesn't present an image so much as translate, on the fly, a set of instructions. And those instructions, being in contact with the pixels and raster of the screen through the buffer of memory, lay the groundwork for a responsive, real-time field of receptivity that allows a person to set themselves down anywhere on the screen, making the graphical screen into a field in which one's will is literally manifest as though without interference. Engelbart, for his part, admitted the interference of the computer as part of a training regimen; Apple brooked no such interference between their graphical field and the feeling of autonomy to be experienced in that field by their users. Here, again, is Gaboury's phrasing of it:

> Ordinary random-access computer memory (RAM) stores everything in discrete pieces—bits at the lowest level. But pictures do not fit well in one-dimensional lists, so a frame buffer stores the picture divided up into rows and columns of what we now call pixels—a 2D array of memory locations. . . . Thus the frame buffer allows for random access to the procedural image, mapping the control structure of the grid onto the linear flow of the television screen through memory. This is the image made digital, the random access image.[42]

The temporality of such an image is key to understanding the valences of the nonrelational for Whitten. "The frame buffer allows for random access to the procedural image."[43] The verbs that animate the materiality of the graphical field are all projective, future-oriented not in the sense of preparing for what's to come, but in the sense of potentiality, an open field for action. Black studies offers a language for the temporality of such an image, hinging on the question of historical priority or what Nathaniel Mackey calls "natal occasion." Thinking about and in such a temporality begins by thinking about how blackness proceeds out of slavery as its product, while also preceding slavery; it is that which surrounds slavery and survives it. Does black creativity exceed and forget its violent past or extend out of it, thus extending it as a kind of memory, what Christina Sharpe calls "wake work"?[44] Fred Moten has parsed this as a question of "anoriginality." Moten is here riffing on Nathaniel Mackey's own sense of a "insistent previousness evading each and every natal occasion."[45] Whitten's process, which is to say, his paintings, responds to such an insistent previousness, echoing it while issuing it. The procedure he invented and iterated over years to "make" rather than "paint" was part of his attempt to force painting to remember making, not in the mode of action painting and the trace of forceful, manly action, but in an ongoing attempt to dissolve, to distribute and dispossess, the self of the maker. Which is why we might also say that Whitten's sense of the nonrelational was nearly synonymous with Whitten's sense of blackness, his ongoing if obliquely pursued allegiance to black politics vectored through procedure, through paint and painting, through photographic speed and automaticity, and through his thinking, at turns both materialist and spiritual, about computer screens and the informatic milieu in which they have played such an outsize role. "Allow the paint as material to take care of the black thing" (studio log, October 8, 1998).[46]

When Whitten made the decision to get his hand out of painting, he was simultaneously making a decision to pursue black being, the process of being a black artist, through nonrelational means. Pursue it not, in other words, through the exertion of will, the arrogation of an individualized freedom, the possession of will and its deployment as possession, where will is assumed to be the only way to manifest human freedom. His blackness, his black past, his childhood in what he referred to as apartheid Alabama—all an insistent previousness that evades each and every natal occasion of his painting: present of course, but nonrelationally. This is not a blackness we can locate in gesture, through hermeneutics, through iconography, through recovery of something marginalized, or through exposure of the object of violence that would precede and so explain every action brought thereafter into representation.[47] Instead Whitten has us approach the question of his blackness, of blackness, which is to say, of the human, through the implements of his procedure, meaning, through his work. Labor's insistent previousness. Whitten was exploring what it meant to even talk about personhood, about racialization, when the screen was to be the space in which that manifestation of self was to be materialized, manifest, encountered. No longer a human manifestation, but neither fully machine; gathering but also dispersing in a raster: a random-access person. Were there possibilities here? Or just more traps? Whitten's answer was ultimately: both. And the difference between the two answers is sometimes hard to discern.

This is all no more or less true of Whitten's Black Monoliths, even if the sense of the raster and pixel feels more literalized in those canvases. Created across a wide swath of his career, the Black Monoliths are homages to important black historical figures, many, but not all of them, artists, many, but not all of them, friends. *Black Monolith IV for Jacob Lawrence* (2001, plate 14) divides, by a single stark red line of tiles, a jutting figure in white from a shimmering, chaotic grid of tiles in blacks, grays, and greens. An outline that holds the two fields of color at bay, containing one, limning the boundaries of another, while asserting an insistent previousness to both fields by the memory they contain of the slab they once were. The red outline is made from a single row of tesserae, red tiles. At 96 × 96 in., or 8 × 8 ft., the figure towers. If we're thinking about gesture in the sense that Whitten left behind in the sixties, gesture as relational, then nothing could seem further from the speed of Whitten's previous slabs than the methodical slowness of his monoliths, some of which he has said took him over a thousand hours to complete.[48] But the insistent previousness that evades the scene of laying down tile is the scene of breaking tile, generating the bits that will eventually encode the painting. And that moment of generating the tiles flashes back to, remembers, a previous liquidity, the pour of acrylic setting the pool that becomes the slab that will scatter into tiles.

On the day Whitten finished the Jacob Lawrence painting, March 31, he remarked, "It went much faster than I expected. Truly, Jake was with me!" The next day, in his studio log, he writes this: "In order to do what I am doing in painting, the painter must be able to go beyond the notion of self. They must take care of identity issues first, just as I did in the 1960s. Only then can one penetrate a higher plane."[49] Selfhood is aligned with identity in this line of thought, but these are precisely not things left behind in order to move forward; they are things that must be taken care of first, before anything else can happen, and so they accompany whatever happens next, another insistent previousness. Whitten refers here to his first years in New York City, after relocating from Alabama to attend Cooper Union. He has spoken often of those final years in Alabama as formative ones: the depth of violence he witnessed, the depth of white hatred of any manifestation of black resistance or even black life, the ways that even the most minor manifestation of black freedom, whether individual or collective, brought down violent retribution. He had marched with civil rights protesters there, and so had witnessed the police brutality that accompanied any assertion of black collective presence. He never said much more about those years of identity reckoning, except to say that they were extremely difficult, and that his art would need to emerge from those years as a kind of crucible.

Situated precisely at this point of emergence, for Whitten, was Willem de Kooning and his wrist, his gestural work, and the relational painting that de Kooning emblematized for Whitten—relational painting with its primary relationship to the self, a self that secures all the individuated marks in and as a unified field. The self emerges (e.g., as personality, as artist, as signature, as style, as value) from the chaotic field of the de Kooning canvas because the coherent self is thought to anchor those relations as a kind of self-possession. Like Gaines in the next chapter, Whitten objected less to the results of that painting than to the process by which the self seems to be imported into the painting in order to secure it. In this process, the self becomes extractable from the painting, almost its primary product, the individual distilled. Maybe Whitten objected to the way that, in de Kooning's relational painting, the self seems always to precede the painting, with the artist (or discourses of the artist) working to block the insistent previousness that enters Whitten's work by way of all the distantiating processes he invented to make room precisely for such a torqued temporality. It is hard to know what role, if any, the biographical de Kooning played in this process. But it certainly had to do with the secure relationship between whiteness and the kind of self-inscription and self-possession that whiteness both allowed and perpetuated, of which the artist was only one manifestation.

Whitten sought other modalities of selfhood. First, he needed to invent a process for making painting that would open up possibilities for who an artist was, using the "container" of artist to explore what kind of human could be invented. But he also was both inspired by and wary of coming digital technologies, most urgently (if we take the record of his own work as a guide) screen technologies. To think about how screens manifest images was an extension of his interest in how cameras manifest images, and this in turn grew out of his contrapuntal understanding of how an artist like de Kooning seemed to create his paintings. In that sense, his developer was always as much about scanning technologies as it was about photo technologies (although as Kyle Stine argues, those two image technologies were intimately connected[50]). And all these questions were undergirded by a driving sense of how to create space and possibility for black being, for what it could mean to be a black man, working in New York City, whose particular modality of work was painting. The screen was the place that Whitten returned to again and again to ask these questions and survey whatever answers would appear on or, better, *as* the canvas. In this sense, his earlier slabs seem to focus on the scanning process that occurs in the CRT screen while the later Black Monoliths, in a sense, zoom in on the relationship between pixel, image, and labor. *Apps for Obama* makes all these interests fluoresce brightly, as though Whitten were looking back and concretizing the problem that he had, after all, been inhabiting since the 1970s.

But a question nags: why shouldn't we think of what Whitten is doing as just composition by another name, either done extremely quickly (as with the early slabs) or extremely slowly (as with the Black Monoliths)? And if it is composition, doesn't the self enter back into the picture? Hasn't it, in the belated fame that Whitten has received? Hasn't this Whitten, now the subject of solo exhibitions, become the generator of the work, standing as the origin of the work? To watch a video of Whitten creating a Monolith is to believe, or find plenty of evidence for the idea that Whitten meticulously creates these paintings, and that in all the time it takes him to make them, he must have been thinking about conventional stuff, de Kooning stuff, relational stuff: composition, the allover field, the building of a world in paint, etc. But this is to misunderstand, or misapprehend, the collectivity of Whitten's work, the collectivity of the tesserae in relation to the final Black Monolith, and indeed, in relation to Jacob Lawrence or to Barbara Jordan or Édouard Glissant or any other of Whitten's dedicatees.

I think it's no accident that the identity issues that Whitten had to confront after his departure from Alabama, or in the later and consequent work of finding something beyond the self, were also, centrally, urgently, and concertedly, about collectivity—about trying to apprehend a form of collectivity that could coalesce around something other than the violence that galvanized the civil rights struggle or the freedom that seemed to be that violence's only proper corrective. A collective form that could coalesce around some other organization of black being. The graphical screen, for its part, occasioned a concomitant exploration of the possibilities for new forms of collective being—harder to see for that field's intensive focus on the individual, the personal, the autonomous knowledge worker as the node of a networked collectivity, but no less a kind of collective fantasy for all that. Whitten must have perceived this.

Engelbart's vision for the graphical screen was, in fact, the product of his attempt to think about a kind of protonetworked worker. The worker connected to other workers not via direct collaboration or dialogue, but because the graphical field promised to become a space where people could relate to one another through information. When Engelbart spoke about teamwork, he meant, first and foremost, the man-machine dyad.[51] Engelbart configured the screen as an open space so that individuals could generate and interact with information space in their own way, but always connected to other knowledge workers by a two-way channel: information flowing from their work, and information flowing from others to inform the individual's work. While part of the technical marvel of his famous demonstration (discussed in the introduction) was its networked quality, what Engelbart was also demonstrating was the capacity of the individual to exist inside an information network. The human becomes the node; other humans augment that node's capacity to work in the information space created by their collective copresence but manifest only for the individual working at a single computer terminal.

By the time Apple transforms the graphical screen into the default space for all computing and instantiates the graphical field of that screen as the space not just for knowledge work but for life itself, this networked collectivity had become attenuated to such an extent, and the figure of the individual worker so mythologized and enhanced precisely by their working relationship with the personal computer, that it would be hard to remember these beginnings of the graphical screen . . . until the internet came along to literally link all personal computers. But the graphical field had always been the internet's training place, where people would learn how to find themselves amid networks of information, where traces of other people's labor were rendered as resources for the self. It's not, as has often been said, that there is no society under late twentieth-century liberalism, or neoliberalism; it's that the self enters into relation with others precisely as a self-sufficient node of information, the links between them instrumentalizable, disposable, and reroutable.

Perhaps seeing that issues of collectivity were entailed in any exploration of the self, Whitten also discovers a form of protocollectivity in a collaboration with machines that was part of a larger and longer attempt to rework the self and its relation to labor. The developer, as he has so often said, was part of his procedure for turning himself into a camera. The camera stood for an automaticity that, through speed, expunged the presence of the self in the final work, or anyway, radically attenuated the way that the self might otherwise come to inhere in the work under the guise of a proper name. In his early slab work, Whitten begins to create the conditions for a form of black being that might inhere not in violence or in any of the defensive postures one is forced to take to survive violence (e.g., freedom from), but in a disappearance of the self into the fields in which it comes to remember and be remembered by an insistent previousness, the random-access image. But rather than disappearing to later reappear as an individualized node of production, augmented and enhanced, Whitten works toward a disappearance that scatters the self across reconfigured historical fields, where jazz and African sculpture displace the postexpressionist artist in a technologized modernism, where the self obtains a self-obviating form of control (e.g., over his own dissolution) while being unburdened of freedom and its ghost of freedom *from*. Here, blackness becomes less the name of a collective identity that a working practice, a form of making, something operative rather than substantive.

Whitten the carpenter. Whitten the camera. Whitten the pourer of paint. Whitten the developer, straining against friction to produce speed, to get out in front of the self in order to also lag behind it. His work is reduced to these actions; no, it expands out into these actions, a capillary movement, filling a space left open once the usual pathways to and from the self have been blocked. The first slab experiment to be entered into Whitten's catalog, *Untitled* (1970), was acrylic on linen and relatively small: 25⅝ × 23¼ in. Browns, blues, blacks, whites, orange . . . these make up the acrylic pool of the slab. From the evidence of the results, the developer raked over the surface quickly and without too much interference (interrupters would come later). Something caught and delayed the developer at the bottom of the canvas, just right of center, where a jagged upward curve in the developer line seems to drive in the direction of up and out. Once noticed, such jags appear all over the canvas, evidence of the resistance that the drying pool of acrylic did offer. After his first slab experiment, the implement attached to the edge of the developer must have gotten much finer (or the pressure applied, far lighter). The grooves disappear, dissolve into a finer resolution. One result is that the painting, already made in one pull, a single gesture, is even less divided into parts, rows or furrows. The painting now seems to take on a high-resolution blur, a field whose component parts are too small to be reckoned with individually. The color palette shades far more to browns in *Second Testing (Slab)* (1972): white, some pink, orange, light blue. Muted. Here again, distinct color zones are evident. They are there for themselves, but they also inevitably invoke something being worked up and out through resolution and irresolution, an image remembered by its parts, coordinated and mapped more than composed.

I say "inevitably" because resolution (rather than composition) was precisely the effect Whitten was after with his developer. Resolution is a nonrelational artifact. It's not put there and it's not an effect of perception; it's an effect of a particular congregation of bits, of parts, and the machinery organized to make those bits appear upon receipt of certain instructions. *Testing (Slab)*, from later in the same year, 1972, has fewer distinct color zones. It reads as a kind of smeared red-brown, with the developer picking up a few stray lines of white near the top of the canvas, dragging them horizontally at a seemingly perfect right angle to the canvas's edge. In October 1972 Whitten writes: "I JUST WANT A SLAB OF PAINT" (studio log).[52] Here there are so many horizontal lines that they are now not lines but pulses, something too fast for geometry. Later in the 1970s Whitten would begin to gouge his slabs before developing them, leaving jagged areas where the substrate layers of paint aren't surfaced by being drug across the surface, but are rawly exposed—skin is what Whitten would sometimes call this effect—"keloids," a scarring.

As Whitten often notes in his studio log, the process of preparing a slab was complex, laborious and time-consuming. It was the first and most intensive locus of experimentation. Back-breaking, in fact, and Whitten's later move from the floor to the wall with his tesserae works was in part a concession to what his body could take, a softening or accommodation, a gentleness introduced to the process—just as Howardena Pindell's video drawings and Alma Thomas's grids are themselves concessions while also signaling a willingness to move with and in constraint. But before this, before the body gave way to something else, much of his time was spent on the floor—all of his time really. In the end, it was always the developer that made the painting, if by "end" we mean that point in the process most intensely harried by persistent previousness. Whitten was after a nonconscious process but still a kind of control, where that control would be leveraged entirely toward the dissolution of the self and all of its old habits of control as self-possession. That apparent paradox would never leave Whitten's work or his thinking about it. To give up on gesture and relationality and the self was not to give up on a measure or form of control. Control was the condition of possibility for what he would, time and time again, refer to as freedom. His was never a selfless art, even if he wanted to disintegrate the self in every painting. The idea was to see what possibilities might be opened up when the self is buffeted by technologies, while feeling out the associated dangers. "In all truth, this blackness is my major asset: my survival in the modern technological society depends upon it" (studio log, January 14, 1999).[53]

In the move to what he once called "acrylic mosaics" (studio log, November 14, 1991), Whitten commented: "I am investigating a concept of digital automatism" (studio log, January 4, 1992).[54] And later, speaking of the same procedure: "Each of my chips of paint is a note carrying both sound + light" (studio log, October 3, 1997).[55] It's striking that Whitten should refer to automatism in relation to these works, seemingly the least automatic paintings imaginable. How to imagine an automatism sustained over the thousand-plus hours it could take Whitten to complete a "digital mosaic," as he sometimes also called them? But to stay with that thought will force us to more directly confront the temporality of labor in these paintings, and in all of Whitten's work, and should once and for all interrupt the suspicion, if one is lingering, that these are Whitten's most laboriously composed works. Do we have to imagine an artist thinking meticulously and compositionally during those hours, willing the painting into being through a kind of determined labor? Or do we have to imagine the rote self-abnegation of a conceptual practice, the artist submitting himself to the rules of a procedure and following it out? Actually, while art history has tended to figure these as the choices available to an artist in the sixties and seventies, an often starkly and polemically defended difference (e.g., Michael Fried's antitheatricality and literalism), they both point to a related model of the self. The first defines the self through creative labor, with each act another freedom, manifest in a kind of self-conscious willfulness that composes the self as ineluctably as it composes a picture. The second alludes to this figure by its negation, its (often unwitting) hypostatization and recrudescence in something like Idea or Concept.[56] Fred

Turner's work, first discussed in the introduction, shows us how this antinomy ramified far outside the art world. Turner's work does not show—although it does allow us to notice when read in conjunction with Grace Kyungwon Hong, Jodi Melamed, and others—how this very choice defined the boundaries of a mode of white racial personhood that could imagine itself to have expanded beyond race and other identity markers precisely in being able to make this choice.[57]

Whitten spoke often and brashly about the giants of modernism—Andy Warhol, Willem de Kooning, Franz Kline, Clement Greenberg, Sol LeWitt—about wanting to make them obsolete, about beating them at their own game. But his real contribution might have been to invent modes of being that avoided this impasse of the conceptualist self versus the painterly self. Both modes are invested in an aggrandized and ultimately individuated self, and thereby in a kind of liberal mentality whereby self is the product of will, decision, choice, style, and, increasingly, an isolation from others relieved only by the conscious or nonconscious exchange of information. Here, finally, we find the means to think about Whitten's move to his digital mosaics as something other than a move away from automatism to painstaking composition. Whitten's turn from his early slabs to his later Monoliths and digital mosaics now reads like someone subjecting his own methods to a stringent test: would the dissolution of selfhood accomplished in the early slabs, the developer, the scanning procedure, hold up under the radically distended time frames of the mosaics? Could the self continue to dissolve, the slab still operate as a coordinate field for such a dissolution, in an achingly slow time frame? This is one reason why it matters that the monoliths are dedications: they are for another. They dissolve Whitten in that other, in his debt to them, but by extension, they dissolve culture itself into that debt. They position James Baldwin, W. E. B. Du Bois, Barbara Jordan, Ralph Ellison, Jacob Lawrence, Lena Horne, Muhammad Ali, and others as debtors to the world. In this, we glimpse the contours of a speculative version of (black) collectivity envisaged by Whitten's works. The relation of pixel to field, tessera to painting, pull to slab models this vision, lets Whitten enter it and experiment with it. The Monoliths extend this thought out into the black intellectual and artistic diaspora, and so make it apparent that blackness already exists inside the technologies Whitten explores, though it is seldom acknowledged there, except as various excluded remainders (the wrong side of the digital divide, the body that facial recognition can't recognize, the skin that medical devices can't read, etc.[58]).

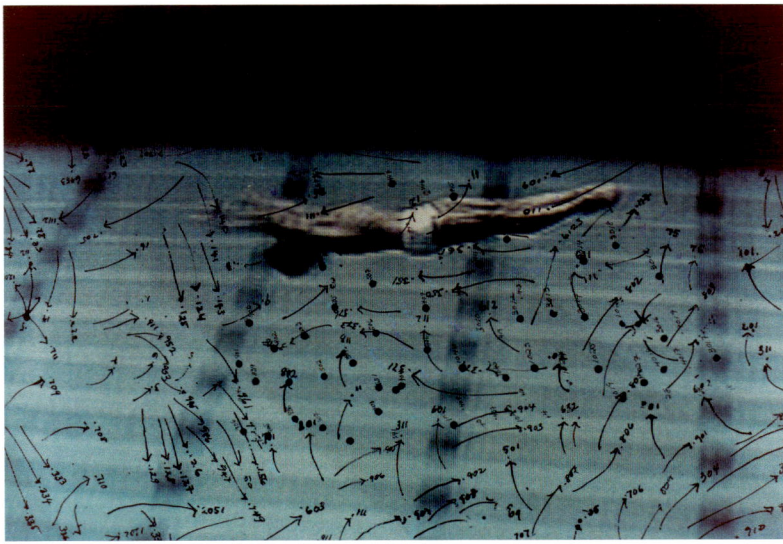

1 Howardena Pindell, *Untitled*, 1973. Ink on paper collage, 17½ × 90⅜ in. Signed and dated, lower right (Inv# PINPP088).

2 Howardena Pindell, *Video Drawings: Swimming*, 1975, 14 × 16⅛ in. Collection Museum of Contemporary Art Chicago, Anixter Art Acquisition Fund 2016.6. Courtesy of the artist and Garth Greenan Gallery, New York.

3 Alma Thomas, *Mars Dust*, 1972. Acrylic on canvas, 69¼ × 57⅛ in. (175.9 × 145.1 cm.). Whitney Museum of American Art, New York. Purchase, with funds from the Hament Corporation. Inv.: 72.58. © 2025 Estate of Alma Thomas (Courtesy of the Hart Family) / Artists Rights Society (ARS), New York. Digital image © Whitney Museum of American Art / Licensed by Scala / Art Resource, NY.

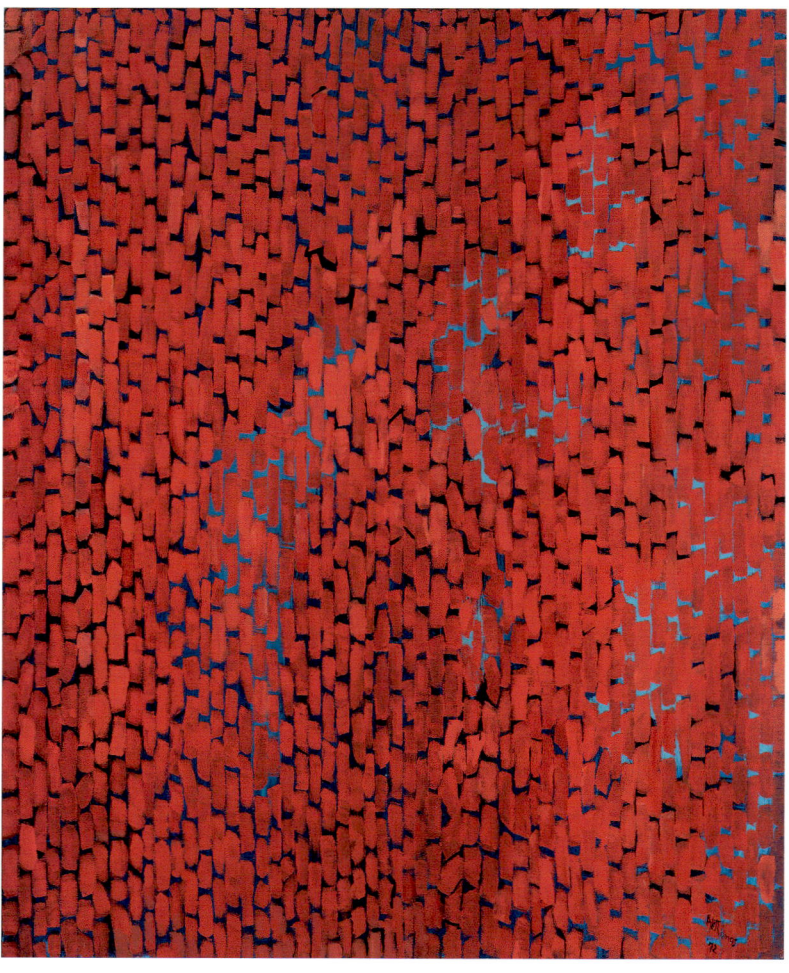

4 Alma Thomas, *Gray Night*, 1972. Acrylic on canvas, 68⅞ × 56⅞ in. (175 × 144.4 cm.). Smithsonian American Art Museum, Washington, DC. Museum purchase. 1972.147. © 2023 Estate of Alma Thomas (Courtesy of the Hart Family) / Artists Rights Society (ARS), New York. Photo: Smithsonian American Art Museum, Washington, DC / Art Resource, NY.

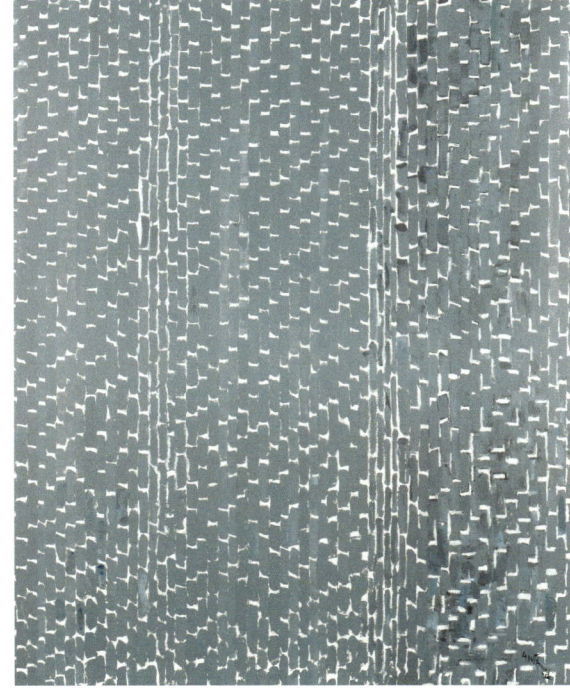

5 Alma Thomas, *Arboretum Presents White Dogwood*, 1972. Acrylic on canvas, 67⅞ × 54⅞ in. (172.5 × 139.5 cm.). Smithsonian American Art Museum, Washington, DC. Bequest of the artist. 1980.36.6. © 2023 Estate of Alma Thomas (Courtesy of the Hart Family) / Artists Rights Society (ARS), New York. Photo: Smithsonian American Art Museum, Washington, DC / Art Resource, NY.

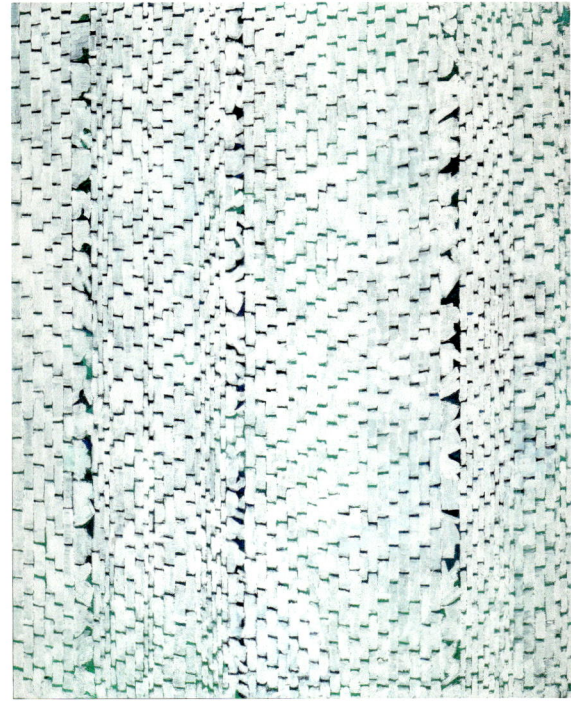

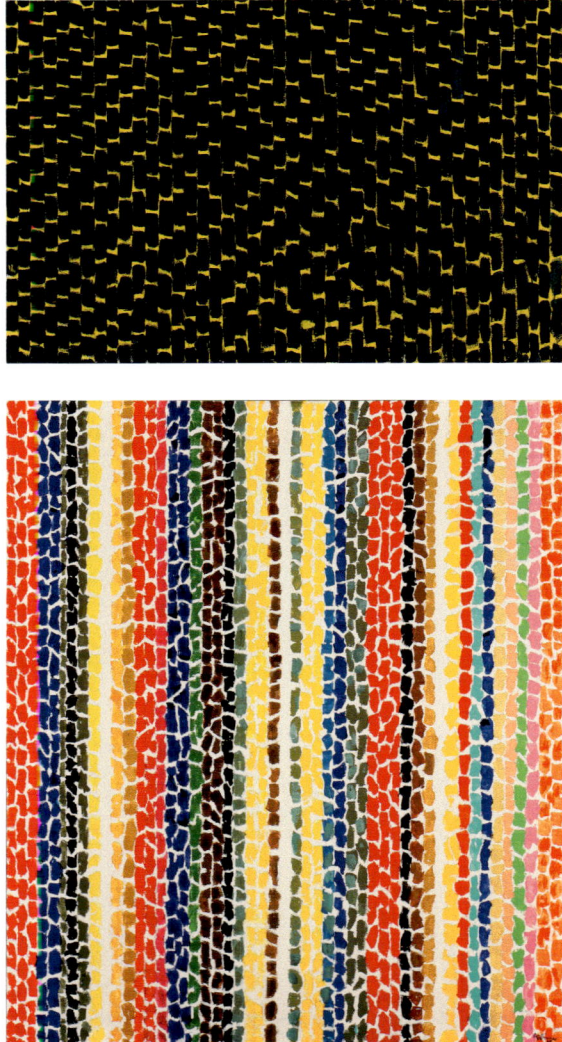

6 Alma Thomas, *Late Night Reflections*, 1972. Acrylic on canvas, 28¾ × 44 in. (73 × 111.8 cm.). Collection of the Nasher Museum of Art at Duke University, Durham, North Carolina. Museum purchase and bequest of Marjorie Pfeffer, by exchange; 2010.13.1. © Estate of Alma W. Thomas. Courtesy of the Nasher Museum of Art.

7 Alma Thomas, *Breeze Rustling Through Fall Flowers*, 1968. Acrylic on canvas, 57⅞ × 50 in. The Phillips Collection, Washington, DC. Gift of Franz Bader, 1976.

8 Alma Thomas, *Grey Night Phenomenon*, 1972. Acrylic on canvas, 68⅞ × 53⅛ in. (175 × 134.8 cm.). Smithsonian American Art Museum, Washington, DC. Gift of Vincent Melzac (1975.92.1). © 2023 Estate of Alma Thomas (Courtesy of the Hart Family) / Artists Rights Society (ARS), New York. Photo: Smithsonian American Art Museum, Washington, DC / Art Resource, NY.

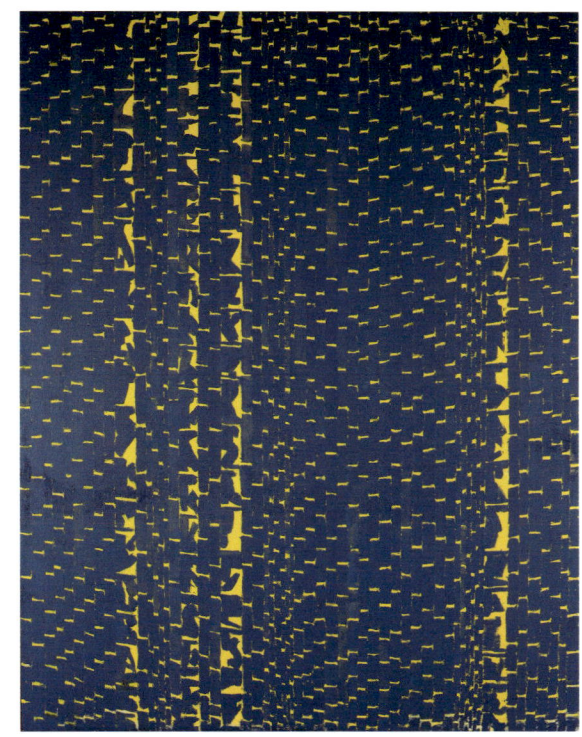

9 Alma Thomas, *Antares*, 1972. Acrylic on canvas, 65¾ × 56½ in. (167 × 143.5 cm.). Smithsonian American Art Museum, Washington, DC. Bequest of the artist (1980.36.13). © 2023 Estate of Alma Thomas (Courtesy of the Hart Family) / Artists Rights Society (ARS), New York. Photo: Smithsonian American Art Museum, Washington, DC / Art Resource, NY.

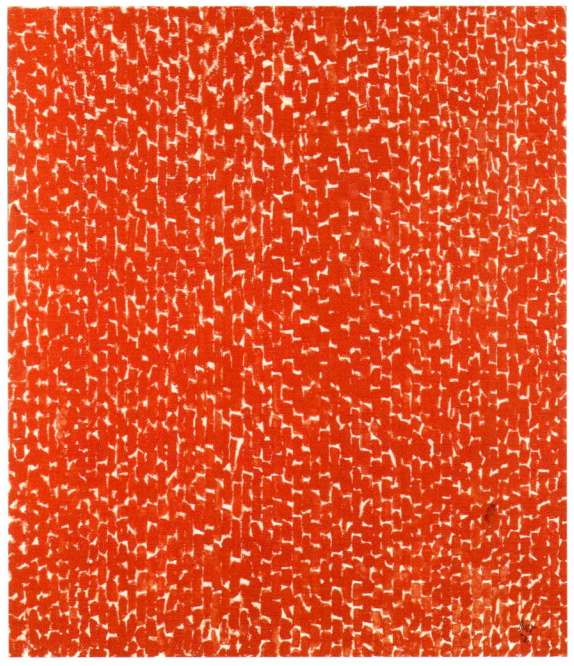

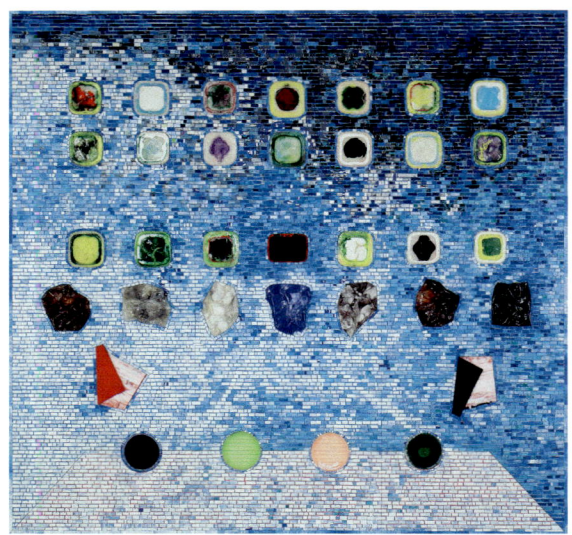

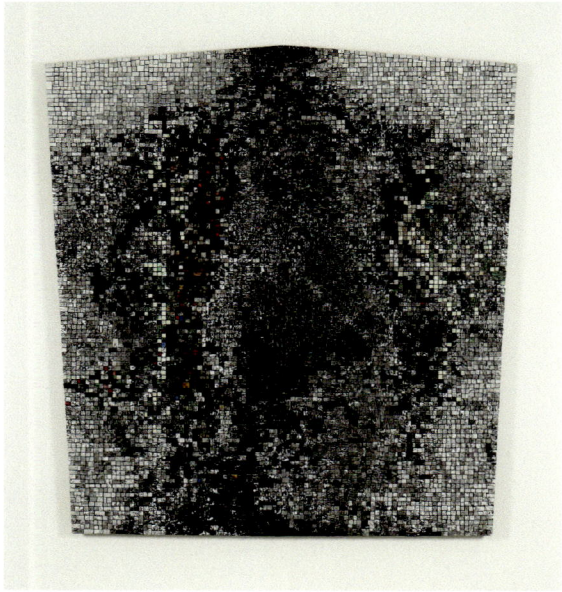

10 Jack Whitten, *Apps for Obama*, 2011. Acrylic on hollow core door, 84 × 91 in. © Jack Whitten Estate. Courtesy of the Jack Whitten Estate and Hauser & Wirth. Photo: John Berens.

11 Jack Whitten, *Black Monolith III for Barbara Jordan*, 1998. Acrylic on canvas, 69 × 65½ in. (175.2 × 166.4 cm.). © Jack Whitten Estate. Courtesy of the Jack Whitten Estate and Hauser & Wirth. Photo: John Berens.

12 Jack Whitten, *April's Shark*, 1974. Acrylic on canvas, 72 × 52 in. (182.9 × 132.1 cm.). © Jack Whitten Estate. Courtesy of the Jack Whitten Estate and Hauser & Wirth. Photo: Jeff McLane.

13 Jack Whitten, *Mee I*, 1977. Acrylic on canvas, 63¾ × 63¾ in. (161.9 × 161.9 cm.). © Jack Whitten Estate. Courtesy of the Jack Whitten Estate and Hauser & Wirth. Photo: Thomas Barratt.

14 Jack Whitten, *Black Monolith IV for Jacob Lawrence*, 2001. Acrylic on canvas, 96 × 96 in. (243.84 × 243.84 cm.). © Jack Whitten Estate. Courtesy of the Jack Whitten Estate and Hauser & Wirth.

15 Jack Whitten, *Head VII*, 1964. Acrylic on canvas, 23⅛ × 21¾ in. (58.8 × 55.2 cm.). © Jack Whitten Estate. Courtesy of the Jack Whitten Estate and Hauser & Wirth.

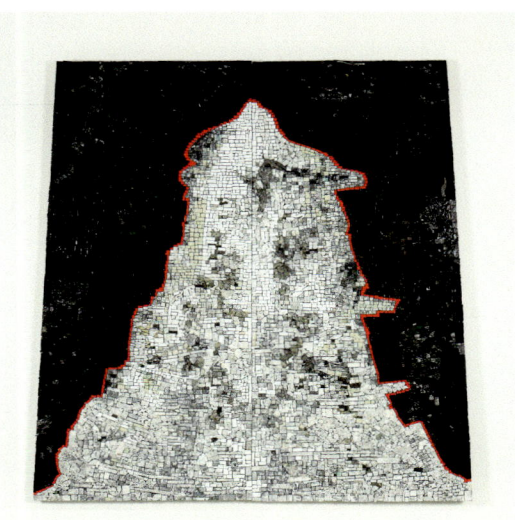

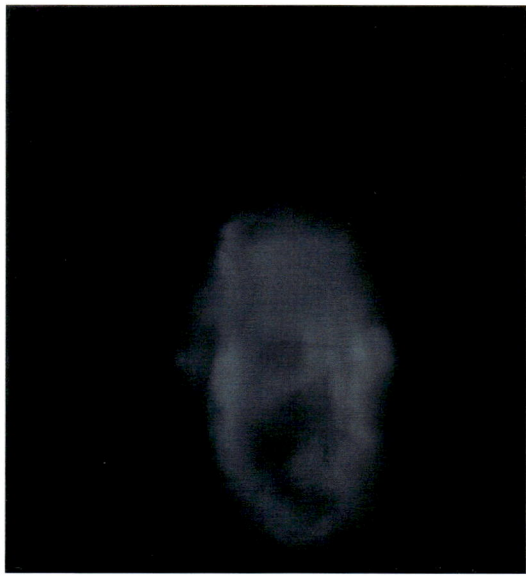

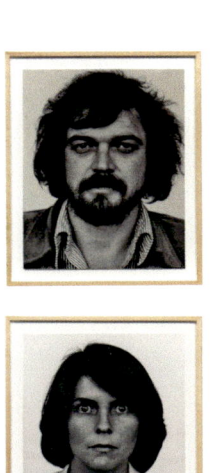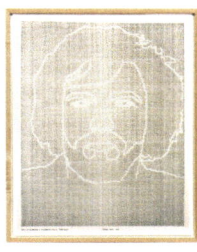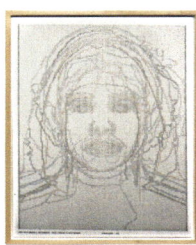
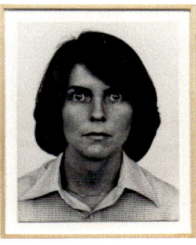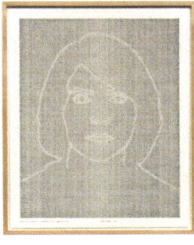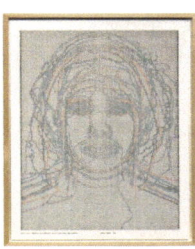
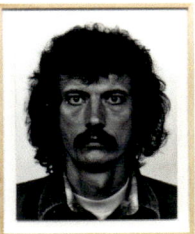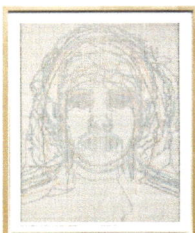
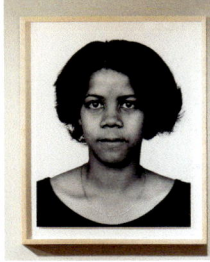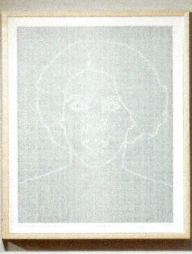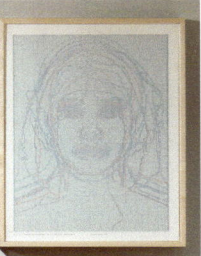

16 Charles Gaines, *Faces* [3 faces]: *Faces, Set #10: Terry Allen,* 1978; *Faces, Set #13: Kerny Callaway,* 1978; *Faces, Set #14: Charles Hanzieck,* 1978–79. All images: Photograph, ink on paper. Three parts: 23 × 19 in. each (framed); 23 × 57 in. (overall). Collection of Dan Fauci. Courtesy of Susanne Vielmetter, Los Angeles Projects. Photo: Robert Wedemeyer.

17 Charles Gaines, *Faces: Men and Women: Set #9, Pam Criswell,* 1978. © Charles Gaines. Courtesy of the artist and Hauser & Wirth.

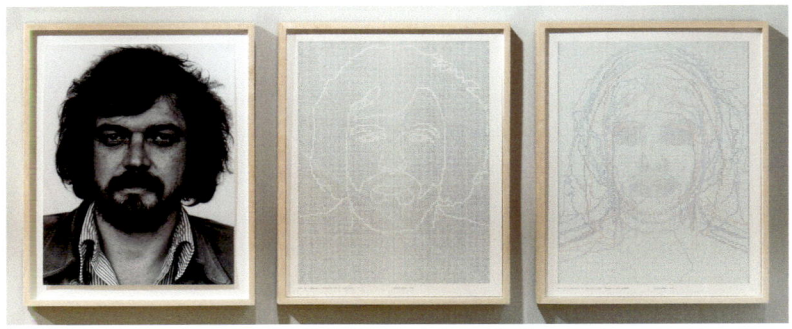

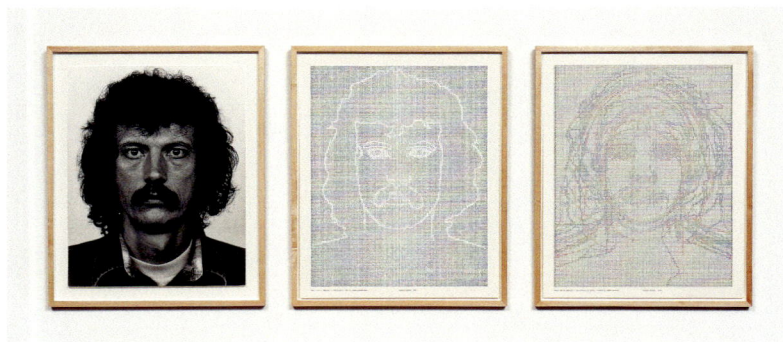

18 Charles Gaines, *Faces Set #10: Terry Allen*, 1978. Photograph, ink on paper, 23 × 19 in. each (framed). Collection of Dan Fauci. Courtesy of Susanne Viel-metter, Los Angeles Projects. Photo: Robert Wedemeyer.

19 Charles Gaines, *Faces: Men and Women: Set #14, Charles Hanzlicek*, 1978. Photograph, ink on paper. Each 24 × 20 × 1½ in. (60.96 × 50.8 × 3.81 cm.); 24 × 64 × 1½ in. (60.96 × 162.56 × 3.81 cm., overall).

20 Charles Gaines, *Falling Leaves*, 1979. Set 6 (detail), 1979. Photograph, ink on paper, framed, 30 × 70 in. (76.2 × 177.8 cm.). © Charles Gaines. Courtesy of the artist and Hauser & Wirth.

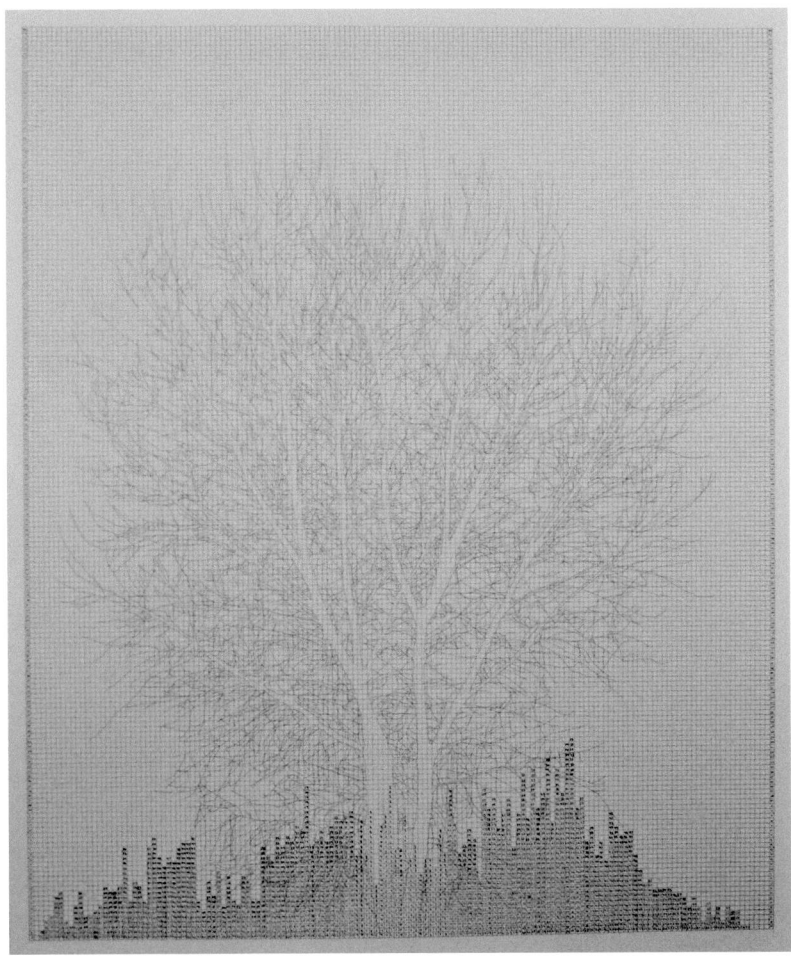

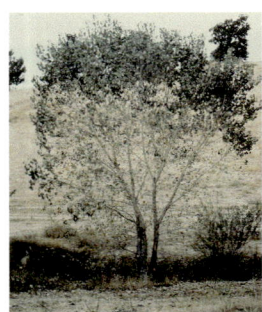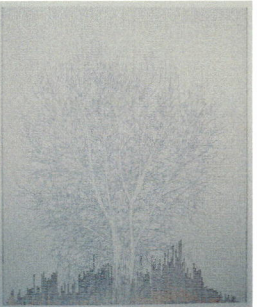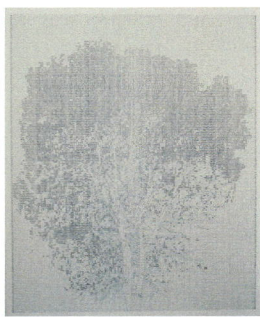

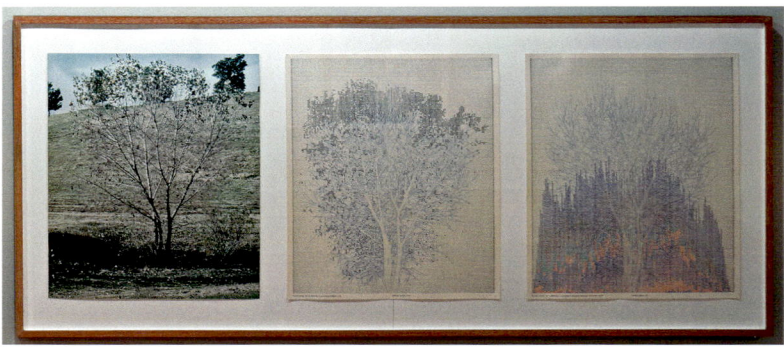

21 Charles Gaines, *Falling Leaves*, 1979. Set 6. Photograph, ink on paper, framed, 30 × 70 in. (76.2 × 177.8 cm.). © Charles Gaines. Courtesy of the artist and Hauser & Wirth.

22 Charles Gaines, *Falling Leaves*, 1980. Set 12. Photograph, ink on paper, framed, 30 × 70 in. (76.2 × 177.8 cm.). © Charles Gaines. Courtesy of the artist and Hauser & Wirth.

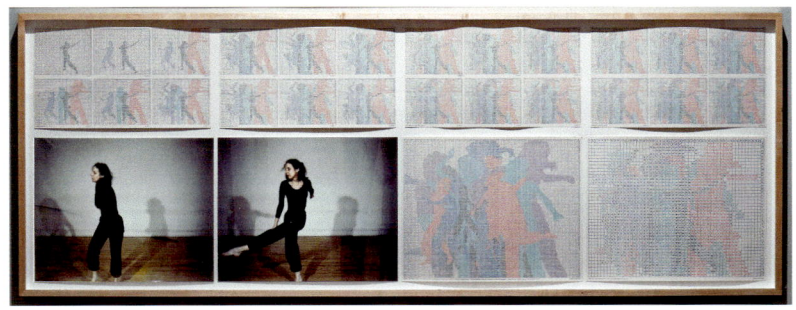

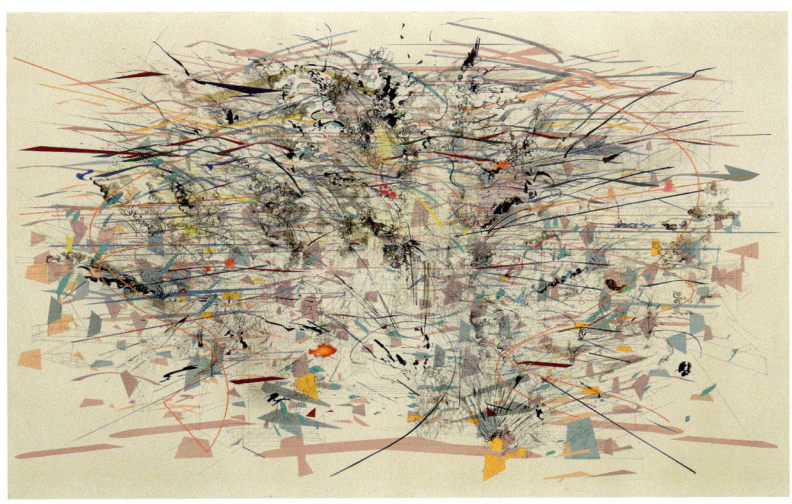

23 Charles Gaines, *Motion: Trisha Brown Dance*, 1980–81. Set 11. Color ciba-chrome photographs, ink on Strathmore paper. A set of eight parts: four small drawings, two large drawings, and two photographs, framed, 31⅛ × 84½ × 2 in. (79.1 × 214.6 × 5.1 cm.). © Charles Gaines. Courtesy of the artist and Hauser & Wirth.

24 Julie Mehretu, *Renegade Delirium*, 2002. Acrylic on canvas, 90 × 144 in. (228.6 × 365.8 cm.). © Julie Mehretu. Photo © White Cube (Theo Christelis).

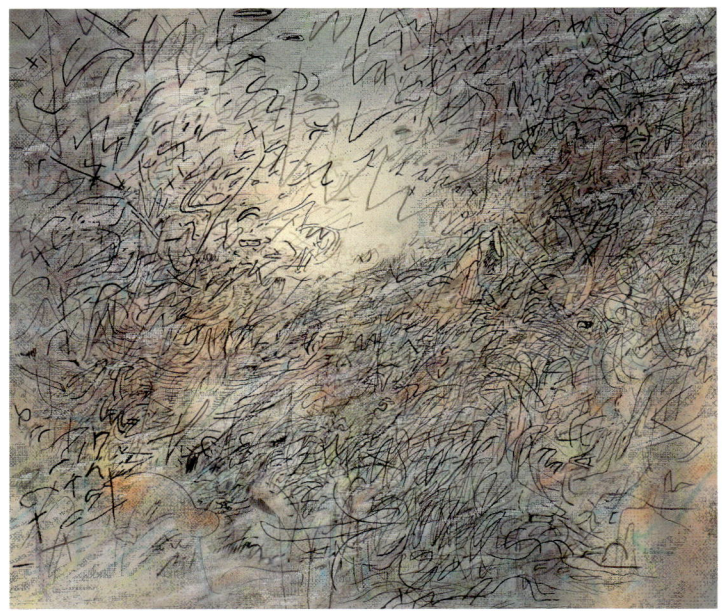

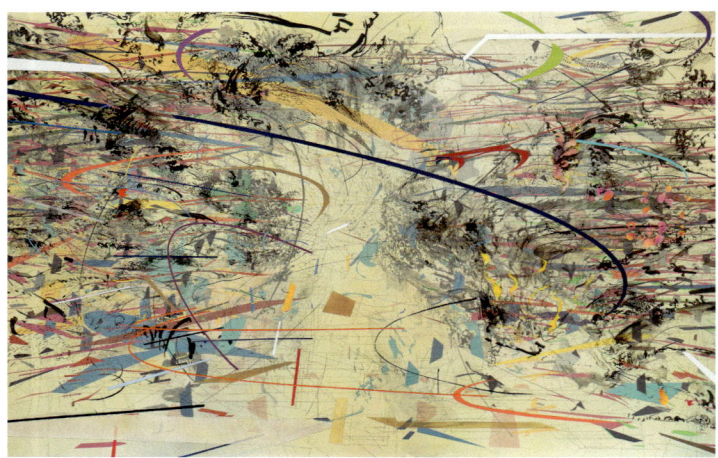

25 Julie Mehretu, *HOWL, eon (I, II)*, 2017. Ink and acrylic on canvas. Each panel: 324 × 384 in. (823 × 975.4 cm.). San Francisco Museum of Modern Art, Gift of Helen and Charles Schwab. © Julie Mehretu. Photo © Tom Powel. Courtesy of White Cube.

26 Julie Mehretu, *Dispersion*, 2002. Ink and acrylic on canvas, 228.6 × 365.8 cm. © Julie Mehretu. Courtesy of the artist, Marian Goodman Gallery, and White Cube.

27 Julie Mehretu, *Black Ground (deep light)*, 2006. Ink and acrylic on canvas, 72 × 96 in. (182.9 × 243.8 cm.). © Julie Mehretu. Courtesy of the artist and White Cube.

28 Julie Mehretu, *Palimpsest (old gods)*, 2006. Ink and acrylic on canvas, 60 × 84 in. (152.4 × 213.4 cm.). © Julie Mehretu. Photo © Erma Estwick. Courtesy of White Cube.

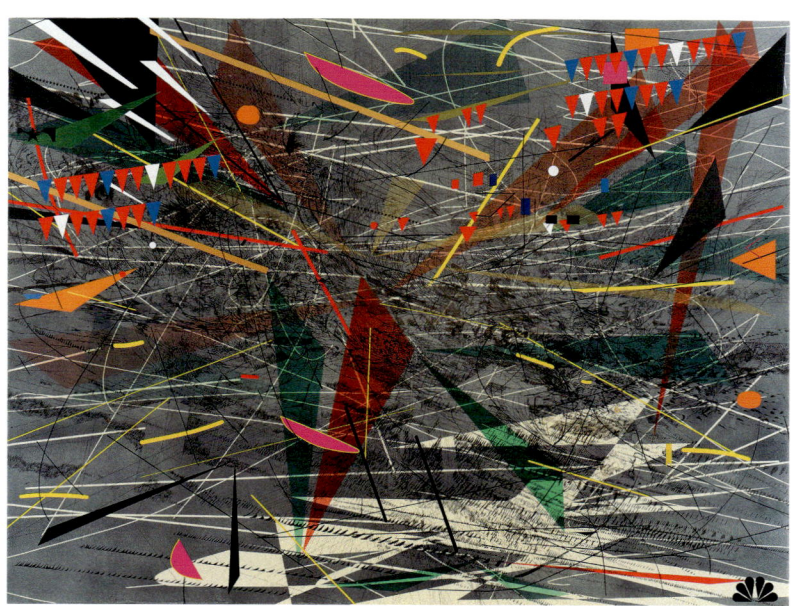

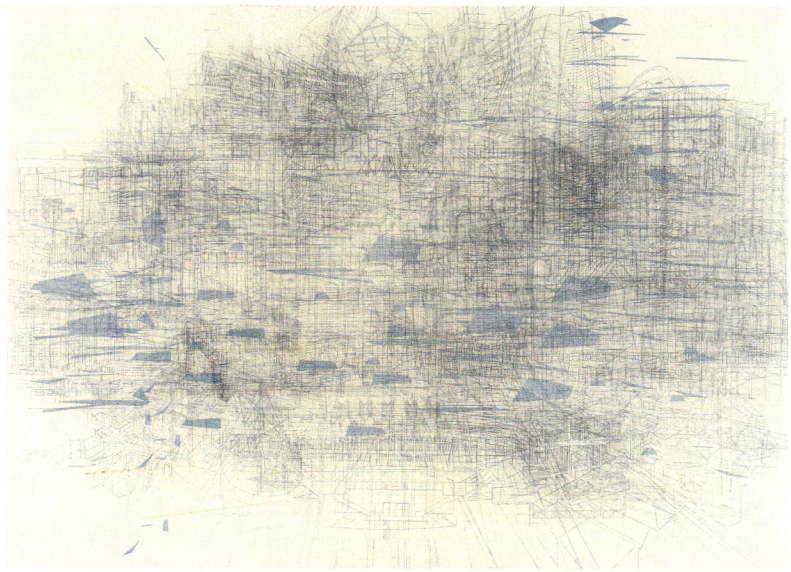

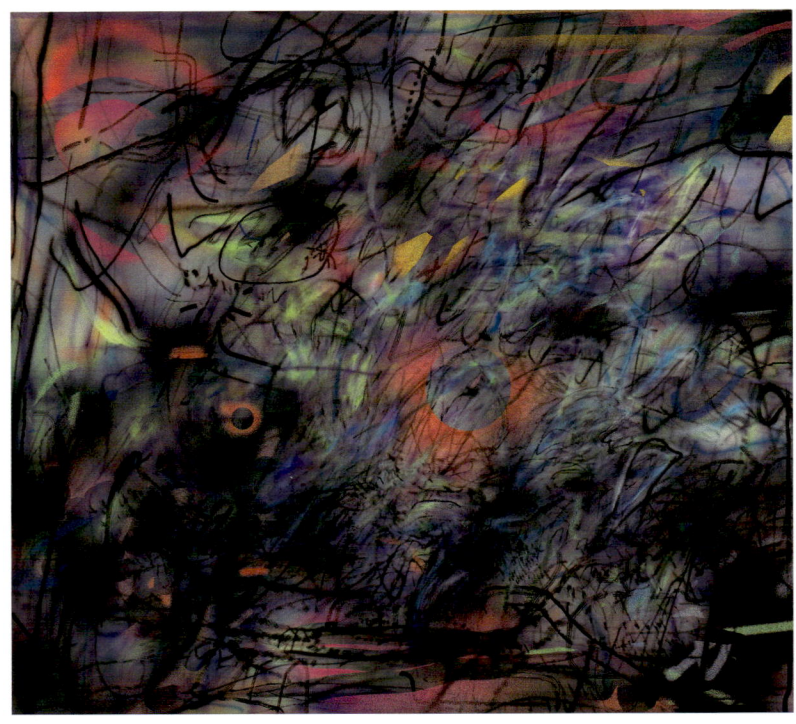

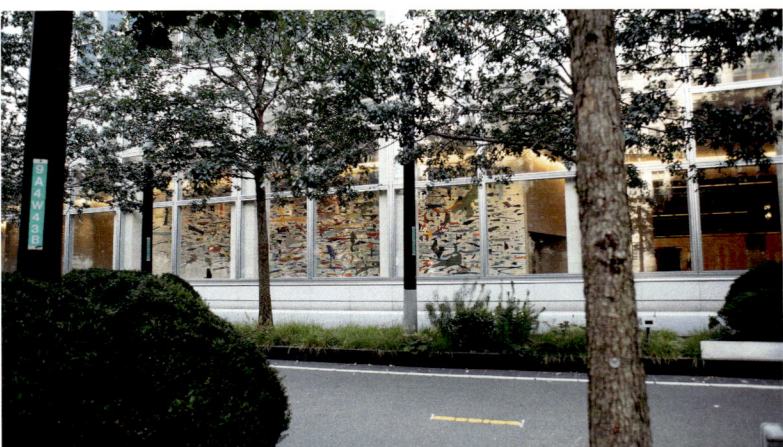

29 Julie Mehretu, *Sun Ship (J. C.)*, 2018. Ink and acrylic on canvas, 108 × 120 in. (274.3 × 304.8 cm.). © Julie Mehretu. Photo © Tom Powel. Courtesy of the artist, Marian Goodman Gallery, New York, and White Cube.

30 Julie Mehretu, *Mural*, 2009 (street view).

But process matters here too: the fact that Whitten never touched the tiles once he started the process of assembling a digital mosaic (he used tools as intermediaries); that the pouring of a slab generated an insistent previousness to the laying down of tiles, always tethering them and each individual tile to a prior moment, each embodying a whole and so generating the field in which they sit; that Whitten in some sense was making himself into a screen or screening mechanism, manifesting images from a set of operating instructions issued by the slab itself, manifesting that image in a coordinate raster that, as the product of a scanning procedure (here done far more slowly than with the developer), becomes a kind of open field for the projection and inhabitation of the figures to whom they are dedicated.

To get here, we have to remember that part of Whitten's project was to invent devices—his paintings—for the insistent dissolution of the self. The control he desired was precisely over the terms and conditions of that dissolution. If he was concerned with the signatory work of the name "Jack Whitten," it was because he wanted to be known as precisely the artist who expanded the vocabularies and machineries of selfhood out past the tether of the expressive, named, liberal self, the distillate of will and individuated action. This is why Whitten could set his sights by neither Pollock nor LeWitt, de Kooning nor Warhol. And that was why he was so concerned about computer screens, seeing there the same drama that was currently being played out in the art world, if in different materialities. Being concerned with the self inhabiting the fields of new technologies such as the graphical computer screen, but equally and at the same time, with the self as a fugitive from slavery and its apartheid future present tenses, Whitten had to move into other vocabularies, other machineries for conceiving the self in relation to a field of others. If not identity, if not that form of black collectivity composed of excellent black individuality, then what? If not expressive selfhood, then what? If not conceptualist rigor, then what? If not the self freed *by* technology or *from* technology, then what? I believe Whitten thought so persistently about digital and screen technologies, the technologies that increasingly saturated and defined his present tense and set the conditions for the very idea of developing a self, because he saw them as both unavoidable (it could only be modernist idealism to try to avoid them) and as harboring a fugitive strain.

If the graphical field of the personal computer could clear space for a person to exist in information space and still feel as though they themselves were the content, that all actions in that field would redound back to them, incarnating a renewed form of white personhood, then maybe this effect could be reversed, or as Richard Shiff voices Whitten's foundational relationship to photography, "everted."[59] Labor, even painstaking, backbreaking, time-consuming labor, could perhaps be made, by way of the technologies of the screen, to scatter the self as so much light refracted in the raster of a mosaic, in the cant of a tile. The experiment was beset on all sides by dangers. To become the machine itself was to invoke the human-machine divide so important to the resurgent humanism of these years. How not to retain that receding shoreline of humanity so longed for by people bemoaning the incursions of technology into life? At the same time, to become the force that disrupted the machine was to do the same, although by way of negation. In any case, black being has never had the luxury of avoiding a machinic past, a past of stolen and experimental humanity, a history of objecthood where the body was used as a production technology.[60] The very conditions of Whitten's life made certain choices unobtainable, or in any case, politically undesirable, untenable. So Whitten would start with an idea of fusion, or becoming, or better I think, indistinction: "The image is photographic. Therefore, I must photograph my thoughts."[61] Oft-quoted, hung always on the wall of his studio, this thought occurred to Whitten in 1964 and puzzled him, while also inspiring him, throughout his life. Who, or where, is the "I" in the question? Rather than the man-machine fusion of augmentation, where both sides of the equation served to enhance and aggrandize the other—the machine becoming more efficient and more dominant, the "man" becoming the same—Whitten wanted a mutually dissolutive relationship.

In a series of small images made in 1964 that Whitten admits he didn't understand at the time, the import or impact of such a mutual dissolution would become, if not clear, then at least palpable. Called his *Heads*, they were created while Whitten was still pursuing various abstract expressionist avenues that he was frustrated to find always led back to the expressive self. Made, as Richard Shiff describes, by applying black-and-white acrylic on canvas, Whitten then "stretched tulle netting, allowing the paint to seep through," and later wiped away the excess.[62] The netting, acting as an extremely fine grid or raster, caused the image to appear, as though photographically, as though without the conscious intervention of any maker, or anyway, any knowably human one. Here again, the language of resolution asserts itself. In the final images—which cannot exist apart from their generating conditions, dogged by previousness, working in an operational temporality—something seems to be made present through irresolution. There is the sense of a thing blurred out, indistinct, ungathered—maybe gathering, maybe atomizing. The field that manifests the image seems to be interfering with the transmission of the image. The field that manifests the image seems also to be producing the image. This field doesn't dictate the role and work of each individual element that makes it up. Rather, the bits generated by the fine mesh of the tulle each constitute a set of instructions that makes manifest a field that is coordinated but not homogeneous, aggregated but not in erasure of the differences that define it, but also not in a way that aggrandizes those differences as anything that can exist in themselves. Neither an index of the tulle, nor a purely transcendent phenomenon, the heads are a product of the coordinate field, this graphical field, working at a distance but not separate from the generating engine, effacing the labor of generation precisely to make manifest a new form of labor, operative exactly and only in that field. The passive voice becomes eerily active here: a head appears.

Latent here somewhere, there was a model for selfhood beyond the self, for the self dissolving into a field of coordinate but not subsumptive likeness—maybe mysterious and irresolute to Whitten at that moment because irresolution was their being, their charge. This is a perceptual phenomenon, but also a procedural one. In *Head VII* (1964, plate 15), a figure seems manifest: ovoid, just off-center, appearing through a dissolute outline, internally rent by resurgences of the black background that read as vacuoles: mouth eye nose. One discerns something seen through interference—the word ready to hand is "blur." At the same time, one sees the tulle weave that creates the effect. Maybe this is standard painterly self-reflexivity, the artwork laying bare the conditions of its own making. Except . . . whether working at the level of the pixel (the digital mosaic) or the scan (the developer and the slabs), Whitten was always shuttling along a procedural chain that kept a certain notion of the self at a distance, distending the laborer as the primary effect of that labor, leaving him spread out along the procedural chain, blurred, dissolving, or coming into being as something else, something nascent. There is, as though in consequence of this procedural shuttling, a restlessness of being, something palpably nonhuman about Whitten's heads. They can seem inexplicable by the usual explanatory apparatuses of art history, or even by the set of techniques art history has cataloged for getting an image to materialize. They feel like emanations—not merely perceptual, not just some trick of the eye, but neither do they seem fully there. There's a James Turrell effect in the way the *Heads* play with the effects of extremely dim light, but a non-phenomenological Turrell. Appearing or dissolving, they seem captured (a visualization more than a creation) while also in process. A figment but also a puzzle, a perplexity. It's hard to imagine the human procedure, or the human, who could have made these. If they registered as photographic to the young Whitten, it was because, at least in part, they seemed to come from some order of being other than the human, to have a different ontology, to be some byproduct of the human mixing with some interfering element, as though the human quotient itself were suspended between states: coming or going, aggregating or dissolving, part of a field and indistinguishable from it.

Dissolving into the screen, the raster, the field composed of bits: it's a description that can serve to describe the fate of the contemporary culture that drove Whitten's practice as well as it can describe Whitten's practice itself. Whitten was not so in thrall to the modernist novelty imperative to avoid borrowing where he could. But if there is to be a homeopathy between Whitten's practice and the technical-cultural forces he set out to confront, born of scavenging where he felt he could, then it matters a great deal what exactly we mean by "dissolve," what the valences of that procedure are, and to what ends it is pushed. Some of Whitten's stated goals were to pursue blackness under the tutelage of African art, to become a "photo machine," to produce materialized thought about the technological age that enveloped his life.[63] The practice he pursued to get there involved composing a field in which an insistent previousness never allowed the parts to be subsumed into the whole, nor to stand out as singular elements. No drama then of foreground and background; none of modernism's worry about illusion. Thinking about screens, about their effects, scavenging what might be useful to him as materializing procedures, Whitten ended up building screens from a parallel universe whose purpose was not to augment the human, not to join a long project of individualizing and responsibilizing the self who would appear there, but to dissolve the human as completely as possible. No wrist, no Idea, no heroism, and no opposition to these either; just stringent, persistent experiments in deploying massive amounts of physical and mental power to dissolve the agent of that labor. The self, especially the creative self, the self reborn and augmented on the other side of the graphical screen, was never going to dissolve in an instant, with a simple pull of the developer. If Whitten's name continued to appear in the vicinity of his paintings, even to gather a modicum of belated fame in the last decade of his life, this, too, was part of Whitten's challenge: how to make the proper name contain so much dissonance that it could only appear, eventually, after an extremely fast or extremely slow process, as the harbinger of a time when proper names, including the improper name of blackness itself, could only voice the sound of its own dissolution. Whitten, at an early moment in the history of the graphical field's emergence as an encompassing cultural and economic force, but also spanning that field's efflorescence, tried to exploit what he perceived as some of its weaknesses, which is to say, its inherent potential for self-dissolution, its capacity for being deployed to that end.

Charles Gaines, working at a later and more foreclosed moment in this same history, would discover in the graphical screen less a latent potential to be exploited than a latent threat. Not, however, the familiar threats to liberal personhood—alienation, exploitation, homogenization—but an older, more foundational fear of human fungibility, transcoded into the new environments that the computer and the graphical screen would make possible. Gaines's work will help us see that the graphical screen, especially in its later, more reified instantiations, was expressly, if not self-consciously, designed to escape precisely this threat of fungibility, and so it was shaped by it.

Modernity and Fungibility: Charles Gaines

4

The Black Arts Movement that immediately preceded Charles Gaines's career actively debated the blackness of abstraction.[1] In these debates, abstraction was framed as a choice, and the willingness to exercise that choice was at the heart of those debates.[2] These were also debates, therefore, about personhood seen in relation to work—the labor of art-making, of self-elaboration, of testing out some ways of working that were ways of living in and with blackness, of challenging and elaborating it.

All the while, a certain other kind of abstraction was coming, one that did not so much exercise choice as harness it. The particular source of abstraction I'm concerned with here is the graphical display of the personal computer (graphic user interface, or GUI)—we can think of it as an abstraction of the body, although really its ambition was to be an abstraction of white personhood.[3] To be involved with modes of abstraction, including conceptualism and systems art (usually considered to be the genres that best fit Gaines's practice), was therefore necessarily to be involved with this coming abstraction, like it or not. Gaines's gridwork confronts this torquing of personhood and the forms it had taken under the impress of the graphical field—if not exactly head-on, then certainly with a committed persistence. Systems aesthetics was the ground on which he met it; it was his starting point for creating a zone of nonexpressive art within the delimited confines of the artwork as system. This was to be a homeopathic aesthetic, pitting the systematicity of computing's bodily abstractions against that of systems art, all set within the frame of a long history of racial violence. The effect was to force open the smallest space for movement between the framing of black abstraction as a choice, as a certain kind of freedom, and the coming abstraction that wanted to generate a feeling of freedom as its object—its product, really. Freedom was to be the key problem, both in its implications for black personhood and in the relatively new promises being made by the graphical field for personal computing.

The works that I will be concerned with most are what the Studio Museum in Harlem has called Gaines's "gridworks."[4] And while the grid is their most basic visual referent, the period in which they were made (from the 1970s to the present), their contiguity within an overall system, and Gaines's abiding interest in related questions of work and personhood render that referent less a grid than a raster. This is a grid put to a kind of use. And it is a system that is often not taken to be a system at all so much as an image technology: the raster-based computer screen. In its form as a graphic user interface, the graphical screen aspired to invent a form of labor best performed by a human who was to be augmented by new forms of freedom, often pitched as a loosening of constraint.[5] In Gaines's investigations of that form of the screen, this technocratic promise of augmenting the human lingers as a broken promise, given flesh or form in a kind of constrained, divested personhood that Gaines referred to as "contiguity."[6] Gaines's systematizations of personhood, collectivity, and creative labor need to be seen in this context, and not just in the universalizing history—the white history—of the twentieth century that has provided the implicit or explicit background for most histories of conceptual art, process art, and systems art.

In the early 1970s, as a recent graduate of the MFA program at the Rochester Institute of Technology (its first black graduate), Charles Gaines stopped painting and started to produce the work that indissociably connected him with systems and process-based work. This work has been a through line in his prolific and varied practice—much of which deals with music, with quotation, and with a history of black protest, as well as with signification, metaphor, and metonymy—extending from the early 1970s to his eponymous exhibition at Paula Cooper Gallery in 2018 to the present. Here's how, in a letter to mentors Carol and Sol LeWitt, Gaines explained this transition from painting to systems: "I dropped painting in 1972.... The problem is the associated discourse surrounding gesture, that is, gesturing was a material manifestation of emotive or expressive intent. And I didn't care for that idea."[7] He did not care, perhaps, for the fantasy of autonomy that was encouraged by the discourse of gesture, the feeling that expressivity could be an analogue to something like human spirit or unbounded imagination. More broadly, Gaines seems to reject any easy coincidence or relay between the laboring body, that body's interiority, and the product of that body's labor. Gaines often called the work that followed from this rejection "systems work," a common enough idiom at the time, although here put to some unexpected uses. Most unexpected, perhaps, is the fact that systems do not, in Gaines's work, constitute an antinomy or opposition to gesture and expressive intent, even if they do work to escape the gravity of those subjective emanations.

One of the most approachable of Gaines's early systems works, *Faces* (1978–79, plates 16–19) — a work he would reprise for his 2018 exhibition at Paula Cooper — employs a transposition system like all of his other gridworks, moving from one imaging system to and through others.[8] The full work comprises sixteen triptychs. Each of the individual, framed images (forty-eight in total) is 23 × 19 in. The triptychs all follow the same transpositional pattern, with each triptych a kind of process in itself: in the first or leftmost image, a photograph; next, its outline in negative; and finally, a composite image that gathers and overlays each of the previous outlines from the second image onto the same image plane. In the first triptych, then, the rightmost image contains only one outline, one face; in the rightmost image of the sixteenth triptych, there are sixteen superimposed outlines. Each individual triptych is titled with the legal name of the subject photographed. All are Gaines's friends and associates; they are also people who were not widely known (in contrast to his reprisal of *Faces* for Paula Cooper in 2018, in which all of the subjects are famous historical figures).

The fourth triptych is called *Faces: Set #4, Stephan W. Walls*. It pictures a young black man, photographed frontally and close-up. As if to immediately announce the project's intention to tarry with some protocols of representation, the first image of every triptych in the series is a black-and-white portrait photograph — a close-up with the face arrayed frontally, as though for "our" examination (the artwork makes that collective pronoun possible, if not equally inhabitable for everyone). It invokes a kind of overseeing collectivity precisely in its frontality and the history of surveillance and incarceration that it evokes — a variety of technologies, in fact, for indelibly inscribing identity onto body. In this sense, Gaines's system moves in at least two directions: along this violent trajectory that wants to inscribe identity onto the body of its victims, but also along speculative trajectories that want to free the body from such compulsions to speak, to be legible, to be fungible precisely in its identifiability. Both of these are black histories. But in the second image of the triptych, the face, first given in extreme, even forensic detail, now becomes an outline hollowed out of a fully activated raster—as though its representational protocols are starting to fray, or to become something else. Into each of the grid squares, Gaines has inscribed numbers in black ink, leaving empty squares to articulate the face's barest outline. This use of the activated or unactivated raster to materialize an image is why many refer to Gaines's images as "pixelated."[9]

The rastered images in the middle and right images of the triptychs, as in all of Gaines's gridworks, are numbered along their X and Y axes. This numbering system begins with zero in the exact center of the image plane. Zeros are written in black ink in each grid square, forming a vertical column extending from top to bottom of the image, except where Gaines has articulated one pixel or unit or bit of the outline of Walls's face. From this center line and extending horizontally out to the sides of the image, the numbers ascend to sixty-six, again, except where Gaines has left a blank square to articulate some part of the outline of the face. Gaines stops this numbering system one column short of the leftmost column. In that column, he has used the letters of the English alphabet to give coordinates to the grid squares, this time starting from the bottom at A and extending to the top at 7M, cycling through the alphabet six and a half times. So, this is not just a grid space but a coordinate space.

I call a grid square with a number inscribed in it *activated* and an empty square *unactivated*, but this is arbitrary. The language of *activated* and *unactivated* is accurate to the raster display system employed here, but there is nothing in the logic of that system to say that one state is "on" and the other is "off." In fact, as Gaines's images show quite clearly, there are really only two states of "on" formed by the contrast between those two states. While the second image presents the body in negative, the third presents the body in positive, with numbers inscribed in squares (and not the absence of numbers) materializing the outline of the face. But here, too, the language of *negative* and *positive* is a heuristic, an artifact of photographic technologies that are actually *not* the historical precursors of the raster display system used here. Both images present the body schematized, mathematicized for configuration on *this* particular surface, a raster that seems designed to block any fantasy of free movement, gestural or expressive, through the body of the artist or the space of the image while at the same time decidedly manifesting an image out of the traces of rote labor visible in the handwritten numbers.

In the third or rightmost image, the face appears as the barest outline with the surrounding raster left empty or blank. In the final accumulation and intercalation of faces in the raster of the third image, the different colors in which Gaines has written the numbers of each outline allow one to distinguish individual faces, but barely and only with difficulty. Otherwise, accumulation moves toward indistinction, with facial features clustering in rough zones—evoking the surveillance technology not of photography but of facial recognition. This precise effect is repeated in Gaines's 2018 show at Paula Cooper, this time extending across the twelve images of the series so that, in the final image, the faces of twelve thinkers—Aristotle, Maria W. Stewart, Karl Marx, W. E. B. Du Bois, Malcolm X, Jacques Lacan, Dolores Huerta, Michel Foucault, Luce Irigaray, Edward Said, Molefi Kete Asante, and bell hooks—overlap, intercalate, and gather in interference and irresolution along jagged lines of what is nevertheless a kind of contiguity.

While so much like Gaines's other gridworks, the objects of his system here are human faces, many of them black or brown, and this has allowed commentators to discuss *Faces* in the context of identity politics.[10] As one might imagine, there is far less talk about race or identity politics in Gaines's other gridwork: *Regression* (1973–74), *Calculations* (1975), *Walnut Tree Orchard* (1975–2014), *Color Regression* (1978), *Falling Leaves* (1978), *Incomplete Text* (1978–79), *Shadows* (1978–80), *Motion: Trisha Brown Dance* (1980–81), and *Numbers and Trees* (1986–89). So maybe the first kind of work that systems have performed in Gaines's oeuvre is to erect an obstacle to talking about race or identity. This is understandable, but it's also a mistake, reliant on the assumption that race is primarily a technology of representation.[11] Race is not only that in Gaines's work, nor is that what it becomes in graphical systems, though representational forms can be easily overlaid onto graphical systems. This, in fact, is one of the reasons why graphical screens have been so attractive, have felt so usable, for so many people. Rather than a negotiation with a computer, the graphic interface lets the user engage with their own creative instincts such that the work produced in that space can serve as a kind of self-representation.[12] While Gaines was likely *not* thinking about this precise articulation of freedom, he *was* interested in harnessing graphical systems to engage a rhetoric of freedom seen in relation to raced personhood, as we will see.

Most of what I have written about systems so far is commonplace for studies of systems aesthetics.[13] But writing about systems (like abstraction and conceptualism) can suffer from a lack of precision. Systems discourse is often deployed as a totalizing framework, collapsing significant political and aesthetic distinctions under the sign of technology, itself both metonymized by and condensed inside the discourse of systems. Nizan Shaked's work has been an important part of a broad reconsideration of the ways that systems aesthetics and conceptualism actively take up, rather than avoid, the particular and the political.[14] Shaked tracks the movement in conceptualism from, as she puts it, "art about art" (Joseph Kosuth) to "art about political art" (Adrian Piper)—that is, from conceptualism to a politicized conceptualism that explicitly takes up identity politics.[15] But the parallel movement, occurring in the development of the computer screen and centrally concerned not just with systems but with subject formation, makes it clear that all systems aesthetics are concerned with identity politics. The question then is: what sort? And in service of what? Gaines's work tracks not just the movement of systems art into identity politics, but the movement of computer systems into identity politics and the machinery of subject formation.

What matters most for my purposes is that we see the graphical interface as an environment for a significant reimagining of the individual, but an individual now seen in relation to (individuated on the basis of) the world reimagined as a vast information-sharing network.[16] In other words, the creators and salespeople of the graphical screen had found a way to make systems—graphical, computational—sit in the service of an American ideal of autonomy, creativity, expressivity. Already, then, when Gaines started working with systems in the 1970s, they were not, as the rhetoric of conceptual art often frames it, antithetical to those ideals.[17] The system of the graphical screen was an environment and engine of this change.

So it is striking—especially within this larger history of how the raster and its arrayed pixels have played such a central role in the augmentation of the self—that Gaines's gridworks are each interested, in a few distinct ways, in forms of de- or nonindividuated life, life tethered and contiguous. In *Faces*, as in all of Gaines's other gridwork, the third image in the triptychs of his series gathers up previous images, accumulating silhouettes of the bodies of people or objects. In a sense, the third image simply gathers each of the individual outlines from the second image in one place, on one plane. But the third image also performs a counting function: counting off the number of bodies in the series up to that point. The series *Faces* accumulates silhouettes of faces. *Falling Leaves* accumulates the total leaves fallen from a single tree over time. *Motion: Trisha Brown Dance* accumulates outlines of single images extracted from the flow of a dance, bodies frozen in space, although retaining a (nonindexical) trace of movement in their ultimate accumulation. *Faces: Identity Politics* (2018) collects the outlines of faces of recognized thinkers, from Aristotle to bell hooks, so that by the twelfth image the famous identities intermingle nearly to indistinction. In his move to systems, Gaines was not just siding against expression, as is often said; he was moving away from, or at least working to radically expand our sense of, the possibilities of the individual. A gathering, something always just more than one, veering away from *one* but not toward more defined forms of collectivity, a collective that is contiguous but never unified: this is where Gaines's transpositions from one representational system to another, his system aesthetics, most insistently and consistently lead.

Falling Leaves (1978, plates 20–22) consists of sixteen sets of triptychs. The system that structures the work documents the rate at which leaves fall from the same tree. In the series, each triptych's first image gives a color photograph of the tree documented in successive states of abscission. The second image transposes that photograph into a line drawing of the tree that proceeds mostly heedless of the grid. Grid squares are activated by Gaines's familiar numbering system, but here the squares correspond to leaves on the tree—one number to one leaf—rather than component parts of a drawing. In the final image we find the same line drawing of the tree, but the activated grid squares now graph where the leaves have fallen from the tree over time, with colors articulating vertical strata of leaves, but also documenting the intervals at which Gaines visited the tree. The final image of the triptych, in other words, aggregates leaves as a function of time.

But in all the gridwork series, including *Faces* and *Falling Leaves*, there is a different kind of collectivity implied in the second image. The first image, a photograph, pictures a specific face or tree: that very one. But the system for producing subsequent images of *that* person, that tree, for transposing that image from a photograph to a numerical tabulation within an enabling raster, could equally well produce such an image of any person or thing. The system is, in a sense, designed to perform just this function—that is precisely its systematicity. In this way, the tree and the singular face, seen in and for their particularity, generate a collective, are already collectives once they enter the system of Gaines's gridworks. This means that the action of the system on personhood (or thinghood) here is not to render it anonymous or faceless as in the Adornian nightmare of modernity—Gaines graphs and so retains the particular shape of *that* tree, *that* branch, *that* nose, *that* hair. It is, rather, to surround personhood with the specter of fungibility. In other words, systems thinking here manifests as a way of materializing bodies and objects that recognizes their individuality—even records it in the *Faces* series's reference to mugshots—but does so in a form constituted precisely to let anyone, anything, anybody step into that space (the formal features of the mugshot perform the same function). While the graphical computer screen would aim to cater to the singular individual, set free inside an unconstrained field, granted the feeling of being alone with their own subjective expression, Gaines's graphical fields interpolate anyone whatsoever, a fact that is as true of their production (once the system is established, anyone could, in the theory of the system itself, replicate it) as it is of their subjects.

Both of these previous forms of collectivity—that of the aggregated pixel field and that of the fungible object—are produced and encompassed by a third form: what Gaines called contiguity.[18] He entrains the images in each series by way of a thematic or morphological unit (trees, faces), and the images in each triptych by way of a numericized extension that starts with the source photo and circuits its way through to the final image, in which all the images in the series up to that point get aggregated. In this way, Gaines makes his systems generate accumulation, indebtedness, contiguity. The point of his transpositional systems often seems to be these contiguities themselves more than any image produced.

Motion: Trisha Brown Dance (1980–81, plate 23) doesn't conform to the patterned three-part structure of the triptych, but there is nonetheless the same accumulative procedure, slowly dissolving the named body into a system, a motion study that records the dancer's (Brown's) movements but that could equally well record any movements whatsoever once the system is established. To initiate the work, Gaines took a photograph every three seconds of Trisha Brown performing one minute of her dance *Son of Gone Fishin'* (1981).[19] Gaines then asked Brown to select images from the larger set for inclusion in his final work.

There are two registers of images in each set of the sixteen-set series of *Motion*: twenty-four smaller, rastered images proceeding horizontally across the top and four larger images across the bottom. In the lower register, the two leftmost images are color photographs chosen by Brown from the complete set: the rightmost image is a plotted enlargement—or, as given in Gaines's title, a "blow-up"—of one of the small drawings on top. And the gridded image to that image's left is another accumulative window, with figures adding up over the course of the series of sixteen.[20] Again, the rastered images are composed of numbers recorded into grid squares. This time, the numbering system that orders the smaller pages proceeds from 1 to 52 moving left to right and from A to 2P bottom to top. Colors code the different poses as they gather. As in many of Gaines's works, bodies accumulate across the rastered upper register, culminating in the final image to the far right. The titles precisely enumerate this accumulation. One such title, the eleventh in the set, is *Motion: Trisha Brown Dance, Photographs and Graphs Sequencing Continuous Movement at 125th/second at 1 Second Intervals. Continuous Graphing of the Actual Sequence and 11 Arbitrary Sequences. Graph of Actual Sequence, Set 11, Photos 1 through 22.*

Here the accumulation doesn't follow the linear logic of the system's transpositional procedure. Instead, it takes its form from two interlinked sets of choices: Brown's selections from the total set of photographs, and Gaines's ordering of those selections according to the chronology of the dance. So while bodies accumulate, both layered and intercalated, in the rightmost image of the upper register, they do so in some relation to Brown's selections, themselves constrained and enabled by Gaines's photographs. Choice, a kind of subjective emanation and constituent part of individuality, finds a place within the terms that shape the work's form, but never far from a set of constraints—invoking Fred Turner's democratic subject following their own path within a lightly managed atmosphere (see the introduction) and seeming to cancel that subject at the same time. Brown chooses, but only after Gaines has made his photographs. Gaines photographs, but only at predetermined intervals. The system here, and in all of Gaines's gridwork, seems less about making systems antithetical to expression and more about producing a series of enchainments where no part floats free, where all parts move in contiguity with those that proceed and follow.

Unlike other of Gaines's gridworks, the bodies here are all Brown's, recorded in different states of movement. In a sense, Gaines's system renders Brown's performance as so many overlapping windows, each a unit of movement given in arrest. Here, among all of Gaines's gridworks, the graphical screen with its accommodation and aggrandizement of the individual, its division of the self into units of labor, all of which appear to be emanations from that self's expressive interiority, and its use of windows as a way of expanding the space in which work can happen, seems perhaps most disconcertingly near.

This machinery of aggregation found in all of Gaines's gridwork flirts with the danger felt by so many in the 1960s and 1970s, documented in Turner's work and elsewhere, of the human-turned-automaton, a true, mimetic product of mechanized factory labor and early IBM-style corporatism.[21] This is sometimes expressed as a fear of anonymity, of becoming nameless.[22] But given Gaines's commitment to transposing the quiddity of his objects, anonymity is not the threat that looms in Gaines's work. Rather, in the lamination of systems to the threat of fungibility, Gaines's work forces a reconsideration of familiar histories of anxiety that coursed beneath various postwar efforts to reassemble personhood inside the new universalism of systems thinking, indelibly marking these as white anxieties, not American or universal ones.

Taken on its own and somewhat ahistorically, the fungible self has been called a neoliberal modality, in which selves become interchangeable within an overall atmosphere of shared inequality, which in turn makes competition into society's dominant collectivizing force.[23] This, in fact, is exactly why some queer theorists have found in fungible personhood a source of cautious optimism, a new politics of negativity in which proprietary individuality might be dissolved in a solution of general equivalence.[24] But seen within a longer history of commoditized labor, fungibility isn't just about a general equivalence. It also involves an asymmetrical structure of intersubjectivity in which white subjects are marked as white by their endowed capacity to imaginatively inhabit the subject position of the black or blackened other—a capacity that is just as available to avowed racists as it is to liberal sympathizers.[25] Saidiya Hartman describes this component of fungibility as it is applied to human subjects traded as commodities.[26] Key to this quietly brutal mode of intersubjectivization is to deny all points of contact, of touch, between subject and other: whether existential, ontological, or political. The violent intersubjectivity of human fungibility does not violate this sequestration; it enforces it. To inhabit someone's subject position, whether through violence or sympathy, one has to feel oneself utterly separate from them, linked, in fact, only by the fickle bonds of sympathy, which is not a linking at all but a delinking, fully asymmetrical. It is a denial of contiguity at a deep, even ontological level.[27]

Putting it this way helps us to see a different fear being warded off by and in the graphical field of the computer screen and elsewhere. Beyond the fear of authoritarianism (Turner's focus and the express focus of so much liberal postwar anxiety across public and private sectors) or the anonymity of the crowd (an early modern fear recast by Turner in the postwar period as a fear of the brainwashed crowd, the subjects of authoritarian aesthetics), the specter of the fungible human hearkens not to subsumed individuality but to a context of stolen life, the history of slavery and all of its poisonously lingering histories.[28]

As Frank B. Wilderson III stresses, to have one's individuality subsumed is to have already been granted, in a framework of universal rights, the privilege of individuality.[29] One's individual rights can be violated only because they existed in the first place, having been granted a priori to some, precisely as a way to differentiate those who were to be included in universal personhood and those whose exemption (not exclusion, not alienation) was to set off and define those rights for their bearers. In its focus on the augmented individual intellect—the creative self working within, but not subsumed by, informational networks—the graphical field should therefore be seen as one part of a far larger and longer defense against what Hartman calls "the fungibility of the captive body."[30] The fungibility of the commodity makes the captive body an abstract and empty vessel vulnerable to the projection of others' feelings, ideas, desires, and values. As property, the dispossessed body of the enslaved is the surrogate for the master's body since it guarantees his disembodied universality and acts as the sign of his power and dominion.[31] Gaines's systems help us to see how the project of the graphical, all along its historical course, has been haunted not just by the anonymizing mass, the fear of which can't but invoke the strong individual as a bulwark against that threat, but by the feared and projected fungibility of blackness.[32] The computer's graphical interface was a space of retreat from and a defense against this threat. This radically changes any attempt to set the individual against the collective within the context of systems and the systematization of life.

We encounter a related problem in the way that Kyle Stine takes up Jacob Gaboury's claim—discussed in chapter 2 and elaborated throughout in my discussions of the graphical as nonrepresentational—that the computer is not an image-based medium.[33] To ultimately reassert the presence of an image logic, Stine points to the way that photographic and filmic technologies are used in the manufacture of integrated circuits and are thus part of the machinery that makes computers possible in their current regress toward infinite speed and infinitesimal size. In this, we can begin to see, as Stine says, how "this trajectory of technical operations beyond human perception... should be understood to be that closure of an epoch of writing that reveals logocentrism for what it always was, a certain guarantee against the threat of techné that all writing in some way returned to the human."[34] This is, if logocentrism once guaranteed that a remainder of humanity would persist after new technologies took their share, that era, Stine argues, is now definitely closed by computational technologies that seem not to need the human at all in their operations—just so many autonomous circuits of data and the images they generate. Stine's question then becomes: what is the product of the new, more tightly wound and rapidly pulsing circuit between image and data? His answer, unlike Whitten's in the previous chapter, will be that this further excision of the human from circuits of writing and voice necessitates a resurgence of the human and humanism as a defense against this very fate.

This is why Gaines's arrangement of the raster for and against the assembly of a fungible collective is important. The raster of the graphical field, like those of Gaines's gridworks, reconfigures creative labor in its relation to personhood and the possibilities of the creative self. The graphical field was designed to produce a form of the individual that was, on the one hand, well adapted to navigating a world turned into an information network while, on the other, able to forge a strong mode of individuality precisely in those spaces. Abetted by the proxemics of the mouse and cursor, set free within the seemingly open fields of the graphical display—its raster transforming the apparently undemocratic rigidity of the command-line interface into the democratic playground of the graphical display's open spaces—the ideal subject of graphic display systems forged a mode of creative individuality not sapped but buoyed by the vastness of an information network and its operating systems.[35]

In Gaines's denaturing of this graphical field, a kind of constraint is emphasized, and into that constrained opening comes an assembly, bodies arrayed together, mutually interfering, indistinct. It was as if Gaines saw the dangers of a certain renewed rhetoric of freedom, ascendant both in civil rights politics and in new technocultures—saw it, perhaps, as a technologized version of what Hartman calls "burdened individuality." With this phrase, Hartman refers to the freedoms granted to enslaved people after emancipation, granted precisely in order to extend their subjugation, this time under the yoke of personal responsibility.[36] In the wake of emancipation and its vaunted freedoms, Hartman says, "The exercise of free will, quite literally, was inextricable from guilty infractions, criminal misdeeds, punishable transgressions, and an elaborate micropenality of everyday life."[37] Call it burdened or call it augmented, this false promise of freedom, transformed but never abated, has left a deep scar across the present tense.[38]

The history of black life in the United States reveals the lie behind both sides of the antinomy often constructed to make sense of systems in general, or computational contexts in particular: on the one side, the system, the machine, the inhuman, all of which have been used to entrap, incarcerate, and immiserate black life from the Atlantic slave trade until now; on the other, freedom, the human, the subjective, the expressive, all of which have also long been used—often by people who feel themselves most sympathetic to equality and civil rights—to circumscribe and burden black life by trapping it within the form of the expressive individual, thereby erasing, even seeming to solve the structural history of racism.

This kind of progressive freedom, manifest in the freedom of the artist's hand set loose from social norms, the freedom of the blank canvas or the blank graphical screen, the trained freedom of the postwar knowledge worker, the authorial freedom of the conceptualist working in service of the idea . . . Gaines wanted none of it. But neither could he simply reject it. The threats to freedom were real, both intra- and interpolitically, among his fellow black artists as well as within various technocratic think tanks that established the political milieu for his thinking about labor and its environments.[39] If freedom for so many people engaged in the project of creating the graphical field invoked a particular form of collectivity built around the antinomy between autonomous individuality and the threat of homogenization, Gaines would make his graphical fields produce forms of collectivity based on indebtedness, contact, contiguity, on indistinction and accumulation.[40] Within a long history of false promises and "burdened individuality," these qualities of Gaines's collectives need not be understood as states of subjection chosen nihilistically or pessimistically, but as tactics for standing down, for ceasing the escalation of the human into more and more powerful technocracies of freedom, self-possession, and control.

Gaines's systems, in other words, are a machine for producing contiguity more than they are an imposed logic or depersonalizing structure. Contiguity, in this sense, short-circuits—rather than negates or opposes—the smooth interior-to-exterior relay of expressivity: what Gaines, echoing Immanuel Kant, has called the "free play of meanings."[41]

Gaines reorganizes the field of his images as rasters, as graphical interfaces, precisely in order to emphasize and extend contiguity, contact, and self-limitation.[42] The selves and things that show up in Gaines's rasters, via system or the projections of viewership, do so as tethered, as indebted. Everything that appears in one of Gaines's gridworks owes its existence, in precisely that form, to another image in the series or the triptych. Key here, especially for the ways in which Gaines's work addresses racial politics after expressivity and its associated modes of representational politics, is the fact that this contiguity is how Gaines supplements—deforms but doesn't negate or erase—the fungibility one sees in the way his systems absorb the singularity of particular selves and particular things. The move here isn't the dramatic one from fungibility to freedom, as though any form of individuality could defend against ongoing forms of racializing violence, as though individuality in all of its updates, including the graphical one, hasn't been the very instrument of that violence. Gaines makes the quieter move to contiguity, an avowed collective form that sees selfhood as the problem not the solution, and so stresses contact without communication, indebtedness without possession, transposition without representation. Fungibility-contiguity is, in other words, a dramatically different historical problem than alienation-individuality. Gaines wrests both conceptualism and the graphical interface out of the latter to show their historical entanglements with the former. The latter is a white history in search of a new universalizing principle, a supremacist history; the former is a black history, which is to say, an American history. If the new subjects of the graphical computer screen were to evade (and so invoke) the threat of fungibility in their exercise of a renewed form of creative freedom, Gaines's graphical systems would raise that threat. They did so not exactly to escape or defeat it, but to show the role that a certain enabling rhetoric of individuality and freedom has always played in both the racializing violence of fungible personhood and in white, predominantly liberal attempts to define itself against those threats.

Infrastructures of Containment: Julie Mehretu

5

I want to think about a particular moment in the making of one of Julie Mehretu's paintings. An early moment, long before completion and display. But some time after a particular work has been set in motion, its trajectories traced and starting to be followed. I'm thinking about work from the early and middle 2000s, where layers and intercalations of tracings sit way back in a painting to project into and interfere with the murmuration of curves, script, and colored planes that more aggressively assert themselves in the visual experience of the work. The layers—many architectural and urban planning schematics—get traced onto a work. A projector, a transparency, a beam of light flipped, inverted, and thrown onto a wall. An arm, a pencil, a face so close to the surface, body angled so that light passes by, sidled up to the bright throw, rubbing up against it close enough that the arm can reach but not so close as to obstruct the light. In process photos, often it is Mehretu's longtime studio assistant X who does this work.[1] In 2010, X had worked for Mehretu for three years. Looked at from a certain vantage (say, that of the museum or gallery, for whom X *might be* a name to be acknowledged, given *some* credit, mostly so that *real* credit can be reserved for the artist with a name, for Mehretu), X assists Mehretu's "vision," sits in the service of it, executes it.

But if Mehretu's work is about collectivity, and it is, then it's about these relationships too: relationships between X, tracing, and projective layers; between Mehretu and X; between X and the final painting. To think of this as background work leads to all the wrong metaphors, and that's because formally, the idea of background cannot describe how the projective layers in the paintings work. Neither can it describe how X sits in the final matrix of the work, nor adequately characterize the form of X's labor in the space of the works. Yes, X is hired labor; we don't need to be naive about that. But are they more than that too? Do the forms of collectivity embodied in Mehretu's paintings, their congeries of marks and elements, colors and materials, vectors and planes, allow X to be more than that, while also being that? There's a relationship between people here that I think vectors through a relationship in form, literal on both sides of that relation. It would be so easy to say that X's tracing exists to allow Mehretu's gestural freedom; X is the manual labor that allows the creative labor of Mehretu's hand to fly, to float, to improvise, to be free. But this refuses the invitation we are given when entering a Mehretu painting to repattern our thinking about the human and what it is set off against, about how value striates humans into the privileged and the disposable. And it would ignore the ways that the graphical computer interface rewires possibilities for freedom. Meaning, it would ignore the parallel ways that the artists whose work I've dwelled with so far have wanted to situate freedom narratives outside of the oppositional framing that would see freedom as opposed to constraint or to dispossession.

This history of the graphical screen that this book has tracked is a history of a particular bifurcation, where creative labor gains a new footing after World War II on the basis of it coming into a new kind of relationship with manual labor, itself now reconfigured. The graphical field is the place where creative labor retreats to gather itself, but not in opposition to the manual labor that thereafter, for a privileged few, gets assigned to the computer, to computing, and to the CPU. Rather, creative labor now would be subtended and supported (if invisibly) by that computing power—*augmented* in Douglas Engelbart's language. In the graphic interface, the power of the computer was harnessed to allow new forms of creative labor, based in the abstraction of making connections, to come to prominence. We see one form this rewiring of creativity takes in Lisa Nakamura's work on Navajo women working in the Fairchild Semiconductor factory, where their labor to construct circuits was claimed as creative, as cultural, by way of an exoticizing connection made between traditional Navajo weaving and the work of constructing a circuit.[2] Creativity came thereby to reside in the work of wiring those connections—presaging the kind of extractive relationship that diversity efforts, later in the twentieth and early in the twenty-first century, would have to black and brown workers. Vannevar Bush, in 1947, speculatively imagined this situation with his memex, where information work is understood as the work of making associations. Engelbart implemented this vision of creativity in the associative matrixes of his Augmented Human Intellect project. The open field of the graphical screen, unstriated, gridded precisely to obviate the feeling of a grid's constraints, both metaphorized and materialized this space of connectivity, of information being brought into contact with other information, nested in windows, generated in association.

To see how Mehretu's paintings help us understand some of the deeper implications here, it's important that we are precise in the way we imagine and describe association in Mehretu's paintings. Her works are often likened to networks and screens, although these claims usually rest on a question of visual likeness—that Mehretu's paintings *look like* computer screens, or somehow visually evoke the scale of networks. Such visual associations might be correct, but are often misleading or beside the point in computational environments. I do, however, think Mehretu's canvases share certain operative logics with the graphical field. Both work a particular relationship between containment and infinite expansion, between the potentiality for anything to exist *in* and the particularities *of* a specific assembly. And in this thought—encouraged by the tense proximity of Mehretu's canvases and the graphical fields they cite, inhabit, mock, and slyly reproduce—the figure of X tracing projections is an important guide, a reminder not to zone our thinking, where connection would only come to exist as an art form when it is set off against, zoned in extraction and isolation from, an act of making that is understood to be merely functional, computational, manual, programmed, automatic. Or as Andrianna Campbell puts it, questioning the contrast that so frequently appears in writing on Mehretu's work: between "media- and handmade marks."[3]

It's not the oppositional pole that matters here. It's the definition of something *in extraction from* in order to be positioned *in opposition to*. Because there is, of course, a reality of the market, where labor is extracted, zoned, and valued. X certainly exists in the lesser-valued part of that market. But part of the extractive work of that kind of market is to sap our imagination for how forms of life that exist there can be anything more, or anything else. So while I don't discount the reality in which X's work is zoned in order to be less highly valued, I do want to suggest that here, too, even in the context of a very well-known and justly rewarded artist and her assistants, we need to think about what else the associations built in Mehretu's studio can be. Mehretu's work enters into this kind of thinking and so demands it of us. It does so because of its proximity to, but not perfect coextension with, the graphical, where the graphical is itself a space, perhaps the central or at least the densest space for the reorganization of association as a specific form of collectivity. The graphical computer screen provides the field in which association would be lived, mouse in hand, cursor as one's proxy, the single, creative human isolated within networks of information that can only be glimpsed tangentially or in blur from one's situation there. Mehretu's and X's associative logics help us see that fact as a question of containment and infrastructure.

X and Mehretu meet at the intersection of an informational space, extend themselves through those vectors, touch through the laying down of lines, come together in the movement of improvisational marks over and across the canvas with its girding of tracings, plans, schemas. The field in which they work, X and Mehretu, tracery and murmur, contains that flight while making its extension imaginable. As we learned from Jack Whitten's work, improvisation is not the exercise of an unconstrained freedom, and freedom is not the expression of an uninhibited liberty. The price of these fantasies of freedom can also be a forgetting, a severing of self from history. Freedom as autonomy is what one gets offered only in exchange for taking responsibility for oneself, for isolating oneself in responsibility. The improvisation Mehretu practices moves instead through constraint. This was Alma Thomas's lesson too. The grid didn't set her free; the grid also did not impinge on her creativity. The grid was the set of constraints through which she had to move to see her world differently. In accepting constraints, she was accepting the partiality of her self, her being as something singular but less than or more than individual, more or less than individuated. The fragile, animated, sometimes enervated, sometimes bristling grid of Thomas's imaginative flights indicates an acceptance of limitation, where limitation means that one needs ballast, histories stolen and reclaimed, the work of others, even if that work takes the form of a bureaucratizing, mathematical logic, which is one history of the grid itself.[4] If the history of black life after the transatlantic slave trade is in part a history of mathematics, as Katherine McKittrick says, then Thomas commits, with her use of the grid, to working through that math to come out somewhere else. In a field of flowers, in outer space, never leaving her kitchen table studio, never ceasing the work of teaching.

Mehretu's grids take the more postindustrial, flexible form of the plan or project, a set of instructions to be followed, instructions encoding a vision for structure, an ordering of the events of painting. But as in Thomas's work, a grid's appearance in the overall matrix of Mehretu's work is not simply something that she supersedes or overcomes through flight. The plan exists at the level of the city, the city square, the building, architecture, public space, nation-space, but it also exists inside the relationship between Mehretu and X. So the fact that Mehretu hires assistants to trace those urban grids is itself not proof that Mehretu divides her work process into creative and noncreative parts, more and less skilled, artistic and non-, that she is now too famous to bother with such manual labor.

There are two Mehretu paintings that present very little but intercalated plans, all superimposed, vibrating and interfering together, jostling each other's orderly procession. These are *Projects* from 2008 and *Berliner Plätze* from 2009. In the case of *Projects*, X was one of the assistants who worked between projector, projection, transparency, plan, wall and canvas, and between that series of exchanges and Mehretu. The name would matter not because we must give a proper name, and thereby dignity, to the unsung laborers or, in Gregory Sholette's terms, the "dark matter" of the art world. It would matter because the more names we can pile into the crowded space of a Mehretu canvas, the less those names attach to individuals by way of possession, and the more the canvas—despite all of the best work of the art world to single out, name, and individuate the artist it needs—can be seen as an interruption of the processes of individuation that the art world doesn't know how to do without.[5]

Is this individual that the art world needs the same as or a historical extension of the individual as it has been reshaped by the graphical field? Mehretu's work, perhaps more forcefully than any other artist in this book, forces this question. Its scale alone places this question about persons in the milieu and atmosphere of information; in Mehretu's work, one has to speak about information to get to a vocabulary of persons. The sheer scale, the intensity of labor that seems to be embodied by works like *Projects* forces one either to superinflate their notion of the individual artist, or to give up on that ideal altogether in favor of an account set more in the collaborative, managerial atmospheres of the artist's studio. Those conversations about the studio—about outsourced labor, about armies of assistants, about the artwork as a set of instructions—often veer toward the vocabulary of conceptualism to recuperate a valued Idea from what appears to be a scene of debased or recessive labor. Or else they take on a melancholic tinge precisely because so many people, for so many reasons, don't want to give up on the artist as individual—the individual whose artisanal values and small scale can provide a last desperate kind of bulwark against the persistent encroachment of capitalist realism into the artist's studio.[6] Art lovers get depressed when that ideal seems to give way to something like fame. It's as though works at this scale, especially for artists who work at Mehretu's level of visibility, demand a language of capitalist realism where the artist inevitably ends up looking like a project manager, or whatever is the art world's avatar for dominant capitalist labor at that moment.[7] And while the labor critique of the project manager and management is real, it also hides a shadow commitment to the individual, as though what's been lost in this move to a period of project management is precisely the autonomous individual, the solo artist. That's often the only form of the human to which people know how to attach any ideal of freedom. One of the operations of liberalism in the United States—especially relevant to all the artists in this book—continues to be the need to isolate black individuals as exceptional in some way.[8]

Projects anticipates this conversation, not least for its title. What if we see in Mehretu's paintings, in their scale, in the way they supersede the individual, not another opportunity to bemoan the loss of the autonomous, artistic individual, lost either to fame or to the conceptualist gesture, but a chance to exit the very choice between the heroic individual and the individual succumbing to their own fame by farming their work out to an army of assistants? A chance, that is, to leave behind that idea of the individual as the type of person we want or the type of person we want in having lost? Such individuality was never anything but toxic for the black history in which Mehretu works and lives. The very promise has always been a guarantee that whatever the predations of America's racist history, black people from now on would be understood in the eyes of the state and so many of the state's "natural" citizens as now, finally, on equal footing, responsible for themselves.[9]

Projects doesn't evoke the graphical field of the computer screen because it looks like such a field, but because it tempts with the promise of the individual whose status grows in time with the hyperinflation of their capacity to work with and inside networks of information. Mehretu's *Projects* seems, in this sense, not to provide a visualization of Vannevar Bush's memex, which anticipated the graphical field, but to invoke the skill set of the person Bush imagines sitting in front of his memex:

> The lawyer has at his touch the associated opinions and decisions of his whole experience, and of the experience of friends and au-

thorities. The patent attorney has on call the millions of issued patents, with familiar trails to every point of his client's interest. The physician, puzzled by a patient's reactions, strikes the trail established in studying an earlier similar case, and runs rapidly through analogous case histories, with side references to the classics for the pertinent anatomy and histology. The chemist, struggling with the synthesis of an organic compound, has all the chemical literature before him in his laboratory, with trails following the analogies of compounds, and side trails to their physical and chemical behavior. The historian, with a vast chronological account of a people, parallels it with a skip trail which stops only on the salient items, and can follow at any time contemporary trails which lead him all over civilization at a particular epoch.[10]

Associations, skip trails, analogous case histories, side references, syntheses, chronological accounts . . . a vast array of associations that, in Bush's account, aggrandize the individual working in isolation at the terminal. X has been working with Mehretu, in her canvases, across those fields, for over twenty years now. What resources don't we have for understanding those associations, that span, and a canvas like *Projects*? The graphical field, while being the site of such promiscuous association, has also been the site of the particular impoverishment by way of which we don't quite know what to do with X and their presence in, through, and beyond the associative fields, the skip trails, analogies, side references, and chronologies of these canvases.

With Mehretu's canvases and their particular operation of the graphical field's logics, we open onto a world of dynamic interchangeability, association, and containment as a play of *anything*, rather than something. Recall Steinberg from chapter 1: "The flatbed picture plane makes its symbolic allusion to hard surfaces such as tabletops, studio floors, charts, bulletin boards—any receptor surface on which objects are scattered, on which data is entered, on which information may be received, printed, impressed—whether coherently or in confusion."[11] Anything goes in that container. The work of the container is precisely to hold anything and so offer the feeling that all is available. So we need to learn more about *forms of* containment, which prop up the projective sense of *anything* over the concrete determinant of *something*.

In Mehretu's painting from 2002, *Renegade Delirium* (plate 24), a cursory inventory of objects includes flat planes of color, straight or gently bent vectors of color, migratory tracery marks, filigree curls in black that sometimes explode out into linked rays with a common source, washes of a diluted black that register as gray or haze, faint wisps of black ink as though someone had it in mind to sketch smoke rising, flat planar colored circles, lines carved in negative out of thick hedges of lines, and a color palette that feels dominated by pink but is punctuated with royal blue, accented in yellow, and subtended and surrounded by black. And of course, all of this is undergirded by what seems to be, or feels like, a bottom layer of architectural plans rendered in line drawings with a precision that approximates printing. There is no evident shading, no modeling, nothing volumetric. Space isn't painted so much as implied or given as an aftereffect of the intervals between layers.

Writing about Mehretu's work is replete with such lists. A list doesn't bother with relations except insofar as it is itself a light touch mode of relation: a relationship built in the absence of stronger or more evident modes of relationality. In Engelbart's famous demonstration (the so-called "Mother of All Demos"), the list featured prominently as the form of data collection most amenable to displaying the affordances of a graphical organization of the screen. Famously, and invoking the cozy domesticity that would become the hallmark of the marketing of the personal computer, Engelbart manipulates a grocery list that he says has been given to him by his wife. She created the list. He imposes order on it, sorting it into categories that might match the shopping patterns of an efficient shopper. The graphical screen allows this imposition of order, aggrandizing the efficiency of the person who can impose order in, and because of, that open graphical expanse—creating associations, skip trails that align with ways that grocery stores are often themselves ordered. But a list, before this imposition, tames profusion by capitulating to it. It takes the form of profusion; it gives up on organization in favor of just getting it all down in one place. This is how the entry on Mehretu in the *Remote Viewing* exhibition catalog begins: "Her work incorporates everything from . . ."[12] And in the same catalog, Katy Siegel writes that Mehretu has been creating "inventories" of her own marks since 1997, early in her career. The items that proliferate in such inventories Mehretu sometimes calls "characters."[13]

A list and an inventory are both forms of gathering. And Mehretu's paintings are gatherings, that much is clear by the prevalence of the list form. But what is the form of that gathering? Layering is one form that it assumes. So it matters how that layering is arranged. In HOWL, *eon (I, II)*

(2017, plate 25), installed in 2017 in the lobby of the newly reopened San Francisco Museum of Modern Art (SFMOMA), the layers produce depth, but not illusionistically—not by representing depth through, say, perspective. It's not a dimensional depth beyond the barest, most schematic sense in which one thing, added *after* another, looks to have been added *atop* the other. When these layers are seen through, as Mehretu almost always lets one do, the layers acquire sequence and priority. In HOWL, an outer scrim of Benday dots has been printed on top of several underlayers of painting and printing. But Mehretu never leaves the priority of these levels alone, which means we can never rest assured that the layers correspond to particular forms of content, even if those forms are all modes of abstraction. In HOWL, therefore, it's never the case that the traces of race riots, street protests, and nineteenth-century depictions of the American West stay securely and stably beneath the rest of the content, which means we can never say something like Mehretu's more manual marks, the gestural marks of black paint, keep their distance enough to comment on or caption the distorted photos.

HOWL is built up from two composited landscapes of the nineteenth-century American West: one by Frederick Church, the other by Albert Bierstadt. Both are merged with more recent news images of protests in the wake of fatal shootings of black men. If these particular concrete images register in the overall matrix of the canvas, it is not as themselves. They are not perceivable or sensible and are therefore not referential in the usual sense. You more know they're there; one can study the idea of them and their presence, but not study them in their particularity and singularity. They've been too thoroughly integrated. Their containment by the canvas doesn't address a viewer as an individuated interpreter; that path is blocked, at least visually.

This confusion of layers, and therefore of depth, is exacerbated by Mehretu's habit of sometimes simulating depth, simulating the visual results of seeing one thing through another. Sometimes one really does view one mark through another. In HOWL, one often sees underlayers through the spaces between Benday dots. In some instances of seeing through, the layer that registers as bottommost does so because it appears grayed out, faded, as though seen through a translucent but not transparent screen. But looking very closely at HOWL, a view that the SFMOMA central lobby staircase affords, one can see that Mehretu also paints some marks on top (or late in the painting) but precisely to look grayed out, as though they are submerged beneath something. These are nearly impossible to distinguish from the blurring or graying out where one thing was actually painted over top of another. Here, the layering *is* illusionistic. One isn't seeing a form grayed out because something else is interfering with the passage of light to one's eyes. A form is sometimes grayed out because Mehretu has painted it that way, *as though* seen through something else.[14]

Why do this? Why produce depth or priority or firstness in two distinct ways that are so difficult to notice as distinct? Because however slight the differentiation, this proliferates modes of nesting things in a cramped space that threatens never to contain what it presents. Their coexistence flirts with dramas of containment and as such are modes of togetherness. As the graphical field has always been and has always aspired to be.

The chapter on Jack Whitten begins with a painting that seemed to directly represent a graphical computer screen (that of an iPhone). This chapter begins with a series of works that, like Alma Thomas's paintings from the first chapter, look very little like graphical screens. Although others, commenting on Mehretu's work, have seen them differently. David Joselit, in a review of a Whitney Biennial in which Mehretu's *Empirical Construction, Istanbul* (2003) appeared, says: "Mehretu, too, in her spectacular compositions reminiscent of giant scrambled computer screens, lays down marks and forms in as many as six translucent layers, creating a compressed but spatial, or expanded, surface."[15] Or Christopher Miles: "Mehretu builds the paintings from misty transparent and translucent layers, each with its own set of marks and imagery—something like hand-painted versions of the collapsed strata utilized in graphics and imaging software."[16] Such likeness notwithstanding, the fact that the graphical computer screen is only secondarily or epiphenomenally visual, a host for representation but not foundationally representational, should encourage us to seek out other axes of comparison. In other words, as I argue in each chapter, the graphical field needs to be tracked not through a series of visual correspondences, but through a series of resonances with its operational logics, with the ideas that made it possible. What shows up most clearly in relation to Mehretu's work is the fact that the graphical field is an experimental infrastructure of containment whose temporality is always about the thing to come, about what's next. Leo Steinberg's work on operational processes predicts this (see chapter 1), and Jacob Gaboury's work articulates it as a specifically graphical logic.[17]

But this confusion between the visual and the graphical, as I refer to it, is instructive, both conceptually and historically. The graphical screen, as this book emphasizes, is not fundamentally an image-based platform, even if its actual structure allows it to host images as one kind of interactive form—allows it, in fact, to be marketed as more picture than text, intuitive like an image is intuitive, and therefore more personalized and personalizable than text-based input systems.[18] The graphical field is not, in any easy way, analogous to the canvas. Or wasn't, until Leo Steinberg's attempt to reorient our thinking toward the canvas as itself not primarily a container for images, nor even an object primarily addressed to the eyes, but an operational space, a container for data, a place where information flows intersect and interfere (see chapter 1).

Here, as Steinberg hints, perception obtains a weird status. In Mark Hansen's or Brian Massumi's terms, the perceiving body always envelops the digital and the computational. This is what Massumi means when he insists on the "superiority" of the analog, and it's why Hansen insists on the primariness of embodiment.[19] But Massumi's and Hansen's insistence only makes sense when seen in relation to the thought or feeling or fear that computers might make the body come second, become a mere product of the computational environment. And certainly the graphical field feels like this, with its prostheses for hand and eye aligning in the cursor's crosshairs, with its shaping of the free play of the imagination, or what Engelbart unabashedly calls *training*. Consequently, it's easy to imagine that the operational canvas is the space where human perception, in its humanity, goes to die. And so to imagine that that is where humanity must be defended or resuscitated. I do think Engelbart thought this way about the computer interface, and that the Metropolitan Museum of Art thought this way about their postwar graphical art exhibitions (see the introduction). But both stories, of decline and resurgence, share an assumption that Steinberg importantly does not make: that the figure, the point in space addressed by the operational field, canvas or screen, can be assumed to be a human, can as such be assumed to share human traits, traits like embodiment, like perception. This is why Steinberg gives this thought the form of a question: "Is he a man in a hurry? . . . [T]here is a proposition here . . . it is unclear."

It is on this point, precisely this confusion, that Mehretu's canvases and the graphical field of the personal computer most densely intersect and most vehemently diverge. We can think of them as involutions of one another. From the site of the same fissive impasse, Mehretu intensely follows the path of black thought and black study in refusing to accept any compensatory modalities of the human, given in autonomy, in freedom, in responsibility. In the face of her canvases, the aspiration to be such a thing becomes hopeless; one floats in proximity to the experimental infrastructures for being that are on offer, becomes deracinated, makes due with quasi containments.[20] The graphical field, meanwhile, follows out the parallel logic of a certain technoliberalism, reinvesting in the individual, but now not as a defense against the homogeneity of the crowd, but as the new container for both the self and the self's routing through populations, which is to say, data fields, homophily, algorithmic assemblage . . . places where individuality becomes the site for dis- and reassembly, where the self becomes operationalized.[21] The graphic field is the space of this operation and prepares the way for its efflorescence.

I have wanted to get at the ways that a graphical interface catches people up in its fields, transforms them, and so begins to alter the very idea, or anyway, the practical operation, of the human. The graphical screen is a labor technology first; its visual manifestation was always in service of its aim to transform labor for an informational milieu. It was never, in any case, meant simply to be looked at and described formally. Performative language suits the space better, as Brenda Laurel predicts with her thinking about "computers as theater."[22]

Like all the artists I've considered, Mehretu's work is diverse, divergent. So, as in other chapters, I'm selective about the works I treat, looking to characterize a set of historical relations more than characterize anything like Mehretu's oeuvre. For my purposes, there are a few repeated gestures that undergird what I have to say, and these are worth at least provisionally generalizing. Scale is the first, and is an oft-remarked feature of Mehretu's work. Their massive scale has invited metaphorical comparison to the scales at which contemporary technologies seem to operate— although too often commentators on contemporary networked technologies have conflated complex and difficult to understand with large, and in doing so make some odd, though familiar, assumptions about the form of the human who is supposed to be the measure of these things. Here's one example: "The conflation of multiple perspectives and levels of information creates a kaleidoscopic configuration that recalls the cacophonous experience of everyday life in an urban environment."[23] In this vein, the idea of "networks" comes up frequently, even though, again, it's not clear that scale measured on a spectrum from micro to macro is the best way to characterize what electronic networks are and do. They are, just to name one complicating relation, both micro and macro, able to address a single individual while aggregating that individual with innumerable others. Big data is big precisely so that it has the potential to work at such microscopic scales of address.[24] Likewise, I think it is not clear that characterizing Mehretu's scale as "large" fully takes their measure, or describes how and in what registers they operate. And in any case, large doesn't always mean overwhelming, where an individualized, "normal" human body is needed and presumed for that attribution of scale. Mehretu's 2002 painting *Renegade Delirium* is 90 × 144 in. (7½ ×12 ft.). This is not an exceptional scale for her work. Her *Mural* (2009) for the lobby of the Goldman Sachs headquarters is far larger, as is her diptych installation for the SFMOMA, *HOWL, eon (I, II)*, where each panel is 27 × 32 ft. The latter two don't fit within a predefined space so much as they quite literally assume the scale of the architecture that houses them. *Large* is therefore one way of putting it, but there are other ways. For example, to say her works become architectural more than they fit inside any architecture, even while they live inside various buildings, is to say that they become infrastructures in and of themselves.

Besides scale, perhaps the feature that most characterizes Mehretu's work—certainly the one singled out by both of the critics quoted above and most of Mehretu's commentators—is the way she works in layers, often with many layers of plans and drawings undergirding many more layers of mark, gesture, accident, and incident. It is often the case, although not always, that the mechanical drawings—projected, traced—appear to occupy the background or earlier levels of her works while the hand-based modes of mark-making inhabit the upper or later registers. Although, as we've already seen, the way the layers interact confound any simple, stable attribution of depth and surface.

Mehretu herself has given a vocabulary to the profusion of incident and information in her works: she refers to "characters" as a way to talk about the groupings, the collectives of marks that inhabit distinctive layers in her works.[25] *Characters*, referencing their narrative function, gets at a sense of repetition, the way certain marks recur across a canvas, and even across different canvases. Early Mehretu works such as *Character Migration Analysis Index* (1997) and *Timeline Analysis of Character Behavior* (1997), both ink on mylar and under six inches on a side, depict these characters as kinds of informatic displays. Given the dense referentiality of Mehretu's canvases—and this is the third generalized quality that I'll list—her works often seem to be about something clear and articulable, despite their abstraction and the ways their own elements and layerings interfere with the ability to identify and name anything in the works. Her installation for SFMOMA can thus be said to be about "the complex leg-acy of nineteenth-century westward expansion, including the Bay Area's deeply embedded histories of colonialism, capitalism, class conflict, social protest, and technological innovation."[26] Or *Mural* for Goldman Sachs (discussed in the coda) can be said to be about a history of finance capi-talism.[27] The reading of HOWL is authorized by the photographs Mehretu used as a basis for the painting. But in the final product, those referents are divorced from any physical or phenomenological sense, as they can hardly be perceived at all, and certainly not at the distance the works in-sist on between themselves and their viewers.

Mehretu, across her career, has produced paintings and drawings while also working in a variety of photo-mechanical reproductive tech-niques, the latter both discretely in stand-alone works and in many of her paintings. She has taken many high-profile public commissions, includ-ing the ones for SFMOMA and Goldman Sachs, and she has had residen-cies with a master printer resulting in the touring exhibition *Excavations: The Prints of Julie Mehretu*. She resides and shows in the United States. But she has also shown as a representative of Ethiopia where she was born (*Julie Mehretu: The Addis Show*, Gebre Kristos Desta Center—Modern Art Museum, Addis Ababa, Ethiopia). We could accumulate biography data, but in the end we would still have to say that Mehretu has no given relationship to birthplace, home, nation, or for that matter, race, although her personal history is often cited (including by Mehretu herself) as a con-ceptual foundation for her work.[28]

But these generalizations, while they label salient formal features of Mehretu's work, can seem, in the art-historical register that they echo, to lead only and always to oeuvre, and thus back to artist as the subject of history—and so to Mehretu as the representative black artist. I don't think Mehretu makes those kind of claims for herself. Actually, I think her work actively militates against those claims to the extent that it works at and to-ward other ways of plotting the human into a field. This is why the conver-sation about her work can lead us to the graphical interface as something that produces or anyway nudges subjects of history into a particular form. And for that to happen, we need a different orienting vocabulary.

I've been building to this: that Mehretu's works can be understood as experimental infrastructures for the contingent reorganization of life.[29] The phrase means to register four displacements: to say "experimental infrastructure" is not to say image space; that is not their address (neither where they live nor how they exist to be encountered). To say "contingent" is not to say subjective; they don't address themselves to individual vicissitudes. Instead, they catch individuals up in their folds and deposit them elsewhere, estranged from sense and meaning as hermeneutic activities, as the plumbing of depths. To say "reorganization" is not to say transformation or enlightenment or edification or even defamiliarization; they don't exist to change minds and hearts. They aspire to reorganize the human form in which the mind or heart come to reside. And to say "life" is not to say "viewer," not to say a being contained in a porous subjectivity available for critical intervention or the aesthetic pleasure of, as Lauren Berlant puts it, being spanked a little by art.[30] Life inside what I referred to in the first chapter as an operational process takes the form of something both less and more than a subject; it is both more molecular and more global, more diffuse and less well organized, less well known because less an object of knowledge than of quantification and experiment.[31] These displacements land us in the field of the graphical, as they have been its work.

Building on Leo Steinberg's work (see chapter 1), I'm proposing that what so often gets registered in Mehretu's work as complexity can, in an operational milieu, be thinkable as a psychic address to a thing we don't yet believe ourselves to be, to some contingent organization of life that we don't inhabit or don't inhabit yet and maybe desperately want not to inhabit, all the while knowing or fearing we might already be living there. Graphical fields, and the information networks they predicated, are harrowing because they catch up not subjects (preformed, e.g., as audience) but life (unformed) in a mode of address that is misrecognizable for sure (as friendly, as angry, as bewilderingly complex and reassuring). But they also, whatever the ways people know how to feel recognized, address themselves to beings, forms of the human, that haven't existed yet because they are actively, right now, being generated.

This is a less outlandish proposal when we remember that the horizon of this book and the history it considers is the extraction and compression of life into the confines of a screen, a labor space with particular characteristics, features, and affordances; a screen designed to accommodate anything and everything; a space made coherent only in the freedom of the creative subject that it was designed to make possible; which is to say, only in the reconstruction of whiteness not as essence or history condensed in a particular region, but as diversity or difference itself, as what others have called postracial.

The history of the graphical field has always predicted Julie Mehretu's work. Not, of course, its specificity or special incisiveness or unique range of interests. But the dark potential of glut and its infinitely expanding folds of containment. The promise of the graphical screen was always that it could contain everything, from grocery lists to a life remembered in social media. Mehretu works at the edges of that promise. And so, in her work, the dramas are no longer about pixel and resolution, field and bit, as they have been up to this point. They expand to layers, each coeval and coequal, a set of intercalated windows or projects, set in relation, moved through in a kind of manic multitasking. This is precisely where the figure of the studio assistant lives—it is what they assist in manifesting. Mehretu thus addresses the kind of labor that has come to exist in the graphical field, because of the graphical field, seen as a space of reconfigured personhood.[32]

There is agreement among Mehretu's critics that she has invented a kind of space unique for its capacity to contain, for its delamination of line from figuration, for its multiple discordant representational regimes, and for the ways that a profusion of marks and characters makes the fact of containment a wonder. In this way, Mehretu both lyses and overpopulates her canvases. This drama of profusion and containment is a key dynamic in her work as well as in the literature on her work. This is where the form of the list comes in handy for people endeavoring to capture something of that profusion in prose. And the profusion that cannot be contained but that can only be intimated by the list, in turn, spawns metaphors in the literature on Mehretu's work: data, information, electronic networks . . . all contemporary forms that seem themselves to suggest profusion of the sort that no one knows yet how to contain.

This dynamic between profusion and containment then leads to another line of thought: an emphasis on her layers as spacers, organizers of space and profusion. On a basic technical level, Mehretu separates her layers by laying down a transparent film of acrylic and silica between each, allowing her to draw on and in those intervals, while allowing a kind of visual access, sometimes direct, sometimes occluded, always by way of transparency, to the levels beneath. This is why Mehretu and her critics often speak of strata, working the geological metaphor, bolstering a case for linking the scale of Mehretu's canvases, along with their profusion, to something planetary in scale. But as I note in my description of HOWL, there is a great deal of play between otherwise discrete layers, with marks often juxtaposed in such a way that, if only in those moments, the layers seem less discrete than intercalated, but always unevenly, unsystematically. This shifts the emphasis of the works from the layers themselves to movement between layers, and thus to the work as a kind of contingent infrastructure: infrastructure in the sense of being labile, occasional, subject to change.[33]

And this leads, finally, to the tension that gets set up between what are perceived to be the two major types of information or data contained in the works: on the one hand, the engineering and architectural drawings, the planographic renderings, the institutionalized forms of information presentation, what Mehretu in an interview once called the "language of Rationalism"; and, on the other, the gestural marks that scatter across the surface, interpenetrating and flying over (sometimes through, but mostly over) the previous.[34] We have to note here that "the language of Rationalism" is executed by her assistants while the gestural marks are executed by Mehretu herself. In this particular kind of containment, the artist would seem to confront something "rational." And whatever drama occurs in the canvas would occur across the poles of this defining, structuring tension. This zoning of the human (artist) as distinct and separate from the rational (technological, industrial) has also, not coincidentally, been a useful narrative for people wanting to describe the social and political impacts of technology while reserving a cherished place for the human in that schema.[35] But whatever the graphical field's investments in rationalism, this is precisely the narrative that the graphical field set out to overturn so that whiteness could gather itself in a different field of play.

Profusion/containment, layers, the rational versus the human: these dynamics are all over Mehretu's work. Mehretu sometimes employs more muscular structures for containment, where containment almost reaches to the edges, almost tames profusion. One such structure, especially prominent in her early work, is the vortex, a violent ascension or descension of matter usually centered on the canvas, thus centering the canvas itself. Centrifugal, centripetal, a force that sweeps, carries, organizes in chaos. Her characters in *Renegade Delirium* (2002), *Stadia II* (2004), and (in negative) *Dispersion* (2002, plate 26) seem to swirl around some absent center in vertiginous motion. Containment, of course, doesn't necessitate order or rationality; it simply implies a gathering, without saying much about what galvanizes or stirs that gathering.

Occasionally things rise up from out of the welter of a Mehretu painting and seem, often fleetingly, to organize the whole, to provide an interior mode of containment. In works like *Stadia III* (2005) and *Black*

Ground (deep light) (2006, plate 27), the NBC logo appears in the lower right-hand corner of the canvas. In each case, that logo stands out from the profusion, unobscured by other layers of information, visibly atop those layers, and so relatively isolated. In the case of *Stadia III*, the logo is nothing more than an outline, a stencil. In *Black Ground*, the logo appears filled in, a silhouette in black. That mark, placed in that location, iconic and referential when most of Mehretu's marks are just iconic (or simply unplaceable, abstract in this sense), remakes the entire canvas as a TV screen. Much like Whitten's *Apps for Obama*, discussed at the start of chapter 3, this literalizes my book's project, making the canvas function like a kind of screen—this one televisual rather than computational, but still a cathode-ray tube (CRT). The logo establishes an imagined or invoked frontmost transparent screen, behind or inside of which the action of the painting seems to take place. This, then, is another figure of containment, and one that I'm sure won't seem out of place in the oeuvre of an artist so associated with media and mediation, and with visual technologies that seem defined less by medium and more by their resistance to the specificity of medium, their capacity to screen anything. It is the special purview of the screen to aspire to greater and greater scopes of containment. Less an image-medium than a container, the graphical screen was always conceived this way.

This trajectory is especially evident in a series of three paintings (*Stadia I, II,* and *III,* all from 2004) widely accepted to be about mass spectacle. Their titles come from the architectural renderings of three famous, massive sports stadiums that sit more or less in the anchoring center of each canvas. All were conceived in the run-up to the 2004 Summer Olympics and during the US invasion of Iraq, events experienced, for those who weren't targets of the bombing, exclusively through television.[36] Mass spectacle itself is a term for the containment of profusion that is also a channeling of profusion and a marketing of it. But the TV screen has cuts, multiple cameras, splicing, voice-overs... all manner of technology for letting profusion expand into other frames, still contained, so that profusion might feel manageable, meaning watchable: the nightly news, a sports event. Genre, in this sense, offers containment as relief from the very profusion for which it is also the occasion.

Relatedly, one of the problems computer interface designers had to face was how to fit everything in the world onto a single screen. The graphic interface is the solution to that problem for the personal computer; information theory is the grammar of that solution.[37] For Engelbart and his team, inspired by Vannevar Bush, *everything* meant all the information produced by scientific researchers, encoded in a form that allowed it to travel with maximum dispersion and rapidity.[38] They didn't think much beyond scientific information, even if in the famous Demo from 1968 Engelbart illustrated some of the graphical screen's wider capacities by organizing a grocery list. But here, even a grocery list becomes information optimized to interface with the worlds of its dispersion and circulation, helping the list-maker move through a physical grocery store, but also, more slyly, through the containers of gendering. That was the point of Engelbart's grocery list. Windows were the most overt way in which the graphical screen was designed to contain profusion.[39] And there is a sense, both technical and practical, in which "layers" in Mehretu's work function like windows in the graphic interface.

But the graphic screen was built for containment in a far more fundamental sense. By eschewing any one natural language or coding, such as the text in a command-line interface, the graphic screen could traffic in any manner of sign or sign regime. This is maybe what most fundamentally defines a graphical screen *as* graphical. Many have tended to think about this as an image space—that is, as graphics. But that is less accurate than it is evidence of a reflex to oppose image and text (if the screen isn't text-based, then it must be image-based).[40] A graphical interface is no more aligned with images than it is with text.[41] It is strictly agnostic about what it contains and the languages in which it operates—it inherits a tenet of information theory in that sense, the strict separability of form and content so that form could be agnostic about content, treating all forms of content equally.[42] That is the primary meaning of *graphical* in this context. And this, as is emphasized in previous chapters, is so that the graphical field can eventually come to feel as though it is nothing more and nothing less than a practical manifestation of the will of the user: one's own space, optimized for efficient working, but personalized in all of its particulars. Blank, precisely so it can be filled by a particular I, the graphical then becoming a manifestation of a particular first person pluralized (many I's all occupying the same space without any interference between them).

In Mehretu's work, *layers* is a term that refers equally to her work process as to the topology of her surfaces. *Layers* is an apt term for describing the graphical field as well, where *layers* might refer equally to the windows into which users compartmentalize their projects, or the levels of mediation that separate and connect computer and user. In the intercut of intercalation, layers might also describe a form of selfhood, or the process by which that selfhood is explored, opened up, and turned outward, as in a painting, or as in a process of reckoning with the violent sedimentations of history. As Hortense Spillers argues, "In order for me to speak a truer word concerning myself, I must strip down through layers of attenuated meanings, made an excess in time, over time, assigned by a particular historical order, and there await whatever marvels of my own inventiveness. The personal pronouns are offered in the service of a collective function."[43] These layers are the accretions of historical dominance—of American democracy, law, and society making the black body and the black population into what it needs again and again, over time, so that black is made an excess in time. Spillers enumerates the names by which history has made her desperately knowable, locatable, available when needed—thrown to the margins when not. Above all, containable. And yet, Spillers leaves no space, no buffer, neither in life nor in grammar, between these layers and herself. The "marvels of her own inventiveness" are invoked in confrontation with the self, her self. The layers await her, a kind of bastard inheritance, her "prepossession." They are, in this sense, a sedimented layering that black life, in its inventiveness, its work "in the hold" of such layerings, must create experimental infrastructures to endure, survive, exceed.[44] "The personal pronouns are offered in the service of a collective function." An experimental infrastructure is a collective function. And so, all of the dizzying, disorienting complexity that Mehretu seems to both assert and somehow, for many critics, offer refuge from, doesn't just reference contemporary information society or the economic networks of finance capitalism or intimate extimacies of globalization, but the structure of black subjectivity "made an excess in time." The reasons for this coincidence, of canvas to subject, graphical field to person, are not coincidental.

"Her work incorporates everything from . . ."[45] Layers are how Mehretu holds all of this profusion together, one strategy of containment. Transparent, sanded acrylic sits between the layers, separating and connecting, allowing each subsequent layer to both give access to the one below while also obscuring it. There is erasure in Mehretu's canvases—not least in a work like *Dispersion*, but more obviously and overtly in *Palimpsest (old gods)* (2006, plate 28), where she has literally erased a passage in the center of the canvas. But even when the predominant strategy in a Mehretu canvas is erasure, e.g., in the three infrastructures of density in *Disperson*, erasure still rarely operates through simple occlusion, at least not affectively. As in *HOWL* and its subtending but invisible photographs, everything is or feels available in a Mehretu canvas. There is the feeling that, with enough time, it could all be seen, described, accounted for. There is noise and amassing, the noise of amassing, but always something contained, even a kind of clandestine restraint at work in Mehretu's adherence to a cast of recurring characters, in the wash of repetition across her massive canvases, in their overall form that is usually a form in repeated motion. This is the stark hopefulness of a Mehretu canvas, seeming to flatter the human and its vaunted powers of perception. But it also describes their almost aggressive stance toward that figure of humanity: a kind of challenge or dare, an ironic excess of such a human figure mirrored in the work precisely so that viewers come to feel that they can never live up to it. I think this is, in part, how to account for Adrienne Edwards's striking claim that Mehretu's works, especially her gray paintings (2012–17), "are remarkable for what they withhold, for their ability to insist upon the brink of invisibility and ravishing of their intense proximity to the abyss as muted tones, soft yet dense chromas, and bizarre radiance."[46]

But something changes in Mehretu's paintings after 2016. Where before was line, delineation, layer, transparency, shape, assembly through geometry, profusion in containment, after 2016 Mehretu's canvases are aerosol and obstacle, tracery, cloud, and saturation. Her 2018 *Sun Ship (J. C.)* (plate 29) is an example. Sprays of purple, green, and yellow; geometries given in the negative of an object removed, so that the painting seems to remember all the objects that are no longer in it; a latticed tracery of black scrawl, thick, thin, meandering, densely associated. The layers are still here, but now register as depth seen through liquid, their edges watery. There is so little that draws more attention than anything else. And so there is very little that organizes the 108 × 120-in. expanse of canvas. There are two circles sprayed in negative, one large, one small. Both lay across the central meridian of the work. And floating somehow both above and below the pool of the work is a lime-green wisp of cloud that is also the product of aerosol application.

The works I've discussed so far, made prior to 2016, build worlds from line and point, bit and field; these more recent works need a vocabulary of liquidity. There are things we can know by reading wall labels and reviews, although this rarely becomes a phenomenological knowing (it's not something we can perceive in the work): that, for instance, these paintings are built up from photos sourced from Associated Press and Reuters; that, like Whitten's work, they move with the photographic as a machinery of image generation (not a realist claim, but an operationalist one); that any such referentiality is buried or blurred by way of aerosol into the matrix of the painting. The subject of a specific image, referencing a specific event, is not abstracted in the sense of lost, a tease of presence and absence. Abstraction here is more like a transcoding, reminiscent of Charles Gaines's images, a process whereby one thing, one materiality, one address to a body, is transformed into another. Mehretu's aerosol paintings are the result of that transformation, but they are also a document or registration of it. All operational processes are both an effect and a record of the steps through which that effect was reached, even as the effect gives way to new processes. Operational processes don't cease, never fuse into a final image. This is where Mehretu's recent paintings mark a significant difference over the works described previously: being liquid, they are even harder to resolve than Mehretu's previous paintings. While the plans embedded in previous work imply the potentiality of the build, construction, and capacity, even repeatability, these more recent works seem to have internalized that motion of potentiality, not as a distant future possibility but as something volatile now . . . or nearly now.

Under close examination, face pressed nearly to canvas, there are three types of surface saturations in *Sun Ship (J. C.)*, plus every possible form of diffraction between them. There are the stenciled, shaped areas in which aerosol stipples the surface in such fine patterns of dots that it only really resolves itself at the nearest proximities. Here, tight patterns of points cluster, sometimes huddling close, sometime spacing out—where points now are generated out of the geometries of gravity and surface tension, each a force of containment on a liquefied and airborne substrate. Does an aerosol stream produce a grid pattern or the point where a grid gives way to some other organization? The aerosol passages seem to ask this question. There is also a network of black lines, each a tracing, laid down by implements held like writing tools. These pass under and over and through the aerosol dispersions. And yet, they are not autonomous entities as, say, in a Jackson Pollock. These lines give way to the hard boundaries of stencil or simply to the logic of another part of the painting. They yield, like the aerosol yields to the edge of the object that interrupts the spray of paint. The lines sometimes get truncated, motion not stilled but ceased. The final form of surface saturation, in this provisional and partial listing, are the nebula of green and purple. These seem not to be marks at all, seem not to have been laid down or applied or sprayed in any identifiable way. They seem rather to simply be there, in and as the painting's undergirding and interstice. No matter how close you get, you can't get close enough to make these passages resolve into any process that made them. They float in a permanent distance. Not even background, because with backgrounds, there is an imaginable progress to a foreground, a bridgeable space. These stains, these cloud formations are either indistinguishable from the weave of the canvas or they sit at an impossible distance from it, as though one unlikely space is being viewed through another, but by way of disconnection. There are places where these dissociated areas roughly mirror the stipulations of aerosol, as though what had been aerosol has been washed out by water, transferred through capillary motion out and away from the point at which paint contacts surface. As though aerosol, already aerated, has now been further dispersed in liquid: the expansion of air, the expansion of liquid, two states of matter mimicking each other. But there are other passages in purple and green that float free of this form, perhaps having nothing to do with it: where expansion gives way to something so stretched that we can no longer get back along the processual path. When seen from afar, these areas fluoresce, which further confuses their spatial and material relation to the rest of the canvas. Alma Thomas's prepositional aesthetics reassert themselves here: those fluorescent zones float free *from*, while floating *inside* the matrix of the work. They seem to speak from another state of matter altogether: as though ultraviolet light were, at the same time, to appear within the visible light spectrum. Visibilities and invisibilities commingling. But Mehretu's pictures have never just been about vision, just as they have never been only pictures.

An important aspect of any attempt to write about Mehretu's works, and especially these more recent paintings, is that it is extremely difficult to write about any specific coordinate location in the painting's expanse. Words and phrases can attach to patterned phenomena, provisional generalization. But to isolate any single coordinate location in the oversaturated field of the canvas, to share looking in that way with a reader, seems to overtax language. Or else, to turn language itself into a kind of coordinate space that must be overlaid on the canvas but that isn't otherwise resident there. Without this the canvases are all zones of play that maximize the possibility for misunderstanding, and so minimize the possibility for writer and reader to successfully coordinate with one another. The effect—of the expanse of the canvas, the profusion of marks, the withdrawal from reference, all of it—is to make it nearly impossible for writer and reader, in sharing a common canvas, to share a common point of reference. We slide all around the canvas, in pursuit of one another, or else, we accept our togetherness in estrangement, never quite able to find each other while still never quite floating fully free from the gravity of the overall work. The paintings create spaces that in their operational temporality force a loose togetherness, always foiling any fantasy of equality while likewise never allowing any fantasy of autonomy or freedom from one another or from the work of finding each other, which is always pestered by the work of losing each other. One doesn't belong in a Mehretu canvas, and so one can't be excluded either. One operationalizes the self, volatizes the self's relation to the shapes, geometries, passages, saturations in which others find themselves in being lost there.

So we could say that Mehretu's paintings constitute a series of experiments with creating infrastructures of fragile and loose togetherness, of holding things together but in diffusion, dispersion. The process of reckoning with her works requires stripping down through the layers, and there awaiting whatever marvels of inventiveness would allow someone to live there, rather than working hard to decipher, tease apart, to categorize and sort, to try to impose order. An experimental infrastructure is a space invented to house or capture life. Michelle Murphy shows how the attempt to house life has been possible through a logic of population management that has been visible, for instance, in humanitarian and NGO interventions in Africa. Saidiya Hartman shows how, for a time in the early twentieth century, black girlhood operated as an infrastructure to contain life (in police logs and social work ledgers) and, at the same time, an infrastructure by which life's containments were forever exceeded, a way to make the space between subjectivity and personhood into a riot.[47] The riotousness was the infrastructure: a tenuous, courageous, willful experiment with life itself, with how to steal time, steal life. But that infrastructure, so subject to change, so contingent, so fragile, so vulnerable, also created the feeling and reality of volatility, of destabilization that the infrastructure was also, and at the same time, a way of surviving.

An infrastructure is a form of collective life, of gathering life, for better or worse, thick and thin. It is also, therefore, a way of gathering whatever counts as parts of a life: human or inhuman, selected or dysselected. The graphical interface was an infrastructure in both of these senses, although perhaps more rigid and structural in design than infrastructural. And yet, the very idea of the graphical screen was to free a user into a space of creativity, of expansive selfhood, unbound by textual or technical strictures. An infrastructure then, in a precise sense, if only an affective sense, given that it was also, of course, a way to train the human to inhabit certain new structures of work where productivity would be determined by and in the encounter with information. Infrastructures are pedagogies too; they aspire to foster both learning and unlearning.[48]

To call Mehretu's canvases experimental infrastructures and thus forms of lightly galvanic togetherness is not a metaphor. I don't mean that they represent such processes as they happen elsewhere, or that they might give people ideas for how to improvise better infrastructures from within the space of actual life. Their immersiveness, their scale, their cacophony are all markers of the actualness of Mehretu's infrastructures. Infrastructures such as activist organizations, marches, or hashtags are no more easy to inhabit, no more actual or available. They all require active propping up, a collective agreement to endure through whatever, to work out the terms of one's engagement at the same time as one is working out the terms of the structures through which that engagement finds form, solidarity, and containment. Here is Lauren Berlant:

> I am redefining "structure" here as that which organizes transformation and "infrastructure" as that which binds us to the world in movement and keeps the world practically bound to itself; and I am proposing that one task for makers of critical social form is to offer not just judgment about positions and practices in the world, but terms of transition that alter the harder and softer, tighter and looser infrastructures of sociality itself.[49]

What keeps Mehretu's paintings bound to themselves? What keeps the graphical interface as an operational surface or picture plane bound to itself? Strong galvanic forces such as genre or medium have little or no purchase here. Mehretu's work has never simply or easily been painting; it sits, for instance, always somewhere between drawing and painting, map and plan, diagram and list, print and canvas, tracing and improvisation.

Likewise, the graphical screen coheres through neither text nor image; those structuring regimes have to exit the picture in order for the user to take up full residence there, for the interface to become transparent, intuitive, modeless . . . all of those terms the graphics industry has invented to reassure its potential users that the computer will always take a back seat to a certain petrified, hallowed version of the human. Apple was explicit about wanting to free its users into a space of infrastructural dwelling and improvisation, precisely by bracketing, or harnessing, the structuring power of the computer and its languages. Think different. We could therefore say that this version of the human—sovereign, creative, self-possessive to the extent that one is creative and creatively empowered precisely by the graphic screen—is the desired structure (meaning, output) of the screen, while the graphic form itself is the infrastructure, its enabling, expansive containment.

When the scene is as labile as an infrastructure, as permissive and uncontained as a graphical interface, what does it even mean to think about or desire resistance, another way of organizing life or allowing its disorganization? The coda turns its attention fully to this question, which has, after all, stalked every chapter from the shadows.

Coda:
Resistance and Standing

Many of the dynamics that play across this book, and across the history of the graphical field, come to a kind of crux at best, and an impasse at worst in Julie Mehretu's *Mural* (2009, plate 30).[1] *Mural* is a commissioned work installed in the lobby of the Goldman Sachs building in downtown Manhattan. The massive painting is visible to credentialed employees after they have cleared the turnstile and are headed for the elevators. But it's visible from across West Street as well, even if it can be seen only from behind glass and landscaping and traffic.[2] The work is practically a billboard: twenty-one feet, ten inches high and eighty feet long. In accepting $5 million to realize a large mural for the lobby of one of the world's biggest and most corrupt builders of economic networks, Mehretu seems, as Andrianna Campbell puts it, "to disavow the radical politics espoused by Orozco and other muralists of the Red Decade (1930s)."[3] Few people say so outright. Many people, I imagine, think it or can't not think it or wish they could unthink it. Calvin Tomkins's review for the *New Yorker*, "Big Art, Big Money," dances around the accusation, seems always on guard against it, lest it be thrown back at him for being taken in by such a work.[4] "Julie is not a market artist," says art dealer Jeffrey Deitch, summing up this tension by trying, finally, to defend against it.[5]

Mehretu herself takes a different tack. Speaking about Goldman Sachs, she says, "I don't see it as an evil institution, but as part of the larger system we all participate in. We're all part of it."[6]And not one mile away lies the public marker for the slave auction site once located in Lower Manhattan, on Wall Street between Pearl and Water, itself a node in its own brutal global network. It's hard to think that this proximity wasn't on Mehretu's mind when she accepted the commission.[7] Hard not to think that the preposition *inside* was never the structure of containment for her that it would become for people wanting to comment on the work and its relationship to its host institution.

In fact, it's only partially true to say that *Mural* is installed *inside* the Goldman Sachs lobby—true only of the part that has to do with ownership. It also exists for someone walking on the other side of 200 West Street. Looking across four lanes of traffic, a hedge of trees and shrubs, a bike lane, and a kind of circular drive for the Goldman Sachs building itself, *Mural* is there too. From that distance, it exists as an oddity or anomaly in the otherwise smooth, impenetrable surface of the steel and glass building. Some blocks of color, a hint that something chaotically connects those blocks, very little sense of how far those colored shapes float from the glass through which one sees them, or whether they are pressed flat to that glass. One looks through multiple frames, brackets, containers: the staccato rhythm of moving vehicles, the spacing of the trees, the tops of parked cars in the driveway seen over the shrubs, and finally the walls of the building itself as they space themselves around the large panes of glass. Whatever the blocks of color are, they span these containers, apparently running behind them, establishing a brief continuity. Sometimes employees pass by the windows of the floor above. Sometimes taller delivery trucks block the shapes entirely. Unless one knows it's there, there are few hints that this is a painting. On the other hand, many corporate buildings half-display art behind the panes of ground-floor windows that both admit and block. Maybe this is the same: art stored behind glass, a corporate investment in a differently materialized coagulation of wealth. Of course, we know it is.

The view from the near side of the shrubs, our vantage having now moved across traffic, hints more at the filigree lines that connect and move between the prominent blocks of color. Rarely does Mehretu's work get to exist in such long views, but one has the sense that the paintings might always invite it and sometimes reward it. Thin colored lines with dimensionality, planks or rays, jut and divide. It eventually becomes clear that whatever this is resides on a wall, or is that wall, and that the edge of the painting is marked by the end of that wall. The thing is large, massive, but not as long as the lobby of the building. It fills something like six panes of glass, depending on one's angle of approach. There are busier areas and sparser ones. Goldman Sachs workers on break smoke and scroll. Joggers and bikers moving at different paces slide past on the multiuse path that crosses directly in front of the building. Some check watches that are phones that are computers. It's relentlessly abstract at any distance, where abstract here only means never cohering into something for which there is ready language, a name or concept. At some angles, containment isn't really even in play; the painting's shapes and struts occupy some looser form, something that spreads out, extends, moves across panes, antic. There is a sense that the shapes, too, are on the move, vectoring somewhere but nowhere in particular. Nothing, no sign, announces that this is the Goldman Sachs headquarters.

Only right next to the building does it become palpable that the painting is also tall, more or less the height of the entire first floor. There are turnstiles at the left of the wall, elevators to the right. *Mural* sits somewhere between entrance and ascension, becoming background for whatever is left of the distance between citizen and worker. In this sense, too, *Mural* isn't just *in* the lobby. As with all the works in this book, and endemic to the graphical in general, prepositions gets scrambled here. Now a tracery of black lines, lines with almost no dimension, becomes evident, although their location, their situation remains ambiguous. They can seem to pulse in front of and behind the prominent colors' areas, the shapes. A net of tracery, large areas of opaque color, slightly dimensional vectors and arcs of color: these are Mehretu's characters. Aside from the language of geometry, the tracery is the only character for which there are ready names: plans, architectural drawings, planographic renderings, something traced rather than drawn, a type of mark that admits the studio assistant into the discussion by admitting them into the work.

What if we say not that Mehretu chose to put her painting in the lobby, but that the painting is a kind of infrastructural blueprint for the blackness that was already there? Blackness, indeed, has always been in that lobby. Every white-collar employee who walks through the turnstiles benefits from it. Blackness has been there not just by way of its exclusion at the level of demographics, or marginalization on the lower rungs of the corporate ladder (each type of zoning allows for blackness's later selective inclusion under very particular conditions). It has been there because speculative finance has always experimented on black bodies, as so many discussions of the slave trade have made powerfully clear.[8] When Goldman Sachs targets vulnerable communities for predatory loans or to track when those populations tend to default and thus better predict downturns in the economic cycle, they extend a practice as old as the United States. That practice sometimes gets confused for a more contemporary practice called finance capitalism.[9] Goldman Sachs would not exist except for its inheritance of this history of speculation that preys on black populations that they operationalize as vulnerable. But Goldman Sachs also inherits and fosters the era of what Jodi Melamed calls "official antiracism" by commissioning the work of a prominent black artist for its lobby.[10] Such forms of inclusion want to sever the institution's relationship to the history of antiblack speculation and place its activities in a scene of financial speculation operating in the "free market," a scene whitewashed by periodizations that find no role in their account for histories of racialization.

Discussing *Mural* and specifically its "rational" structures, Mehretu mentions the importance of architectural plans for banks and other "brick and mortar" financial institutions worldwide.[11] In this, Mehretu references the work of her studio assistants. So this is a painting about the structures of finance capital: the architectures that have enveloped those practices in the appearance of timelessness, of stability, of locatedness; the reassurances against the risk inherent to money that in being financialized becomes volatized, dependent on global flows of information; the national borders that are made porous to such flows; the states that take it as their job to keep those kinds of borders wide open.[12] If buildings are the brick to finance capital's balloon—the heaviness of stone and gold that belies the lightness of finance, in Fredric Jameson's language for it—this is not because financial and information flows, the kinds that the graphical interface was designed to carry and foster, emerge in contradistinction to the brick of institutional architecture and the mortar of real estate.[13] It is because financial institutions have always been merely the facade for a series of motile flows that might today assume the airy, if ominous, form of the high-speed financial transaction, but that once took the form of the slow-speed expropriation and flow of human bodies across the Atlantic. Black bodies, shipped, killed, claimed as insurance. The brick and the balloon; blackness and global currents. But unlike in Jameson's periodization of finance capital, the liquidity of blackness surrounds the bricks of institutions. Blackness comes first, as the appropriated, the expropriated, stolen life, and then last, as the infrastructures that fragilely supported life, survival, culture, love, and care inside those brutal structures.[14]

First and last, blackness doesn't suddenly appear in the lobby of Goldman Sachs once Mehretu's *Mural* appears there. It was always there, in the long history of the brutal imaginaries that made Goldman Sachs possible in the first place. The aqueous aesthetics of Detroit techno and Afrofuturism have both registered these dynamics, these same histories.[15] Thinking operationally, it is better to say that Mehretu joins her *Mural* with the black history that was always there, the very bricks and glass, all the hard reflective surfaces of that building, just as she joins her labor with that of her assistants. If, in this historical framing, one finds humanity on both sides of the financial line, both subjects and objects, mover and thing moved, then humanity is not what we can rely on as a bulwark to the predations and inhumanity of finance capitalism. And humanity is not what Mehretu's *Mural* is going to rescue from Goldman Sachs or whatever someone thinks Goldman Sachs stands for in this context. In its drama of containment, of trying to hold together an impossible profusion, *Mural* functions less as critique, as drawer of boundaries, than as an operational process.

This question of what *Mural* is doing in that lobby is a question of standing. This is exactly the problem Elizabeth Alexander raises and condenses into her title's question, "Can you be Black and Look at This?"[16] Alexander's essay title is quoting mixed-media artist Pat Ward William's 1986 artwork *Accused, Blowtorch, Padlock*. In both contexts, the titular question is refracted through the videotape of Rodney King's beating at the hands of the LAPD. And in both contexts, that question is about how *being* black is both modulated and reinforced whenever one watches violence done to black people who are thereby rendered as so many black bodies, mere numbers. "I am talking," Alexander says, "about what it is to think of oneself, in this day and age [this was 1994], as having *a people*." How, in other words, to think about belonging when belonging is impossible, intractable, historically unavailable and yet one needs to invent it anyway.

Alexander's question volatilizes the question of standing, of the situation in which one finds oneself when one comes into encounter with another person, or an artwork such as *Mural*, or a video selling black death. Where does Mehretu stand, in this sense, when her work inhabits this particular lobby? Alexander will teach us an easier lesson and a harder one: that *Mural* doesn't suddenly manifest blackness in that lobby, so that it now includes it; but neither, and for the same reasons, is it right to say that *Mural* stands against, opposes and subverts whatever it is we take Goldman Sachs to represent.

Of course, one might well wish for some violent retribution. After all, it was in 2007 that Goldman Sachs issued and underwrote mortgages and securities that had been backed by residential loans given, knowingly, to customers who were unlikely to be able to repay those loans. And this was part of a long history of extraction from vulnerable populations accompanied all along by the invention of forms of citizenship and personhood that make it possible to blame those vulnerable populations, and very concertedly, black populations, for these problems. Ruha Benjamin, in fact, would refer to Goldman Sachs and their innovations in predatory lending as a kind "NextGen" racism, or more prosaically, post-racism. "Government-sanctioned redlining," Benjamin says, "is succeeded by predatory lending."[17] This is the company whose money Mehretu accepted, whose lobby her art adorns. But "Julie is not a market artist," says art dealer Jeffrey Deitch, who represents Mehretu, as if the market was something, a condensation of power, toward which one could simply strike the right pose.

In fact, that very idea of attitude as a politics—which undergirds the fantasy of modernist autonomy from commodities and their logics—has been expressly a prerogative of whiteness, a kind of benefit that accrues to whiteness because the powers of choice and will and self-determination have been so palpably available to that particular population of the chosen and self-selected. For anyone not of that privileged population, Alexander's question—"Can you be black and look at this?"—marks a preexisting proximity, something always too close. A closeness predicated on being not just alienated or excluded, where better representations might help, but absolutely fungible. Fungibility scars the surfaces of Charles Gaines's work, the subject of the last chapter; it is the undertow of every other chapter in this book because it is the undertow of the graphical itself.

Viewing Rodney King, surrounded by cops and the violence that their presence always implies, the black viewer, Alexander says, is already inside that violence—always was because they always *could be*. The black viewer is operationalized into violence in this way. Not only in that moment of viewing, but in all the future moments that that violence marks as possible, even probable—a looming threat. Just because Goldman Sachs practices a particular form of sanctioned and slow-motion violence doesn't mean it has been any less devastating a part of the violence Alexander describes.

So one answer to Alexander's question is that one can't be black and look at that video, or any scene of violence, because it marks all black subjects as objects of violence, never just its witnesses. One is made to witness precisely to mark black subjects' susceptibility to future violence. One is never simply looking. To answer no in this way is to understand that the Rodney King video works through something we could call an operational logic and not just a representational one. It actively marks its black viewers as already living inside a particular structure of violence, one that that very video and its moment of witnessing enforces, reinforces, exacerbates.

This means that the answer to Alexander's question is also yes: looking at the video makes certain viewers black, reminds them, targets them, but also marks that blackness anew as something fragile and susceptible, lest one forget for even one moment. I'm saying that these opposed answers, seen together, get us closer to the standing of Julie Mehretu's *Mural* in the lobby of Goldman Sachs. And also to what it means to inhabit the graphical computer screen and the graphical containment of life generally. Alma Thomas's wayward prepositions continue to haunt here: *in* or *of* the lobby? Contained by or preceding the graphical screen? Which means that no model of simple co-optation is going to be adequate to describe the predicament *Mural* finds itself in. For one thing, these models grant the artist a kind of autonomy that Mehretu herself would not be granted in almost any other space: a form of autonomous individuality that whiteness offers to others as a kind of ersatz freedom—precisely the modality of freedom for which the graphical field was designed to be the infrastructure. The Rodney King video is but one of the many reminders that such an offer can't actually contain blackness; it can only destroy it. "Can you be black and look at this?" Yes, because the looking operationalizes blackness itself as subject to violence. No, because there can be no relation of distanced witnessing when one looks while black.

I think it is truer to the world in which Mehretu's work is situated to start from this situation of being too much inside that lobby and never inside enough, contained and container. This does not mean positing Mehretu's own embodied experience as the model for conceptualizing such a situation. It instead requires displacing, as a starting point for thought about the human embedded in complex systems, the unmarked subject, the autonomous subject as yet untouched by power—which is to say, the white subject, or whiteness as such. This is why telling the history of the graphical, as a container and infrastructure for life, has required a long and winding engagement with whiteness and its transformations; why it has required an engagement with modernism where the dominant problems are not conceived as various threats to a presumed individual autonomy; why, rather than massification, anonymity, crowds, and co-optation, the artists we've followed have led us to think about constraint, nonrelation, fungibility, and containment... each as threats to life but also as conditions for life's endurance and infrastructural transformation. In each of these dynamics, individuality cannot be assumed; in fact, the assumption is that it was never secure, or, was always a trap. Its defense was never the goal; the freedom drive never moved only in that direction. The conception and implementation of the graphical field, across the twentieth century, was driven by these threats of fungibility and containment, a mania that shows up precisely in the urgency of its flight from them. This, above all, is why the graphical is historically bound up with the renovation of whiteness; not because its goal has been self-consciously racial, but because the threats it has been designed to avoid, and the powers it has tried to grant to the human in service of that avoidance, have always been infrastructures of black life in the United States. The renovation of whiteness in the United States in the late twentieth century has required a multivariate flight from blackness, one instrument of which has been the dematerialization of race itself. To tell the story of the graphical has entailed a reframing of modernity that isn't based in the (white) fear of homogeneity, fascism, authoritarianism, or other strong forms of mass address, but that is based in and motivated by the fear of becoming a number, a bit in a field, which has long been both a form and a specter of blackness.

But there's another reason why that old story of cooptation as the threat to modernist autonomy isn't adequate to tell the story of this particular lobby, or the story of the graphical that finds an uneasy home there. This has to do with representational politics. On the one hand, it's clear that *Mural* is not representational, even if it exhibits some identifiable elements. But to then call it abstract doesn't get us very far if we have to think that representational and abstract constitute some sort of polarity. Along with all the cases in this book, there is something importantly nonrepresentational about Mehretu's work. And this in turn has to do with the presence, even dominance, of substantially nonrepresentational powers of subjectivization at work in the world, trafficking in spaces that can feel awfully representational. Yes, digital capitalism, or data-driven capitalism. But also racism in all its familiar and mutated forms that now route through data populations. Goldman Sachs's own tactics for profiling the victims of its predatory mortgages are themselves not *just* representational.

Goldman Sachs is still in the subprime lending market. Why? To better predict the next credit cycle. In other words, people with bad credit will most predictably default on loans, and so offer the fastest and most accurate prediction for when the next booms or busts are coming. Their interest in, say, black populations, isn't about their blackness per se, or even any quality they might attribute to that population as a form of cryptoracism, e.g., their so-called vulnerability. It's about their capacity (*as* a population) to generate a predictive model of the future. Here we find, again, the operational processes that Alexander locates in the act of looking at the Rodney King video, and that Leo Steinberg and Jacob Gaboury help us see as an integral part of graphical interfaces.

Representation, in the sense that these scenes both mutate and evade, means a few things: made in advance to suit a future context (and this could be either as radical tactic or marketing ploy); made by either those empowered to generate public images, or those who would try to take that power for themselves, in order to generate better images, better representations; actions, whether dominant or insurgent, whose power comes precisely from their capacity to operate in a world of images and representations. Black studies—and Alexander's argument is a perfect case—has long sustained an awareness of where representational politics isn't enough, where it already presumes too much about the standing of the subject. Saidiya Hartman and her thinking about burdened individuality in *Scenes of Subjection* is about how a representational logic of personhood was actually opened up to black citizens in the aftermath of abolition precisely to make race and racialization the responsibility of the racialized themselves.[18] Cedric Robinson's "black radical tradition" is a disparate collection of lives and life worlds that do not take recognition or representation to circumscribe their goals.[19] When Jared Sexton and Steve Martinot describe the absolute exposure of black life to violence, they mean not just that the violence is unrepresentable because it is ineffable.[20] Their point is that the logic of exemplarity, a representational logic, utterly fails to account for the absolute pervasiveness and structural ubiquity of violence in and around black life, where it is both background and example, atmosphere and individual, bit and field—never contained enough.

In other words, the absolute fungibility of black life in American culture can only be disguised and softened by strategies of representation, which presume that instances can be singled out, even need to be ferreted out and brought to light. The nonrepresentational view would say instead that violence and the threat of violence are pervasive, constitutive — operational. Representational logics persist because they are in fact a kind of need that whiteness has: a need to contain the kinds of work that the art, activism, and the pedagogies of black thinkers and makers can do to our ways of conceptualizing, and inhabiting, personhood. But whiteness also found a need, after World War II, to experiment with the nonrepresentational logics of the graphical, often precisely as a new platform for the representational. But not only that.

The vexed standing of the studio assistant in Mehretu's work helps us to see how important it is that we develop resources for conceptualizing the nonrepresentational, in relation to both race and the graphical. The assistant: those who trace. Who do their work inside the light beam of a projector, a container no more or less material than light. Who angle their body, flat to the wall, so that they can work from the information that a beam of light carries while themselves becoming the screen on which that information gets projected. Who glue and paste, align, stand back, converse. Run up ladders, shimmy down. Who layer acrylic, translucent and palpable, containers that can't contain. Who operationalize the rational machineries of works whose proper nouns don't bear their names. Who strip down through layers; who lay down layers; who work in the ephemeral light and heat and noise and smell of the matter of those layers to produce a thickness without a weight. Everyone who works *on* a Mehretu canvas works *in* it too. Or as Fred Moten says of Mehretu's paintings, "Being *with* them, by way of a strange and wonderful alchemy, is being *in* them [italics in the original]."[21] They build infrastructures for our movement and habitation, working in layers. Recourse to art's vocabularies for these relations—artist/assistant, conceptual/manual, gestural/mechanical, free/rational—encodes a wish for an older form of containment, where individuality is secured in visible features of the body, in zonings of geography like the nation form, all scenes where representational politics find purchase.

By way of proximity to and divergence from a common history, Mehretu's paintings teach us that graphical fields play out a drama of containment. The graphical field contains the syntax of the computer in order to free its users into a light self-managerial relation wherein the self's contact with others, rendered as information, becomes a renovated form of autonomy. Here, the individual is recast as a networked entity, contained by the very feeling of being newly set free. The graphical field gives way to the self affectively by functioning as the infrastructure of its digital habitation.

To keep the studio assistant inside the work, without the zonings that would allow the management of their presence there, is a reminder that when whiteness dissolves itself into the graphical openness of an invitation, as an attitude or disposition, those who would refuse its invitation might do so, might even have to do so, not from behind oppositional barricades like the human or the individual, but from amid the shifting infrastructures of a more vulnerable standing—as Alma Thomas, Howardena Pindell, Jack Whitten, Charles Gaines, and Julie Mehretu have been teaching us since before the graphical was operationalized as the container for contemporary life.

Introduction

1   Beckwith and Cassel Oliver, *Howardena Pindell*, 156–57.

2   Beckwith and Cassel Oliver, 147.

3   The idea of the genre flail comes from Berlant, "Genre Flailing."

4   Robinson, *Black Marxism*.

5   See also Ed Clark, Romare Bearden, Tom Lloyd, William T. Williams, Melvin Edwards, Louis Cameron, Jacolby Satterwhite, Aria Dean, Martine Syms, Caitlin Cherry, Sondra Perry, Adrienne Gaither. This list, and the ellipses it implies, doesn't name a trend or movement or style, a categorical grouping that would gather historical meaning around a pattern found inside the art world. It names, rather, an ongoing and iterative yet disparate set of experiments at the interface of personhood, technology, and labor. And insofar as these experiments exist, they exist in resonance and tension with the concomitant history of computing. The spirit in which I offer this list, partial as it is, is a desire to provide resources, other places to look and study. But I regret any sense in which the list form, however open-ended, implies that certain artists don't offer substantial commentary on the historical relationship between personhood and technology. I've long been committed to a view that, in wanting to deliteralize our studies of technology, would see almost any

aesthetic practice as a potential place to learn about technology and the forms of life that are bound up with it. One place to look for a source of this thought is Haraway, "Cyborg Manifesto." See also Cohen, *Never Alone, Except for Now.*

6   Krauss, "Grids."

7   Higgins, *Grid Book.*

8   Coleman, "Race as Technology"; Benjamin, "Innovating Inequity"; Chun, "Introduction."

9   Nooney, "How the Personal Computer."

10   Bardini, *Bootstrapping*; Waldrop, *Dream Machine*; Smith, *Fumbling the Future*; Laurel and Mountford, *Art of Human-Computer Interface Design*; Laurel, *Computers as Theatre.*

11   Mondloch, *Screens*; Friedberg, *Virtual Window.*

12   Franklin, *Control.*

13   Sheets, "Black Abstraction"; Bowling et al., *Energy/Experimentation*; Mercer, *Discrepant Abstraction.*

14   Louis Onuorah Chude-Sokei puts it this way: "How we have come to know and understand technology has been long intertwined in how we have deployed and made sense of race." Chude-Sokei, *Sound of Culture*, 1.

15   McKittrick, "Mathematics Black Life," 17.

16   Franklin, *Digitally Disposed.*

17   Louis Onuorah Chude-Sokei's book importantly rehistoricizes technology as that which has been driven by a fear of blackness. Chude-Sokei, *Sound of Culture.*

18   This is part of the story Fred Turner tells. See Turner, *From Counterculture to Cyberculture*; Turner, *Democratic Surround.*

19   Galloway and Thacker, "Protocol, Control, and Networks"; Browne, "Digital Epidermalization."

20   Here, I'm talking about Saidiya Hartman's discussion of the relationship between empathy and fungibility. See Hartman, *Scenes of Subjection.*

21   Césaire, *Discourse on Colonialism.*

22   Berlant, "Slow Death."

23   Ramon Amaro has written a series of essays about this temporality of computation and racialization, all of which have been important resources for what follows: Amaro, *Black Technical Object*; Amaro, "As If."

24   Hong, *Death Beyond Disavowal*; Melamed, *Represent and Destroy*; Hu and Goding-Doty, "Race After Representation"; McKittrick, "Mathematics Black Life"; Du Bois, "Sociology Hesitant."

25   Melamed, *Represent and Destroy*; Hong, *Death Beyond Disavowal*; see also Ahmed, *On Being Included*.

26   This paragraph thinks with the work of Hartman, *Scenes of Subjection*; McKittrick, *Dear Science and Other Stories*.

27   Wynter, "Unsettling the Coloniality of Being."

28   Wynter, "Unsettling the Coloniality of Being." But see also Krista Thompson's *Shine*, which pays so much gorgeous attention to a category of the dysselected that she refers to as "African diasporic aesthetic practice"; Thompson, *Shine*.

29   Ford, *Think Black*.

30   Crawford, *Black Post-Blackness*; Collins and Crawford, *New Thoughts on the Black Arts Movement*; McKittrick, *Dear Science and Other Stories*; English, *How to See a Work of Art*.

31   Stiegler, "Discrete Image"; Galloway and Thacker, "Protocol, Control, and Networks."

32   Wynter, "Unsettling the Coloniality of Being."

33   Liu, *Laws of Cool*, 159.

34   Liu, *Laws of Cool*, 159.

35   Liu, *Laws of Cool*, 160.

36   Liu, *Laws of Cool*, 161.

37   Galloway, *Protocol*.

38   Gregg, *Counterproductive*; Gregg and Andersson, "Lillian Gilbreth's Management Desk."

39   *Taylorization* is the study, quantification, and scientific management of labor such that the labor process corresponds less to human bodies and more to the process itself, thereby rendering bodies as fragments in service to that process. See Braverman, *Labor and Monopoly Capital*.

40   Gregg and Andersson, "Lillian Gilbreth's Management Desk," 123.

41   The iconic example being Sandberg, *Lean In*.

42   For a different account of the gender politics of so-called flexible or creative labor, see Sianne Ngai's chapter on the zany, in Ngai, *Our Aesthetic Categories*.

43   Culminating, perhaps, in Asia Kate Dillon's nonbinary character Taylor Mason in the TV series *Billions*, whose power in the series comes directly from usurping what is, in the world and in the show, an otherwise entirely white-male prerogative to manipulate technology in the service of financial gain. Mason is better than all the other males in the show at this form of productivity.

44   Turner, *Democratic Surround*.

45   Maxwell, *New Negro, Old Left*; Haywood, *Black Communist in the Freedom Struggle*.

46   Cahan, *Mounting Frustration*.

47   Cahan, *Mounting Frustration*.

48   Turner, *Democratic Surround*, 201.

49   Turner, *Democratic Surround*, 210.

50   Bush, "As We May Think."

51   Bush, "As We May Think," 108.

52   Bush, "As We May Think," 109.

53   Turner, *Democratic Surround*, 202.

54   Gunning, "Cinema of Attraction."

55   As discussed in chapter 3, Stephanie Boluk and Patrick LeMieux have a terrific section of their book on the role that the hand has come to play in videogames, tracing the figure from the first gloved-hand cursor icon of an early Apple operating system to Mario back to Mickey, where they discover the ways that Mickey, and thus the whole trajectory of the cartoon hand, partook of minstrelsy and blackface. Boluk and LeMieux, *Metagaming*, 69–70.

56   On the relationship of whiteness (and its long history of violence) to the Holocaust, see Césaire, *Discourse on Colonialism*.

57   Two books tell this history, from inside the computer industry, through the biographies of two key figures: Bardini, *Bootstrapping*; Waldrop, *Dream Machine*.

58   Hafner and Lyon, *Where Wizards Stay Up Late*.

59   For more design-oriented approaches that are far more attentive to the particularities and metaphorics of the graphical user interface, see Laurel and Mountford, *Art of Human-Computer Interface Design*; Armstrong, *Digital Design Theory*.

60   Dyer, *White*.

61   Turner, *From Counterculture to Cyberculture*; Turner, *Democratic Surround*.

62   Waldrop, *Dream Machine*.

63   Engelbart, "Special Considerations of the Individual."

64   Engelbart, "Toward High-Performance Knowledge Workers."

65   Engelbart, "Introducing Our Thinkpiece."

66   Engelbart, "Introducing Our Thinkpiece," 1.

67   Chun, *Control and Freedom*.

68 Engelbart, "Augmenting Human Intellect."

69 Of course, Apple's marrying of the computer to a putatively intuitive, easy interface has stoked the usual kinds of fears, most common among computer literati, about the mollycoddling of the user, about making people into consumers rather than computer users: a Frankfurt School critique but with optimism for the computer as a utopia, if only it is used correctly. See, for instance, Stephenson, *In the Beginning*.

70 Martin, "Black Poetics."

71 Joselit, *After Art*; Väliaho, *Biopolitical Screens*.

72 See, for example, Turner, *From Counterculture to Cyberculture*; Turner, *Democratic Surround*; Bardini, *Bootstrapping*.

73 Cited from the abstract of Stine, "Critical Hardware."

74 Chun, *Control and Freedom*.

75 Rankine, *Citizen*, 49.

76 Such practices are given one kind of vocabulary by Quashie, *Sovereignty of Quiet*; Sedgwick, "Paranoid Reading, Reparative Reading."

77 The thought about ambivalence is inspired by Jagoda, *Network Aesthetics*.

78 Ahmed argues that in studying whiteness, problematizing whiteness, one must refuse the desire of one's auditors to offer solutions, better habits of being, ways of giving up whiteness, both because those solutions act as if the problem of whiteness could be solved, as if it doesn't need to continually be encountered precisely *as* a problem, but also because that very desire allows white people to position themselves as outside of the problem. Critique is not an escape from complicity; see Ahmed, "Phenomenology of Whiteness."

Chapter 1. Operational Processes: Leo Steinberg

1 Steinberg, *Other Criteria*.

2 Wynter and Scott, "Re-Enchantment of Humanism"; Wynter, "Unsettling the Coloniality of Being"; McKittrick, *Sylvia Wynter*.

3 Later collected as Steinberg, *Other Criteria*.

4 Steinberg, *Other Criteria*, 84.

5 Steinberg, *Other Criteria*, 84.

6 Steinberg, *Other Criteria*, 81.

7 It is well known, for instance, that George Kubler's book *The Shape of Time*, published in 1962, a book that many artists, art historians, and art critics read at the time, was influenced by cybernetics and information theory; Kubler, *Shape of Time*. See also Lee, "'Ultramoderne.'"

8   Vannevar Bush's "memex" famously imagined something like the personal computer, but more to the point, it imagined postwar intellectual labor as occurring in and through a kind of technologically advanced desktop, a literalized premonition of what would later become the dominant metaphor of the computer screen and, to the extent that life happens now inside the screen of the personal computer, of life itself. We might easily imagine that Leo Steinberg knew Bush's article, which was published not in some obscure computer science journal but in the *Atlantic*; see Bush, "As We May Think."

9   Vannevar Bush's protégé Douglas Engelbart knew this and worked hard to make it a reality in his research at Stanford University; see Bardini, *Bootstrapping*. For more on labor and the human, see the introduction to Moten, *In the Break*.

10   This is a central claim in a vast body of literature that has tried to describe what becomes of labor and the laboring self when social media set within a broadly computational milieu becomes a dominant form of labor. See, for instance, Hardt, "Affective Labor"; Weeks, "Life Within and Against Work"; Lazzarato, "Immaterial Labour"; Hardt and Negri, *Multitude*. See, more recently, Beller, *Cinematic Mode of Production*; Beller, *Message Is Murder*.

11   See, for instance, Turner, *From Counterculture to Cyberculture*; Ross, *No-Collar*; Gregg, *Work's Intimacy*.

12   Gregg, *Work's Intimacy*. There is now a cottage industry of complaints about hot desking and what a terrible idea it always was. See, for instance, Duncan, "We've Managed to Invent Something Even Worse."

13   Note that, by contrast, the artist-form that was almost desperately conjured by the "dominant formalist critics," was one with, as was said, "singular purpose." Such artists are conceived as problem-solvers; they mentally encompass art's history to consciously supersede it. Even if they are inarticulate or reticent like Pollock, the artist — strong, autonomous, masculine, white — is still the hero of the story of formalist criticism. Theirs was always an extremely strong, even redemptive, version of the liberal subject: decisive, self-possessed, a product of his own will. This is a key, if often overlooked, aspect of the difference Leo Steinberg marks in his essay. Fried, "Art and Objecthood"; Greenberg, "American Type Painting."

14   Ramon Amaro's work is a great and enabling resource on this idea of potentiality seen in relation to computational technology and race: see Amaro, "As If."

15   I say more below on what I mean (and don't mean) by the nonrepresentational. But some points of orientation for now, if we allow some slippage between nonrepresentational and the antirepresentational,

include Jagoda, *Network Aesthetics*; Galloway, *Protocol*; Cohen, *Never Alone, Except for Now*.

16　But, as Christa Noel Robbins so brilliantly shows, even Harold Rosenberg's "action painter" wasn't the same thing as the "action painter" who was to so populate art histories of later decades. Rosenberg, "American Action Painters"; Robbins, "Harold Rosenberg."

17　Steinberg, *Other Criteria*, 60.

18　Operational processes may, in their estrangements, sometimes feel antirepresentational, or more antagonistically oriented toward familiar categories of experience and reception. But the relationship, as I'll try to show below, is even more distant than that.

19　Browne, "Digital Epidermalization"; Cheney-Lippold, *We Are Data*.

20　Astor, "Your Roomba May Be Mapping Your Home"; Cohen, "Literally, Ourselves."

21　Michelle Murphy has made this point powerfully in their work on "economization." See Murphy, *Economization of Life*.

22　McKittrick, "Mathematics Black Life," 23.

23　In addition to Simone Browne's work, the following works have also made this argument: Beller, *Message Is Murder*; McKittrick, "Mathematics Black Life"; Weheliye, "Engendering Phonographies."

24　On whiteness and racism in science fiction, see Delaney, "Racism and Science Fiction."

25　Murphy, *Economization of Life*, 135. Another important contribution to thought about this overlay of data and race is Noble, *Algorithms of Oppression*. See also Dean, "Notes on Blacceleration"; and Beller, *Message Is Murder*.

26　McKittrick, "Mathematics Black Life"; Browne, *Dark Matters*; Noble, *Algorithms of Oppression*.

27　For a critique of the relationship between representation and the very idea of origins, a critique that moves in the direction of the nonrepresentational, see Moten, *In the Break*; Benjamin, "Work of Art."

28　Foster, *Art Since 1900*, 47.

29　Bordowitz, *AIDS Crisis Is Ridiculous*, 21.

30　Sexton and Martinot, "Avant-Garde of White Supremacy," 175. See also Alexander, "'Can You Be Black?'"

31　Though not about representational politics as such, Jean-François Lyotard's concept of the "differend" provides a powerful way to evoke the confrontation of incommensurable worlds that characterizes representational politics, where the stakes of winning or losing are often collapsed full scale into one world or the other. See Lyotard, *Differend*.

32 This is one way to state how the thought sustained here about operational processes intersects with (historically) and is informed by (conceptually) the work of black studies, including Robinson, *Black Marxism*; Hartman, *Scenes of Subjection*; Marriott, *On Black Men*; Sharpe, *In the Wake*; Spillers, "Mama's Baby, Papa's Maybe." Darby English gets at a related expansion and excess in the discussion of his concept "black representational space" as a kind of discursive and phenomenological sequestration of black life. See English, *How to See a Work of Art*.

33 Steinberg, *Other Criteria*, 90.

34 As will be discussed below, a few vocabularies have been developed to mark and explore this temporality of subjectivization. Mark Hansen's "feed-forward," Shane Denson's "postnaturalism," Anaïs Nony's "preemption," and Ramon Amaro's "hall of possibilities" are four powerful ones. See Hansen, *Feed-Forward*; Denson, *Postnaturalism*; Nony, "Anxiety in the Society of Preemption"; Amaro, "As If," 2.

35 Steinberg, *Other Criteria*, 91.

36 For more on always-on computing, see Hodge et al., "'Touch,' a Video Essay."

37 Steinberg, *Other Criteria*, 91.

38 Duhigg, "How Companies Learn Your Secrets."

39 Amaro, "As If," 2.

40 This is what Hito Steyerl describes in Steyerl, "In Defense of the Poor Image."

41 The logic here is closely related to what Boltanski and Chiapello call "the new spirit of capitalism." See Boltanski and Chiapello, *New Spirit of Capitalism*.

42 Steinberg, *Other Criteria*, 84.

43 See the epilogue of Young, *Making Sex Public*. See also Shaviro, *Post-Cinematic Affect*; and Brinkema, *Forms of the Affects*.

44 Joseph, *Beyond the Dream Syndicate*.

45 Meltzer, *Systems We Have Loved*.

46 Steinberg, *Other Criteria*, 91.

47 Michelle Murphy refers to this larger process as "economization." The point about humanitarianism here and throughout is theirs. Murphy, *Economization of Life*. On the connection between Murphy's work and network processes, see Cohen, "Aggregate Life."

Chapter 2. In, Around, Above, Behind, and Other Forms of Space Flight: Alma Thomas

1   Scott-Heron, "Whitey on the Moon."

2   King, "'Where Do We Go from Here?'"

3   For a more robust literature on the technologization of race, see McKittrick, "Mathematics Black Life"; Weheliye, *Habeas Viscus*; Weheliye, "Engendering Phonographies"; Browne, *Dark Matters*; Dean, "Notes on Blacceleration"; Weheliye, "'Feenin.'"

4   Shiff, "Cezanne's Touch."

5   Gough, "Faktura," 38.

6   Robbins, *Artist as Author*.

7   Foster, *Return of the Real*.

8   An important part of the rewriting of that narrative can be found in Dean, "Notes on Blacceleration." For more on the idea of besiegement and race, see Stefano Harney and Fred Moten on what they call the "surround": Harney and Moten, *Undercommons*.

9   Best, *None Like Us*.

10 Shiff, "Cezanne's Touch," 139.

11 Bush, "As We May Think."

12 Wynter and Scott, "Re-Enchantment of Humanism."

13 Jafa, *Dreams Are Colder than Death*.

14 Wilderson, *Red, White and Black*; Wilderson, "Grammar and Ghosts."

15 Scott-Heron, "Whitey on the Moon."

16 Szwed, *Space Is the Place*.

17 Coney, *Space Is the Place*.

18 There is a conscious echo here of Fredric Jameson's metacommentary and the aesthetic modalities concomitant with that mode of historicization, which tend away from critique and opposition and more toward refractive historicization. See Jameson, "Metacommentary."

19 There are many reasons to be skeptical of critique as an aesthetic modality beyond just the generalized need for new ways of thinking historical problems. Fred Moten and Stefano Harney articulate one when they say that to assume the position of critique is to swallow the assumption that one lacks that which the object of critique has; that one is not enough as one is. Black studies, they argue, refuses this assumption, and in so doing, refuses that which is refused to it. Another reason is something like the exhaustion of critical intervention in the age of accelerating appropriation. Luc Boltanski and Eve Chiapello best articulate the historical

conditions and mechanics of this exhaustion; Boltanski and Chiapello, *New Spirit of Capitalism*.

20 For more on touch, see Hodge et al., "'Touch,' a Video Essay."

21 Thomas, *Alma W. Thomas*, 26.

22 Berry et al., *Alma Thomas*.

23 Alma Thomas herself often spoke of these paintings this way. E.g., "I began to think about what I would see if I were in an airplane. You look down on things. You streak through the clouds so fast you don't know whether the flower below is a violet or what. You see only streaks of color." See Berry et al., 106.

24 Frank Wilderson, working through Hortense Spillers, offers the beginning of an important alternative ontology for the grid in modernity. Wilderson, *Red, White and Black*, 298.

25 Berry et al., *Alma Thomas*, 152.

26 Gaboury, "Random-Access Image," 25.

27 Gaboury, "Random-Access Image," 34.

28 Gaboury, "Random-Access Image," 35.

29 Chun, "On Software."

30 Essays in the edited collection *Post-Cinema*, especially those by Mark B. N. Hansen and Shane Denson, retheorize the digital image in cognate ways: Leyda and Denson, *Post-Cinema*.

31 Krauss, "Grids," 64.

32 As quoted in Cotter, "White House Art."

33 Moten says this in many places, in many ways, but maybe most baldly here: Harney and Moten, *Undercommons*.

Chapter 3. Nonrelational Blackness: Jack Whitten

1 Whitten, *Jack Whitten*, 230. This book collects Whitten's studio log entries. In the rest of chapter 3, I will note the date of a particular studio log entry in the text. This entry is dated September 24, 1994.

2 Shiff, "I AM THE OBJECT," 1.

3 For more on "always-on" computing and labor, see Hodge et al., "'Touch,' a Video Essay."

4 Hodge's reference is to Berlant, "Slow Death."

5 For more on the proleptic temporality of digital cultures, see Denson, *Postnaturalism*; Massumi, *Ontopower*.

6 On the data industries, see Cheney-Lippold, *We Are Data*.

7   For a debate among prominent black male artists on the problems of the expressive self seen in relation to the history of black life, see Bearden et al., "Black Artist in America."

8   This is how Richard Shiff puts it in Siegel et al., *Odyssey*, 167.

9   Whitten, note of October 24, 1979, facsimile in Whitten and Shiff, *More Dimensions Than You Know*, 97, as quoted in Siegel et al., *Odyssey*, 168.

10   Whitten, *Jack Whitten*.

11   "Presidential Approval Ratings."

12   "Jack Whitten Speaks at Museum of Contemporary Art San Diego."

13   Laurel, *Computers as Theatre*.

14   Siegel and Whitten, "Jack Whitten."

15   Derrida and Stiegler, *Echographies of Television*; Du Bois, "Sociology Hesitant."

16   Judy, "Introduction."

17   Judy, "Introduction," 14.

18   Whitten, *Jack Whitten*, 256.

19   Siegel et al., *Odyssey*.

20   Whitten, *Jack Whitten*.

21   Siegel et al., *Odyssey*, 158.

22   Siegel et al., *Odyssey*, 154–55.

23   Du Bois, "Sociology Hesitant."

24   Du Bois, "Sociology Hesitant," 41.

25   Judy, "Introduction," 14.

26   Whitten, *Jack Whitten*, 256.

27   Steinberg, *Other Criteria*, 91.

28   Jack Whitten used a sharp tool to skewer and thereby hold and maneuver each tile, a modified artist's palette strapped to his forearm to hold the cement, and a kind of palette knife to apply the cement to the edge of the tile and then scrape away the excess. In my language of containment and separation, there is a self-conscious echo of John Paul Ricco's work on "shared separation." See Ricco, *Decision Between Us*.

29   Gaboury, "Random-Access Image."

30   Boluk and LeMieux, *Metagaming*, 68–71.

31   Boluk and LeMieux, *Metagaming*, 70.

32   Whitten and Shiff, *More Dimensions than You Know*, 17.

33   Kanjo et al., *Jack Whitten*, 20.

34 Whitten, *Jack Whitten*, 76.

35 Boltanski and Chiapello, *New Spirit of Capitalism*; Ross, *No-Collar* ; Turner, *From Counterculture to Cyberculture*.

36 Whitten and Shiff, *More Dimensions than You Know*, 17.

37 Whitten and Shiff, *More Dimensions than You Know*, , 17.

38 Joseph, *Beyond the Dream Syndicate*; Joseph, *Random Order*.

39 Joseph, *Random Order*, 202.

40 Goldsmith and Whitten, "Jack Whitten."

41 Hartman, *Scenes of Subjection*; Gregg, *Counterproductive*. See also the voluminous literature on neoliberalism and its doubled-down investment in the singularized citizen, e.g., Harvey, *Brief History of Neoliberalism*; Brown, *Undoing the Demos*; Browne, *Dark Matters*.

42 Gaboury, "Random-Access Image," 35.

43 Gaboury, "Random-Access Image," 35.

44 Sharpe, *In the Wake*.

45 Mackey, *Bedouin Hornbook*, 42.

46 Whitten, *Jack Whitten*, 256.

47 I am indebted to Stephen Best's work in this line of thinking, in Best, *None Like Us*.

48 Whitten, *Jack Whitten*.

49 Whitten, *Jack Whitten*, 270–71.

50 Stine, "Critical Hardware."

51 Engelbart, "Memo to Stanford Research Institute."

52 Whitten, *Jack Whitten*, 41.

53 Whitten, *Jack Whitten*, 258.

54 Whitten, *Jack Whitten*, 216, 217.

55 Whitten, *Jack Whitten*, 250.

56 Meltzer, *Systems We Have Loved*.

57 Turner, *From Counterculture to Cyberculture*; Ross, *No-Collar*; Hong, *Death Beyond Disavowal*; Melamed, *Represent and Destroy*.

58 For more on blackness as technology's, and the internet's, excluded part, see Noble, *Algorithms of Oppression*.

59 Whitten and Shiff, *More Dimensions than You Know*, 25.

60 On blackness as always-already technologized, see Weheliye, *Phonographies*. See also Moten, *In the Break*; McMillan, *Embodied Avatars*.

61 Kanjo et al., *Jack Whitten*, 20.

62 Whitten and Shiff, *More Dimensions than You Know*, 25.

63 The major oversight of this chapter relates to Jack Whitten's lifelong apprenticeship to African art and specifically African sculpture, something he pursued largely during his summers in Crete. But the recent publications of his studio logs makes it clear how thoroughly that research subtended all of his work. His sculptural practice constitutes, in a sense, the record of these experiments. Much of this work is still coming to light; to date there have only been a handful of exhibitions. Without a deeper engagement with this sculptural practice, my account of Whitten's work, as well as my conceptualization of screen technologies, is partial at best. Delinda Collier's work would be an important part of that expansion. See Collier, *Media Primitivism*.

Chapter 4. Modernity and Fungibility: Charles Gaines

1 Crawford, *Black Post-Blackness*.

2 Romare Bearden chaired a public conversation among older and younger prominent black artists at just this historical crux. Darby English's book on 1971 reflects on this juncture. Bearden et al., "Black Artist in America"; English, *1971*.

3 For more on abstraction and racialization, see Artist, "Black Gooey Universe"; Artist and Cohen, "Abstraction, the Irreconcilable"; Weheliye, "Engendering Phonographies"; McKittrick, "Mathematics Black Life."

4 *Gridwork* is the Studio Museum's term. Keith et al., *Charles Gaines*.

5 The circular logic here is an artifact of cybernetic thought. Hayles, *How We Became Posthuman*; Franklin, *Control*.

6 Gaines, "Reconsidering Metaphor/Metonymy."

7 Charles Gaines to Sol and Carol LeWitt, 1988, in Keith et al., *Charles Gaines*.

8 The titling convention for Gaines's gridworks, which I follow here, has been to italicize the individual works in a series (there are sixteen in *Faces*) and to capitalize the name Gaines gives to the series itself. Here, *Faces* (1978–79) is the series name, and the sixteen triptychs that make up that series are each given titles in italics.

9 Tani, "Face Is a Politics."

10 Tani, "Face Is a Politics."

11 Best, *None Like Us*; Robinson, *Black Marxism*.

12 Jacob Gaboury stresses, rightly I think, that computer graphics broadly are nonrepresentational, or not fundamentally based in images or pic-

tures; Gaboury, "Random-Access Image." I discuss this issue more fully in chapter 2.

13   Gosse and Stott, *Nervous Systems*.

14   Shaked, *Synthetic Proposition*.

15   Shaked, *Synthetic Proposition*, 17.

16   For a different but, I think, related discourse of freedom in this era, see Brown, *Undoing the Demos*; Foucault, "Birth of Biopolitics."

17   Shaked, *Synthetic Proposition*.

18   Gaines, "Reconsidering Metaphor/Metonymy."

19   *Son of Gone Fishin'* premiered on October 16, 1981, at the BAM Opera House, Brooklyn. This was Brown's first musical collaboration, with original music by Robert Ashley.

20   Shaked, *Synthetic Proposition*, 232.

21   See chapter 1. Turner, *Democratic Surround*; Ross, *No-Collar*; Liu, *Laws of Cool*.

22   Ricco, "Commerce of Anonymity."

23   Ong, *Neoliberalism as Exception*; Duggan, *Twilight of Equality?*

24   Roach, "Becoming Fungible"; Winnubst, "Queer Thing About Neoliberal Pleasure."

25   This asymmetrical structure is what Fred Turner's books never quite consider. Patterson, *Slavery and Social Death*; Hartman, *Scenes of Subjection*; Wilderson, *Red, White and Black*.

26   Hartman, *Scenes of Subjection*.

27   On racializing ontologies, see Warren, *Ontological Terror*.

28   Moten, *Stolen Life*.

29   Wilderson, *Red, White and Black*.

30   Hartman, *Scenes of Subjection*, 19.

31   Hartman, *Scenes of Subjection*, 19. Of course, white subjects have never been truly subject to such fungibility. But part of the very structure of fungibility being described by Hartman is the ever-present capacity to project oneself into the subject position of the black other, to feel what they feel, to fear what they fear, to fear becoming what they are—a liberal subject position that purchases empathy at the cost of obliterating the actual subjectivity of blackness, of rendering it utterly useless, even for its own uplift.

32   Turner, *Democratic Surround*; Turner, *From Counterculture to Cyberculture*.

33   Stine, "Critical Hardware."

34   Stine, "Critical Hardware," 786.

35 Galloway, *Interface Effect*.

36 Hartman, *Scenes of Subjection*, 115–24.

37 Hartman, *Scenes of Subjection*, 125.

38 Sharpe, *In the Wake*.

39 Murray, *Queering Post-Black Art*; English, *How to See a Work of Art*.

40 Charles Gaines's term for the freedom he wanted to resist was *metaphor*; the contiguity he set out to produce he called *metonymy*. Gaines addresses this metonymy/metaphor distinction most directly in Gaines, "Reconsidering Metaphor/Metonymy."

41 Gaines, "Reconsidering Metaphor/Metonymy."

42 For a different take on the raster as a mode of picture-making, see Shiff, "Photographic Soul."

Chapter 5. Infrastructures of Containment: Julie Mehretu

1 At the request of Julie Mehretu's studio, I've removed the proper names of all studio assistants and replaced them with "X" to mark both the presence of the assistant in the work and the removal of the proper name—a citation without propriety.

2 Nakamura, "Indigenous Circuits."

3 Campbell, "Julie Mehretu," 241.

4 But this is only one history. For more on this topic, see Krauss, "Grids"; Siegert, *Cultural Techniques*; Higgins, *Grid Book*.

5 Sholette, *Dark Matter*.

6 Fisher, *Capitalist Realism*.

7 Buchloh, "Conceptual Art 1962–1969."

8 For a history of project management as seen through discourses of data and information, see Liu, "Transcendental Data."

9 Hartman, *Scenes of Subjection*.

10 Bush, "As We May Think."

11 Steinberg, *Other Criteria*, 84.

12 Sussman et al., *Remote Viewing*.

13 Edwards, "Antecedents in Black," 253–54.

14 The latest Apple OS as of this writing, OS X, produces a similar effect by allowing one to see the faded colors and shapes of the desktop image even through certain windows.

15 Joselit, "Apocalypse Not."

16 Miles, "Julie Mehretu."

17 Gaboury, *Image Objects*.

18 Brenda Laurel makes the point by referring to the personal computer, which is to say, the graphical computer, as theatrical; Laurel, *Computers as Theatre*.

19 Massumi, "On the Superiority of the Analog"; Hansen, *New Philosophy for New Media*.

20 Examples of related aesthetic modalities include Quashie, *Sovereignty of Quiet*; Sedgwick, "Paranoid Reading, Reparative Reading"; Behar, *Bigger Than You*; Hu, "Wait, Then Give Up."

21 See Gilles Deleuze on "dividuals": Deleuze, "Postscript on the Societies of Control." On homophily, see Chun, *Updating to Remain the Same*.

22 Laurel, *Computers as Theatre*.

23 Mehretu, *Julie Mehretu*, 23.

24 Boellstorff et al., *Data*.

25 Campbell, "Julie Mehretu," 241.

26 "Artist Talk: Julie Mehretu."

27 As quoted in Shiff, *Julie Mehretu*, "Mural."

28 As Julie Mehretu has said, she considers her work a lifelong exploration of this standing of no standing. See Mehretu, *Julie Mehretu*, 55–56.

29 I'm building here on Michelle Murphy's and Lauren Berlant's ideas about infrastructure, Berlant's being keyed to the exigencies of precarious life, and Murphy's keyed to the informatics of postcolonial humanitarianism. Murphy, *Economization of Life*; Berlant, "Commons."

30 Berlant, *Female Complaint*, 220.

31 This, again, is why various writers have located one generative force of the historical present in the slave trade. See Beller, *Message Is Murder*; Moten, "Blackness and Nothingness"; Warren, *Ontological Terror*; Sexton, "Social Life of Social Death"; Wilderson, *Red, White and Black*; Sharpe, *In the Wake*; Dean, "Notes on Blacceleration"; Hartman, *Scenes of Subjection*.

32 Gregg, *Work's Intimacy*.

33 The thinking about infrastructures here is indebted to Lauren Berlant's "Commons."

34 Museo de Arte Contemporáneo de Castilla y León et al., *Julie Mehretu*, 31.

35 This is a narrative that Donna Haraway, a long time ago, gave us the resources to distrust. See Haraway, "Cyborg Manifesto."

36 Julie Mehretu makes these connections in a video she made for the Virginia Museum of Fine Arts, which had just purchased *Stadia III*. See "Stadia III (Primary Title)."

37 Weaver and Shannon, "Mathematical Theory of Communication."

38 Halpern, *Beautiful Data*.

39 Lev Manovich's language describes the waning of temporal montage and the emergence of spatial montage, first in cinema, then in digital media. As Alexander R. Galloway points out, the more common terms for this, now, is *windowing*. Manovich, *Language of New Media*; Galloway, *Interface Effect*, 5.

40 See, for instance, Friedberg, *Virtual Window*. Or, on image-text relations, Mitchell, *Picture Theory*; Mitchell, *Iconology*.

41 Jacob Gaboury's work makes this point explicitly, though by way of ontology, practice, and the materialities of early computer-graphics labs. Gaboury, "Random-Access Image."

42 Weaver and Shannon, *Mathematical Theory of Communication*.

43 Spillers, "Mama's Baby, Papa's Maybe," 65.

44 Sharpe, *In the Wake*.

45 Sussman et al., *Remote Viewing*.

46 Edwards, "Antecedents in Black," 256.

47 Hartman, "Anarchy of Colored Girls"; Hartman, *Wayward Lives, Beautiful Experiments*.

48 Berlant, "Commons."

49 Berlant, "Commons," 394.

Coda

1 For a view of *Mural* from the street outside the Goldman Sachs building, search for "149 West St, New York, NY 10282" in Google Street View and navigate your way toward the building's glass facade. As of this writing, *Mural* could be seen from across West St., and closer street views were available.

2 For more on *Mural*, see Campbell, "Julie Mehretu."

3 Campbell, "Julie Mehretu," 239.

4 Tomkins, "Big Art, Big Money."

5 You hear this worry as well in writing about Julie Mehretu's less expressly corporate works, e.g., "There is a downside to the 'perfection' of her models, however. In so successfully reflecting these overlaid, competing and chaotic aspects of globalised contemporary culture, Meh-

retu's work both reinforces and suffers from the very condition she depicts." Eleey, "Julie Mehretu's 'Perfect' Pictures," 103.

6   Tomkins, "Big Art, Big Money."

7   Chayes, "Wall Street Slave Market Memorial Unveiled."

8   McKittrick, "Mathematics Black Life"; Browne, *Dark Matters*.

9   Baucom, *Specters of the Atlantic*.

10   Melamed, *Represent and Destroy*.

11   Shiff, *Julie Mehretu*, "Mural," 12.

12   On the alter-materialities of high-speed finance, see Starosielski, *Undersea Network*.

13   Jameson, "Brick and the Balloon."

14   "Stolen life" comes from Moten, *Stolen Life*.

15   Williams, "Black Secret Technology."

16   Alexander, "'Can You Be Black?'"

17   Benjamin, "Innovating Inequity," 2.

18   Hartman, *Scenes of Subjection*.

19   Robinson, *Black Marxism*. For more on the nonrepresentational logic of the black radical tradition, see Best, *None Like Us*.

20   Sexton and Martinot, "Avant-Garde of White Supremacy."

21   Moten, "End of the World Picture," 247.

Ahmed, Sara. *On Being Included: Racism and Diversity in Institutional Life.* Durham, NC: Duke University Press, 2012.

Ahmed, Sara. "A Phenomenology of Whiteness." *Feminist Theory* 8, no. 2 (2007): 149–68.

Alexander, Elizabeth. "'Can You Be Black and Look at This?': Reading the Rodney King Video(s)." *Public Culture* 7, no. 1 (1994): 77–94.

Amaro, Ramon. "As If." *e-flux Architecture* (February 2019). https://www.e-flux .com/architecture/becoming-digital/248073/as-if/.

Amaro, Ramon. *The Black Technical Object: On Machine Learning and the Aspiration of Black Being.* London: Sternberg Press, 2023.

Armstrong, Helen. *Digital Design Theory: Readings from the Field.* New York: Princeton Architectural Press, 2016.

Artist, American. "Black Gooey Universe." *Unbag*, no. 2 (January 5, 2018). http://unbag.net/issue-2-end/black-gooey-universe/.

Artist, American, and Kris Cohen. "Abstraction, the Irreconcilable: An Interview with American Artist." *Open Set*, January 2019. http://www.open-set .com/krcohen/essay-clusters/abstraction-the-irreconcilable-an-interview -with-american-artist/.

"Artist Talk: Julie Mehretu." San Francisco Museum of Modern Art (SFMOMA). Last accessed October 14, 2024. https://www.sfmoma.org/event/julie -mehretu/.

Astor, Maggie. "Your Roomba May Be Mapping Your Home, Collecting Data That Could Be Shared." *New York Times*, July 25, 2017. https://www.nytimes .com/2017/07/25/technology/roomba-irobot-data-privacy.html.

Bardini, Thierry. *Bootstrapping: Douglas Engelbart, Coevolution, and the Origins of Personal Computing*. Stanford, CA: Stanford University Press, 2000.

Baucom, Ian. *Specters of the Atlantic: Finance Capital, Slavery, and the Philosophy of History*. Durham, NC: Duke University Press, 2005.

Bearden, Romare, Sam Gilliam Jr., Richard Hunt, Jacob Lawrence, Tom Lloyd, William Williams, and Hale Woodruff. "The Black Artist in America: A Symposium." *Metropolitan Museum of Art Bulletin* 27, no. 5 (1969): 245–61.

Beckwith, Naomi, and Valerie Cassel Oliver. *Howardena Pindell: What Remains to Be Seen*. Chicago: Museum of Contemporary Art; Munich: DelMonico Books/Prestel, 2018.

Behar, Katherine. *Bigger Than You: Big Data and Obesity*. Santa Barbara, CA: Punctum Books, 2016.

Beller, Jonathan. *The Cinematic Mode of Production: Attention Economy and the Society of the Spectacle*. Hanover, NH: Dartmouth College Press, 2006.

Beller, Jonathan. *The Message Is Murder: Substrates of Computational Capital*. London: Pluto Press, 2018.

Benjamin, Ruha. "Innovating Inequity: If Race Is a Technology, Postracialism Is the Genius Bar." *Ethnic and Racial Studies* 39, no. 13 (2016): 2227–34.

Benjamin, Walter. "The Work of Art in the Age of Its Technological Reproducibility (Second Version)." In *Walter Benjamin: Selected Writings, Volume 3 (1935–1938)*, edited by Howard Eiland and Michael W. Jennings. Cambridge, MA: Belknap Press of Harvard University Press, 2002.

Berlant, Lauren. "The Commons: Infrastructures for Troubling Times." *Environment and Planning D: Society and Space* 34, no. 3 (2016): 393–419.

Berlant, Lauren. *The Female Complaint: The Unfinished Business of Sentimentality in American Culture*. Durham, NC: Duke University Press, 2008.

Berlant, Lauren. "Genre Flailing." *Capacious: Journal for Emerging Affect Inquiry* 1, no. 2 (2018): 156–62.

Berlant, Lauren. "Slow Death (Sovereignty, Obesity, Lateral Agency)." *Critical Inquiry* 33, no. 4 (Summer 2007): 754–80.

Berry, Ian, Lauren Haynes, Frances Young Tang Teaching Museum and Art Gallery, and Studio Museum in Harlem. *Alma Thomas*. New York: Studio Museum in Harlem; Saratoga Springs, NY: Frances Young Tang Teaching Museum and Art Gallery at Skidmore College; Munich: DelMonico Books/Prestel, 2016.

Best, Stephen. *None Like Us: Blackness, Belonging, Aesthetic Life*. Durham, NC: Duke University Press, 2018.

Boellstorff, Tom, Genevieve Bell, Bill Maurer, Melissa Gregg, and Nick Seaver. *Data: Now Bigger and Better!* Chicago: Prickly Paradigm Press, 2015.

Boltanski, Luc, and Eve Chiapello. *The New Spirit of Capitalism*. London: Verso, 2005.

Boluk, Stephanie, and Patrick LeMieux. *Metagaming: Playing, Competing, Spectating, Cheating, Trading, Making, and Breaking Videogames*. Minneapolis: University of Minnesota Press, 2017.

Bordowitz, Gregg. *The* AIDS *Crisis Is Ridiculous and Other Writings, 1986–2003.* Cambridge, MA: MIT Press, 2004.

Bowling, Frank, Kellie Jones, and Studio Museum in Harlem. *Energy/Experimentation: Black Artists and Abstraction 1964–1980.* New York: Studio Museum in Harlem, 2006.

Braverman, Harry. *Labor and Monopoly Capital: The Degradation of Work in the Twentieth Century.* New York: Monthly Review Press, 1975.

Brinkema, Eugenie. *The Forms of the Affects.* Durham, NC: Duke University Press Books, 2014.

Brown, Wendy. *Undoing the Demos: Neoliberalism's Stealth Revolution.* Cambridge, MA: MIT Press, 2015.

Browne, Simone. *Dark Matters: On the Surveillance of Blackness.* Durham, NC: Duke University Press, 2015.

Browne, Simone. "Digital Epidermalization: Race, Identity and Biometrics." *Critical Sociology* 36, no. 1 (2010): 131–50.

Buchloh, Benjamin H. D. "Conceptual Art 1962–1969: From the Aesthetics of Administration to the Critique of Institutions." *October* 55 (Winter 1990): 105–43.

Bush, Vannevar. "As We May Think." *Atlantic,* July 1945.

Cahan, Susan. *Mounting Frustration: The Art Museum in the Age of Black Power.* Durham, NC: Duke University Press, 2016.

Campbell, Andrianna. "Julie Mehretu: The Art of Inclusion." In *Julie Mehretu,* edited by Christine Y. Kim and Rujeko Hockley. New York: Whitney Museum of American Art; Munich: DelMonico Books/Prestel, 2019.

Césaire, Aimé. *Discourse on Colonialism.* New York: Monthly Review Press, 2000.

Chayes, Matthew. "Wall Street Slave Market Memorial Unveiled." *Newsday,* June 27, 2015.

Cheney-Lippold, John. *We Are Data: Algorithms and the Making of Our Digital Selves.* New York: New York University Press, 2017.

Chude-Sokei, Louis Onuorah. *The Sound of Culture: Diaspora and Black Technopoetics.* Middletown, CT: Wesleyan University Press, 2016.

Chun, Wendy Hui Kyong. *Control and Freedom: Power and Paranoia in the Age of Fiber Optics.* Cambridge, MA.: MIT Press, 2006.

Chun, Wendy Hui Kyong. "Introduction: Race and/as Technology; or, How to Do Things to Race." *Camera Obscura: Feminism, Culture, and Media Studies* 24, no. 1 (2009): 7–35.

Chun, Wendy Hui Kyong. "On Software, or the Persistence of Visual Knowledge." *Grey Room* 18 (January 2005): 26–51.

Chun, Wendy Hui Kyong. *Updating to Remain the Same: Habitual New Media.* Cambridge, MA: MIT Press, 2016.

Cohen, Kris. "Aggregate Life." *Apricota,* no. 2 (2019): 113–16.

Cohen, Kris. "Literally, Ourselves." *Critical Inquiry* 46, no. 1 (Autumn 2019): 168–92.

Cohen, Kris. *Never Alone, Except for Now: Art, Networks, Populations*. Durham, NC: Duke University Press, 2017.

Coleman, Beth. "Race as Technology." *Camera Obscura: Feminism, Culture, and Media Studies* 24, no. 1 (2009): 177–207.

Collier, Delinda. *Media Primitivism: Technological Art in Africa*. Durham, NC: Duke University Press, 2020.

Collins, Lisa Gail, and Margo Natalie Crawford. *New Thoughts on the Black Arts Movement*. New Brunswick, NJ: Rutgers University Press, 2006.

Coney, John, dir. *Space Is the Place*. New York: Plexifilm, 1974.

Cotter, Holland. "White House Art: Colors from a World of Black and White." *New York Times*, October 10, 2009. https://www.nytimes.com/2009/10/11/weekinreview/11cotter.html.

Crawford, Margo Natalie. *Black Post-Blackness: The Black Arts Movement and Twenty-First-Century Aesthetics*. Urbana: University of Illinois Press, 2017.

Dean, Aria. "Notes on Blacceleration." *e-flux Journal* 87 (December 2017). http://www.e-flux.com/journal/87/169402/notes-on-blacceleration/.

Delaney, Samuel. "Racism and Science Fiction." *New York Review of Science Fiction*, no. 120 (August 1998). https://www.nyrsf.com/racism-and-science-fiction-.html.

Deleuze, Gilles. "Postscript on the Societies of Control." *October* 59 (Winter 1992): 3–7.

Denson, Shane. *Postnaturalism: Frankenstein, Film, and the Anthropotechnical Interface*. Bielefeld, Germany: Transcript, 2014.

Derrida, Jacques, and Bernard Stiegler. *Echographies of Television*. Translated by Jennifer Bajorek. Cambridge: Polity, 2002.

Doug Engelbart Institute. "Doug's Great Demo: 1968." Accessed October 12, 2024. www.dougengelbart.org/content/view/209/448/.

Du Bois, W. E. B. "Sociology Hesitant." *Boundary 2* 27, no. 3 (2000): 37–44.

Duggan, Lisa. *The Twilight of Equality? Neoliberalism, Cultural Politics, and the Attack on Democracy*. Boston: Beacon Press, 2003.

Duhigg, Charles. "How Companies Learn Your Secrets." *New York Times Magazine*, February 16, 2012. https://www.nytimes.com/2012/02/19/magazine/shopping-habits.html.

Duncan, Allison. "We've Managed to Invent Something Even Worse than Open Offices." *Fast Company*, September 27, 2018. https://www.fastcompany.com/90234986/no-plants-no-troll-dolls-why-im-not-hot-on-hot-desking.

Dyer, Richard. *White: Essays on Race and Culture*. London: Routledge, 1997.

Edwards, Adrienne. "Antecedents in Black." In *Julie Mehretu*, edited by Christine Y. Kim and Rujeko Hockley. New York: Whitney Museum of American Art; Munich: DelMonico Books/Prestel, 2019.

Eleey, Peter. "Julie Mehretu's 'Perfect' Pictures." *Afterall: A Journal of Art, Context and Enquiry*, no. 14 (2006): 98–106.

Engelbart, Douglas C. "Augmenting Human Intellect: A Conceptual Framework." October 2, 1962. Douglas C. Engelbart Papers, 1953–2005, Stanford University.

Engelbart, Douglas C. "Introducing Our Thinkpiece on Man-Machine Communication Means and Automatic Physical Skill Training." March 22, 1961. Box 17, Folder 7. Douglas C. Engelbart Papers, 1953–2005, Stanford University.

Engelbart, Douglas C. "Memo to Stanford Research Institute (SRI), Jan. 21, 1960," 1960. Folder 7. Douglas C. Engelbart Papers, 1953–2005, Stanford University.

Engelbart, Douglas C. "Special Considerations of the Individual as a User, Generator, and Retriever of Information." *American Documentation* 12, no. 2 (1961): 121–25. https://doi.org/10.1002/asi.5090120207.

Engelbart, Douglas C. "Toward High-Performance Knowledge Workers." OAC '82 Digest, Proceedings of the AFIPS Office Automation Conference (April 5, 1982): 279–90.

English, Darby. *How to See a Work of Art in Total Darkness*. Cambridge, MA.: MIT Press, 2007.

English, Darby. *1971: A Year in the Life of Color*. Chicago: University of Chicago Press, 2016.

Fisher, Mark. *Capitalist Realism: Is There No Alternative?* Winchester, UK: Zero Books, 2009.

Ford, Clyde W. *Think Black: A Memoir*. New York: HarperCollins, 2019.

Foster, Hal. *Art Since 1900: Modernism, Antimodernism, Postmodernism*. London: Thames and Hudson, 2004.

Foster, Hal. *The Return of the Real: The Avant-Garde at the End of the Century*. Cambridge, MA: MIT Press, 1996.

Foucault, Michel. "The Birth of Biopolitics." In *Ethics: Subjectivity and Truth*, edited by Paul Rabinow. New York: New Press, 1994.

Franklin, Seb. *Control: Digitality as Cultural Logic*. Cambridge, MA: MIT Press, 2015.

Franklin, Seb. *The Digitally Disposed: Racial Capitalism and the Informatics of Value*. Minneapolis: University of Minnesota Press, 2021.

Fried, Michael. "Art and Objecthood." *Artforum* 5, no. 10 (1967): 12–23.

Friedberg, Anne. *The Virtual Window: From Alberti to Microsoft*. Cambridge, MA: MIT Press, 2009.

Gaboury, Jacob. *Image Objects: An Archaeology of Computer Graphics*. Cambridge, MA: MIT Press, 2021.

Gaboury, Jacob. "The Random-Access Image: Memory and the History of the Computer Screen." *Grey Room*, no. 70 (2018): 24–53.

Gaines, Charles. "Reconsidering Metaphor/Metonymy: Art and the Suppression of Thought." *Art Lies: A Contemporary Art Journal*, no. 64 (Winter 2009): unpaginated.

Galloway, Alexander R. *The Interface Effect*. Cambridge: Polity, 2012.

Galloway, Alexander R. *Protocol: How Control Exists After Decentralization*. Cambridge, MA: MIT Press, 2004.

Galloway, Alexander, and Eugene Thacker. "Protocol, Control, and Networks." *Grey Room*, no. 17 (2004): 6–29.

Goldsmith, Kenneth, and Jack Whitten. "Jack Whitten." *BOMB*, Summer 1994. https://bombmagazine.org/articles/1994/07/01/jack-whitten/.

Gosse, Johanna, and Tim Stott. *Nervous Systems: Art, Systems, and Politics Since the 1960s*. Durham, NC: Duke University Press, 2022.

Gough, Maria. "Faktura: The Making of the Russian Avant-Garde." *RES: Anthropology and Aesthetics*, no. 36 (1999): 32–59.

Greenberg, Clement. "American Type Painting." In *Clement Greenberg: The Collected Essays and Criticism, Volume 3*, edited by John O'Brian. Chicago: University of Chicago Press, 1993.

Gregg, Melissa. *Counterproductive: Time Management in the Knowledge Economy*. Durham, NC: Duke University Press, 2018.

Gregg, Melissa. *Work's Intimacy*. Cambridge: Polity, 2011.

Gregg, Melissa, and Magnus Andersson. "Lillian Gilbreth's Management Desk: Bringing Efficiency Home." In *Deskbound Cultures: Media and Materialities at Work*, edited by Johan Jarlbrink and Charlie Järpvall. Lund, Sweden: Föreningen mediehistoriskt arkiv, 2022.

Gunning, Tom. "The Cinema of Attraction: Early Film, Its Spectator and the Avant-Garde." In *Film and Theory: An Anthology*, edited by Robert Stam and Toby Miller. Malden, MA: Blackwell, 2000.

Hafner, Katie, and Matthew Lyon. *Where Wizards Stay Up Late: The Origins of the Internet*. New York: Simon and Schuster, 1996.

Halpern, Orit. *Beautiful Data: A History of Vision and Reason Since 1945*. Durham, NC: Duke University Press, 2014.

Hansen, Mark B. N. *Feed-Forward: On the Future of Twenty-First-Century Media*. Chicago: University of Chicago Press, 2015.

Hansen, Mark B. N. *New Philosophy for New Media*. Cambridge, MA: MIT Press, 2004.

Haraway, Donna. "Cyborg Manifesto: Science, Technology, and Socialist-Feminism in the Late Twentieth Century." In *The Transgender Studies Reader*, edited by Susan Stryker and Stephen Whittle. New York: Routledge, 2006.

Hardt, Michael. "Affective Labor." *Boundary 2* 26, no. 2 (1999): 89–100.

Hardt, Michael, and Antonio Negri. *Multitude: War and Democracy in the Age of Empire*. New York: Penguin Press, 2004.

Harney, Stefano, and Fred Moten. *The Undercommons: Fugitive Planning and Black Study*. Wivenhoe/New York/Port Watson: Minor Compositions, 2013.

Hartman, Saidiya. "The Anarchy of Colored Girls Assembled in a Riotous Manner." *South Atlantic Quarterly* 117, no. 3 (2018): 465–90.

Hartman, Saidiya V. *Scenes of Subjection: Terror, Slavery, and Self-Making in Nineteenth-Century America*. New York: Oxford University Press, 1997.

Hartman, Saidiya. *Wayward Lives, Beautiful Experiments: Intimate Histories of Social Upheaval.* New York: W. W. Norton, 2019.

Harvey, David. *A Brief History of Neoliberalism.* New York: Oxford University Press, 2005.

Hayles, N. Katherine. *How We Became Posthuman: Virtual Bodies in Cybernetics, Literature, and Informatics.* Chicago: University of Chicago Press, 1999.

Haywood, Harry. *A Black Communist in the Freedom Struggle: The Life of Harry Haywood.* Minneapolis: University of Minnesota Press, 2012.

Higgins, Hannah. *The Grid Book.* Cambridge, MA: MIT Press, 2009.

Hodge, James J., C. A. Davis, and John Bresland. "'Touch,' a Video Essay on the Experience of Always-On Computing." *TriQuarterly*, December 2018. 19:50.

Hong, Grace Kyungwon. *Death Beyond Disavowal: The Impossible Politics of Difference.* Minneapolis: University of Minnesota Press, 2015.

Hu, Tung-Hui. "Wait, Then Give Up: Lethargy and the Reticence of Digital Art." *Journal of Visual Culture* 16, no. 3 (2018): 337–54.

Hu, Tung-Hui, and Christine Goding-Doty. "Race After Representation: Christine Goding-Doty and Tung-Hui Hu in Conversation." *Los Angeles Review of Books*, July 21, 2021.

"Jack Whitten Speaks at Museum of Contemporary Art San Diego." YouTube video, 1:04:35. September 19, 2014. https://www.youtube.com/watch?v=MYkI9felK2M&ab_channel=MuseumofContemporaryArtSanDiego.

Jafa, Arthur, dir. *Dreams Are Colder than Death.* United States: Pumpernickel Films, Very Special Projects, 2014.

Jagoda, Patrick. *Network Aesthetics.* Chicago: University of Chicago Press, 2016.

Jameson, Fredric. "The Brick and the Balloon: Architecture, Idealism, and Land Speculation." In *The Cultural Turn: Selected Writings on the Postmodern, 1983–1998.* New York: Verso, 1998.

Jameson, Fredric. "Metacommentary." *PMLA* 86, no. 1 (1971): 9–18.

Joselit, David. *After Art.* Princeton, NJ: Princeton University Press, 2013.

Joselit, David. "Apocalypse Not." *Artforum* 42, no. 9 (2004): 172–73.

Joseph, Branden Wayne. *Beyond the Dream Syndicate: Tony Conrad and the Arts After Cage: A "Minor" History.* New York: Zone Books, 2008.

Joseph, Branden Wayne. *Random Order: Robert Rauschenberg and the Neo-Avant-Garde.* Cambridge, MA: MIT Press, 2003.

Judy, Ronald A. T. "Introduction: On W. E. B. Du Bois and Hyperbolic Thinking." *Boundary 2* 27, no. 3 (2000): 1–35.

Kanjo, Kathryn, Robert Storr, Quincy Troupe, and Jack Whitten. *Jack Whitten: Five Decades of Painting.* San Diego: Museum of Contemporary Art San Diego, 2015.

Keith, Naima J., Anne Ellegood, and Thelma Golden. *Charles Gaines: Gridwork 1974–1989.* New York: Studio Museum in Harlem, 2014.

King, Martin Luther, Jr. "'Where Do We Go from Here?,' Address Delivered at the Eleventh Annual SCLC Convention." The Martin Luther King Jr. Research

and Education Institute. January 23, 2015. https://kinginstitute.stanford
.edu/where-do-we-go-here.

Krauss, Rosalind. "Grids." *October* 9 (Summer 1979): 50–64.

Kubler, George. *The Shape of Time: Remarks on the History of Things.* New Haven, CT: Yale University Press, 1962.

Laurel, Brenda. *Computers as Theatre.* 2nd ed. Upper Saddle River, NJ: Addison-Wesley, 2014.

Laurel, Brenda, and S. Joy Mountford. *The Art of Human-Computer Interface Design.* Reading, MA: Addison-Wesley, 1990.

Lazzarato, Maurizio. "Immaterial Labour." In *Radical Thought in Italy: A Potential Politics,* edited by Michael Hardt and Paolo Virno. Minneapolis: University of Minnesota Press, 1996.

Lee, Pamela M. "'Ultramoderne': Or, How George Kubler Stole the Time in Sixties Art." *Grey Room,* no. 2 (2001): 47–77.

Leyda, Julia, and Shane Denson. *Post-Cinema: Theorizing 21st-Century Film.* REFRAME Books, 2016.

Liu, Alan. *The Laws of Cool: Knowledge Work and the Culture of Information.* Chicago: University of Chicago Press, 2004.

Liu, Alan. "Transcendental Data: Toward a Cultural History and Aesthetics of the New Encoded Discourse." *Critical Inquiry* 31, no. 1 (2004): 49–84.

Lyotard, Jean-François. *The Differend: Phrases in Dispute.* Minneapolis: University of Minnesota Press, 1988.

Mackey, Nathaniel. *Bedouin Hornbook.* Los Angeles: Sun and Moon Press, 1997.

Manovich, Lev. *The Language of New Media.* Cambridge, MA: MIT Press, 2002.

Marriott, David. *On Black Men.* New York: Columbia University Press, 2000.

Martin, Dawn Lundy. "A Black Poetics: Against Mastery." *Boundary 2* 44, no. 3 (2017): 159–63.

Massumi, Brian. "On the Superiority of the Analog." In *Parables for the Virtual: Movement, Affect, Sensation.* Durham, NC: Duke University Press, 2002.

Massumi, Brian. *Ontopower: War, Powers, and the State of Perception.* Durham, NC: Duke University Press, 2015.

Maxwell, William J. *New Negro, Old Left: African-American Writing and Communism Between the Wars.* New York: Columbia University Press, 1999.

McKittrick, Katherine. *Dear Science and Other Stories.* Durham, NC: Duke University Press, 2021.

McKittrick, Katherine. "Mathematics Black Life." *Black Scholar* 44, no. 2 (2014): 16–28.

McKittrick, Katherine, ed. *Sylvia Wynter: On Being Human as Praxis.* Durham, NC: Duke University Press, 2015.

McMillan, Uri. *Embodied Avatars: Genealogies of Black Feminist Art and Performance.* New York: New York University Press, 2015.

Mehretu, Julie. *Julie Mehretu,* edited by Christine Y. Kim and Rujeko Hockley. New York: Whitney Museum of American Art; Munich: DelMonico Books/Prestel, 2019.

Mehretu, Julie. *Julie Mehretu: Grey Area.* Berlin: Deutsche Guggenheim; New

York: Guggenheim Museum Publications, D.A.P./Distributed Art Publishers [distributor], 2009.

Melamed, Jodi. *Represent and Destroy: Rationalizing Violence in the New Racial Capitalism*. Minneapolis: University of Minnesota Press, 2011.

Meltzer, Eve. *Systems We Have Loved: Conceptual Art, Affect, and the Antihumanist Turn*. Chicago: University of Chicago Press, 2013.

Mercer, Kobena. *Discrepant Abstraction*. London: Institute of International Visual Arts; Cambridge, MA: MIT Press, 2006.

Miles, Christopher. "Julie Mehretu: The Gallery at REDCAT." *Artforum* 43, no. 1 (2004): 277.

Mitchell, W. J. T. *Iconology: Image, Text, Ideology*. Chicago: University of Chicago Press, 1986.

Mitchell, W. J. T. *Picture Theory: Essays on Verbal and Visual Representation*. Chicago: University of Chicago Press, 1994.

Mondloch, Kate. *Screens: Viewing Media Installation Art*. Minneapolis: University of Minnesota Press, 2010.

Moten, Fred. "Blackness and Nothingness (Mysticism in the Flesh)." *South Atlantic Quarterly* 112, no. 4 (2013): 737–80.

Moten, Fred. "The End of the World Picture." In *Julie Mehretu*, edited by Christine Y. Kim and Rujeko Hockley. New York: Whitney Museum of American Art; Munich: DelMonico Books/Prestel, 2019.

Moten, Fred. *In the Break: The Aesthetics of the Black Radical Tradition*. Minneapolis: University of Minnesota Press, 2003.

Moten, Fred. *Stolen Life*. Durham, NC: Duke University Press, 2018.

Murphy, Michelle. *The Economization of Life*. Durham, NC: Duke University Press, 2017.

Murray, Derek Conrad. *Queering Post-Black Art: Artists Transforming African-American Identity After Civil Rights*. London: I. B. Tauris, 2016.

Museo de Arte Contemporáneo de Castilla y León, Lawrence Chua, Kunstverein Hannover, and Louisiana (Museum: Humlebæk, Denmark), eds. *Julie Mehretu: Black City = Ciudad Negra*. Ostfildern, Germany: Hatje Cantz; New York: D.A.P./Distributed Art Publishers, 2006.

Nakamura, Lisa. "Indigenous Circuits: Navajo Women and the Racialization of Early Electronic Manufacture." *American Quarterly* 66, no. 4 (2014): 919–41.

Ngai, Sianne. *Our Aesthetic Categories: Zany, Cute, Interesting*. Cambridge, MA: Harvard University Press, 2012.

Noble, Safiya Umoja. *Algorithms of Oppression: How Search Engines Reinforce Racism*. New York: New York University Press, 2018.

Nony, Anaïs. "Anxiety in the Society of Preemption: On Simondon and the Noopolitics of the Milieu." *La Deleuziana*, no. 6 (2017): 102–10.

Nooney, Laine. "How the Personal Computer Broke the Human Body." *Vice*, May 12, 2021. https://www.vice.com/en/article/y3dda7/how-the-personal-computer-broke-the-human-body.

Ong, Aihwa. *Neoliberalism as Exception: Mutations in Citizenship and Sovereignty*. Durham, NC: Duke University Press, 2006.

Patterson, Orlando. *Slavery and Social Death: A Comparative Study*. Cambridge, MA: Harvard University Press, 1982.

"Presidential Approval Ratings—Barack Obama," Gallup, March 9, 2008. https://news.gallup.com/poll/116479/Barack-Obama-Presidential-Job-Approval.aspx.

Quashie, Kevin Everod. *The Sovereignty of Quiet: Beyond Resistance in Black Culture*. New Brunswick, NJ: Rutgers University Press, 2012.

Rankine, Claudia. *Citizen: An American Lyric*. Minneapolis, MN: Graywolf Press, 2014.

Ricco, John Paul. "The Commerce of Anonymity." *Qui Parle: Critical Humanities and Social Sciences* 26, no. 1 (2017): 101–42.

Ricco, John Paul. *The Decision Between Us: Art and Ethics in the Time of Scenes*. Chicago: University of Chicago Press, 2014.

Roach, Tom. "Becoming Fungible: Queer Intimacies in Social Media." *Qui Parle: Critical Humanities and Social Sciences* 23, no. 2 (2015): 55–87.

Robbins, Christa Noel. *Artist as Author: Action and Intent in Late-Modernist American Painting*. Chicago: University of Chicago Press, 2021.

Robbins, Christa Noel. "Harold Rosenberg on the Character of Action." *Oxford Art Journal* 35, no. 2 (2012): 195–214.

Robinson, Cedric J. *Black Marxism: The Making of the Black Radical Tradition*. Chapel Hill: University of North Carolina Press, 2000.

Rosenberg, Harold. "The American Action Painters." In *The Tradition of the New*. New York: Horizon Press, 1959.

Ross, Andrew. *No-Collar: The Humane Workplace and Its Hidden Costs*. New York: Basic Books, 2003.

Sandberg, Sheryl. *Lean In: Women, Work, and the Will to Lead*. New York: Alfred A. Knopf, 2016.

Scott-Heron, Gil. "Whitey on the Moon." Stereo FDS-131, 33 1/3 rpm, track 9 on *Small Talk at 125th and Lenox*. Flying Dutchman Records, 1970.

Sedgwick, Eve Kosofsky. "Paranoid Reading, Reparative Reading, or, You're So Paranoid, You Probably Think This Essay Is About You." In *Touching Feeling: Affect, Pedagogy, Performativity*. Durham, NC: Duke University Press, 2003.

Sexton, Jared. "The Social Life of Social Death: On Afro-Pessimism and Black Optimism." *InTensions*, no. 5 (Fall–Winter 2011).

Sexton, Jared, and Steve Martinot. "The Avant-Garde of White Supremacy." *Social Identities* 9, no. 2 (2003): 169–81.

Shaked, Nizan. *The Synthetic Proposition: Conceptualism and the Political Referent in Contemporary Art*. Manchester: Manchester University Press, 2017.

Sharpe, Christina Elizabeth. *In the Wake: On Blackness and Being*. Durham, NC: Duke University Press, 2016.

Shaviro, Steven. *Post-Cinematic Affect*. Winchester, UK: Zero Books, 2010.

Sheets, Hilarie M. "Black Abstraction: Not a Contradiction." *ARTnews*, June 2014.

Shiff, Richard. "Cezanne's Touch." In *The Language of Art History*, edited by Salim Kemal and Ivan Gaskell. Cambridge: Cambridge University Press, 1991.

Shiff, Richard. "I AM THE OBJECT: Jack Whitten's Work of the 1990s (Excerpt from a New Essay by Richard Shiff)." *Ursula*, November 2020.

Shiff, Richard. *Julie Mehretu, "Mural."* New York: Goldman Sachs, 2013.

Shiff, Richard. "Photographic Soul." In *Where Is the Photograph?*, edited by David Green. London: Gardeners Books, 2003.

Sholette, Gregory. *Dark Matter: Art and Politics in the Age of Enterprise Culture.* London: Pluto Press, 2011.

Siegel, Jeanne, and Jack Whitten. "Jack Whitten: An African-American and Pollock." In *Painting After Pollock: Structures of Influence.* Amsterdam: G&B Arts, 1999.

Siegel, Katy, Kelly Baum, Aleesa Alexander, Anthony Appiah, Meredith A. Brown, Kellie Jones, Courtney J. Martin, et al., eds. *Odyssey: Jack Whitten Sculpture 1963–2016.* New York: Gregory R. Miller, 2018.

Siegert, Bernhard. *Cultural Techniques: Grids, Filters, Doors, and Other Articulations of the Real.* New York: Fordham University Press, 2015.

Smith, Douglas K. *Fumbling the Future: How Xerox Invented, Then Ignored, the First Personal Computer.* New York: William Morrow, 1988.

Spillers, Hortense J. "Mama's Baby, Papa's Maybe: An American Grammar Book." *Diacritics* 17, no. 2 (1987): 65–81.

"Stadia III (Primary Title)." Virginia Museum of Fine Arts (VMFA). Last accessed October 14, 2024. https://vmfa.museum/piction/6027262-57439008/.

Starosielski, Nicole. *The Undersea Network.* Durham, NC: Duke University Press, 2015.

Steinberg, Leo. *Other Criteria: Confrontations with Twentieth-Century Art.* New York: Oxford University Press, 1972.

Stephenson, Neal. *In the Beginning . . . Was the Command Line.* New York: Avon Books, 1999.

Steyerl, Hito. "In Defense of the Poor Image." *e-flux Journal* 10 (November 2009). http://www.e-flux.com/journal/in-defense-of-the-poor-image/.

Stiegler, Bernard. "The Discrete Image." In *Echographies of Television.* Cambridge: Polity, 1996.

Stine, Kyle. "Critical Hardware: The Circuit of Image and Data." *Critical Inquiry* 45, no. 3 (2019): 762–86.

Sussman, Elisabeth, Caroline A. Jones, Katy Siegel, and Whitney Museum of American Art. *Remote Viewing: Invented Worlds in Recent Painting and Drawing.* New York: Whitney Museum of American Art, 2005.

Szwed, John F. *Space Is the Place: The Lives and Times of Sun Ra.* New York: Da Capo Press, 1998.

Tani, Ellen. "The Face Is a Politics." In *Charles Gaines: Gridwork 1974–1989,* edited by Naima J. Keith, Anne Ellegood, and Thelma Golden. New York: Studio Museum in Harlem, 2014.

Thomas, Alma. *Alma W. Thomas: A Retrospective of the Paintings*. San Francisco: Pomegranate, 1998.

Thompson, Krista A. *Shine: The Visual Economy of Light in African Diasporic Aesthetic Practice*. Durham, NC: Duke University Press, 2015.

Tomkins, Calvin. "Big Art, Big Money." *New Yorker*, March 22, 2010. https://www.newyorker.com/magazine/2010/03/29/big-art-big-money.

Turner, Fred. *The Democratic Surround: Multimedia and American Liberalism from World War II to the Psychedelic Sixties*. Chicago: University of Chicago Press, 2013.

Turner, Fred. *From Counterculture to Cyberculture: Stewart Brand, the Whole Earth Network, and the Rise of Digital Utopianism*. Chicago: University of Chicago Press, 2006.

Väliaho, Pasi. *Biopolitical Screens: Image, Power, and the Neoliberal Brain*. Leonardo. Cambridge, MA: MIT Press, 2014.

Waldrop, M. Mitchell. *The Dream Machine: J. C. Licklider and the Revolution That Made Computing Personal*. New York: Viking, 2001.

Warren, Calvin L. *Ontological Terror: Blackness, Nihilism, and Emancipation*. Durham, NC: Duke University Press, 2018.

Weaver, Warren, and Claude E. Shannon. *The Mathematical Theory of Communication*. Urbana: University of Illinois Press, 1949.

Weeks, Kathi. "Life Within and Against Work: Affective Labor, Feminist Critique, and Post-Fordist Politics." *Ephemera: Theory and Politics in Organization* 7, no. 1 (2007): 233–49.

Weheliye, Alexander G. "Engendering Phonographies: Sonic Technologies of Blackness." *Small Axe* 18, no. 2 (2014): 180–90.

Weheliye, Alexander G. "'Feenin': Posthuman Voices in Contemporary Black Popular Music." *Social Text* 20, no. 2 (2002): 21–47.

Weheliye, Alexander G. *Habeas Viscus: Racializing Assemblages, Biopolitics, and Black Feminist Theories of the Human*. Durham, NC: Duke University Press, 2014.

Weheliye, Alexander G. *Phonographies: Grooves in Sonic Afro-Modernity*. Durham, NC: Duke University Press, 2005.

Whitten, Jack. *Jack Whitten: Notes from the Woodshed*. Zurich: Hauser & Wirth, 2018.

Whitten, Jack, and Richard Shiff, eds. *More Dimensions than You Know: Jack Whitten, Paintings 1979–1989*. Zurich: Hauser & Wirth, 2017.

Wilderson, Frank B, III. "Grammar and Ghosts: The Performative Limits of African Freedom." *Theatre Survey* 50, no. 1 (May 2009): 119–25.

Wilderson, Frank B, III. *Red, White and Black: Cinema and the Structure of U.S. Antagonisms*. Durham, NC: Duke University Press, 2010.

Williams, Ben. "Black Secret Technology: Detroit Techno and the Information Age." In *Technicolor: Race, Technology, and Everyday Life*, edited by Alondra

Nelson, Thuy Linh N. Tu, and Alicia Headlam Hines. New York: New York University Press, 2001.

Winnubst, Shannon. "The Queer Thing About Neoliberal Pleasure: A Foucauldian Warning." *Foucault Studies* 14, no. 14 (2012): 79–97.

Wynter, Sylvia. "Unsettling the Coloniality of Being/Power/Truth/Freedom: Towards the Human, After Man, Its Overrepresentation—An Argument." CR: *The New Centennial Review* 3, no. 3 (2003): 257–337.

Wynter, Sylvia, and David Scott. "The Re-Enchantment of Humanism: An Interview with Sylvia Wynter." *Small Axe* 8 (September 2000): 119–207.

Young, Damon R. *Making Sex Public, and Other Cinematic Fantasies.* Durham, NC: Duke University Press, 2018.

Page numbers in italics refer to figures.

Aristotle, 114, 116
Artaud, Antonin, 93
art criticism, 37, 73; formalism in, 38–39
art history, 5, 7, 9–10, 36, 43, 56–57, 75–76, 107, 165n7, 167n16; formalism in, 38
art world, 22, 56–57, 83, 104–5, 128–29, 161n5; New York, 37–38, 56–57
Asante, Molefi Kete, 114
Ashley, Robert, 174n19
Associated Press, 144
associative indexing, 20
augmentation, 4, 18, 61, 69, 111, 115, 122, 125–26; and the human, 14, 16, 22–30, 59, 72–73, 87, 100–101, 106, 108, 120; racialized, 65
Augmented Human Intellect project, 28, 126
authoritarianism, 7, 16–17, 19, 28, 71, 87, 120, 157. See also fascism
automatism, 96, 101, 103–4, 119, 126
autonomy, 42, 57, 61, 87, 90, 100, 121–22, 129, 145, 160, 166n13; and augmentation, 16; fantasies of, 7, 112, 147, 155; and freedom, 127, 134; and GUI, 27, 95, 115; racialized, 84–85, 94, 156; threats to, 6, 14, 32, 157
avant-garde, 58

Baldwin, James, 104
Baltimore Museum of Art: Odyssey, 82
Bauhaus, 18
Bayer, Herbert, 18–19, 21
Bearden, Romare, 161n5, 173n2
Beller, Jonathan, 44
Benday dots, 132
Benjamin, Ruha, 155
Berlant, Lauren, 76, 138, 148, 161n3, 170n4, 176n29, 176n33
Best, Stephen, 172n47
Bierstadt, Albert, 132
Billions, 163n43
Black Arts Movement, 10, 45, 110
black being, 96, 99–101, 106
black creativity, 96
black death, 154
blackface, 87–88, 164n55
black life, 78–79, 81–83, 85, 122, 143, 158, 168n32; and address, 32;

and experimentation, 33; and fungibility, 46, 159; and numbers/numeracy, 5–6, 9, 44, 127, 154, 157; and self-expression, 171n7; vs. white flight, 52–53, 157; white hatred of, 98
blackness, 32–34, 65, 172n58, 172n60, 174n31; in Alma Thomas's work, 52, 54, 56–57, 68, 70–73; in Charles Gaines's work, 110, 120; fear of, 162n17; in Harlem on My Mind, 21; in Jack Whitten's work, 74–109; in Julie Mehretu's work, 152–58; and numbers/numeracy, 5–6; and space program, 52; transcoding of, 19; violence against, 46
Black Panther Party, 30
Black Power movement, 19, 30
black radical tradition, 3, 158
black representational space, 10
black studies, 38, 96, 158, 168n32, 169n19
black study, 134
bodily abstraction, 62
Boltanski, Luc, 168n41, 169n19
Boluk, Stephanie, 87–88, 164n55
Bordowitz, Gregg, 45–46
Brown, Trisha, 116, 118; Son of Gone Fishin', 117, 174n19
Browne, Simone, 43–44, 167n23
Buolamwini, Joy, 49
burdened individuality, 22, 121, 158
Bush, Vannevar, 20–21, 26, 64, 126, 129–30, 142, 166nn8–9

Cage, John, 93–94
Cahan, Susan, 18, 21
California: Bay Area, 137; Menlo Park, 24; San Francisco, 23–24, 132
Cameron, Louis, 161n5
Campbell, Andrianna, 126, 150
capitalism, 59, 93, 129, 137, 168n41; digital, 157–58; finance, 153–54
cathode-ray tube (CRT), 2, 26, 66, 68, 94–95, 99, 141
Cézanne, Paul, 57–58, 61
Cheney-Lippold, John, 43
Cherry, Caitlin, 161n5
Chiapello, Eve, 168n41, 169n19
choice, 4, 90; artistic, 18, 20, 103–4, 110–11, 118; within constraint,

175n40; *Calculations*, 114; *Color Regression*, 114; *Faces*, 112–17, 173n8, plates 16–19; *Falling Leaves*, 114, 116, plates 20–22; and fungibility, 6, 109–23, 155; *Incomplete Text*, 114; *Motion: Trisha Brown Dance*, 114, 116–19, plate 23; *Numbers and Trees*, 114; *Regression*, 114; *Shadows*, 114; and systems aesthetics, 6, 110, 115; *Walnut Tree Orchard*, 114

Gaither, Adrienne, 161n5

Galbraith, John Kenneth, 52

Galloway, Alexander R., 177n39

Gallup, 80

gender, 10, 57, 142, 163n43; and time management, 14–17. *See also* femininity; masculinity; patriarchy

genocide, 18, 25

geometry, 79, 102, 144–45, 147, 152; Euclidian, 26; geometric spectral works, 82; of history, 12; of whiteness, 21

Georgia: Atlanta, 83

Germany, 18

gesture, 25, 26, 114; in Alma Thomas's work, 61, 63, 66, 74; in Charles Gaines's work, 111–12; in Jack Whitten's work, 75, 77, 84, 90, 92, 96–98, 102–3; in Julie Mehretu's work, 125, 129, 132, 135–36, 140, 159; and lateral agency, 76–77

Gilbreth, Kenneth, 12, 14–15

Gilbreth, Lillian, 12, 14–16, 18, 20–22, 24–25, 32

Glissant, Édouard, 99

Global South, 88

Goding-Doty, Christine, 7

Goldman Sachs, 136–37, 150–56, 158, 177n1

Google, 50

Gough, Maria, 58

grammar, 44, 51, 74, 81, 141, 143; of suffering, 65

graphical personhood, 11, 33

graphic user interface (GUI), 13–14, 16, 31, 34, 50, 75; Apple's, 4, 21, 26–29, 72, 79, 87–88, 95, 100; and autonomy, 27, 95, 115; and computation, 26; and creativity, 7–8, 24–25, 29–30, 71, 80, 114–15; and Douglas Engelbart, 12, 17–18, 20–32, 64, 66, 88, 95, 100, 131, 134, 142; and freedom, 4, 7, 29–30, 69, 71–72, 111, 117, 148; as image of an image, 49; and individuality, 7, 22–23, 25, 29, 69; and racialization, 10–12, 25, 27, 30, 35, 88, 110

Greenberg, Clement, 38, 93, 104

Gregg, Melissa, 14–16, 22, 94

grid, 9, 95, 126, 170n24; in Alma Thomas's work, 55, 57–62, 68–72, 74–75, 102, 127; and blackness, 33, 68; in Charles Gaines's work, 110–23, 173n4, 173n8; in Howardena Pindell's work, 1–3; in Jack Whitten's work, 79, 86, 97, 106, 145; in Julie Mehretu's work, 127–28; and personal computer, 4, 33; Rosalind Krauss on, 3–6, 68, 70

gridworks, 110–23, 173n8

Guerrilla Girls, 45

GUI. *See* graphic user interface (GUI)

Gunning, Tom, 23

Halley, Peter, 3

hall of possibilities, 168n34

Hammons, David, 92

Hansen, Mark, 134, 168n34, 170n30

Haraway, Donna, 176n35

Harney, Stefano, 169n19

Hartman, Saidiya, 22, 94, 119–21, 147, 158, 162n20, 163n26, 174n31

he-man attitude, 16, 43

Hidden Figures, 54

history of the graphical, 5, 14, 23, 33, 58, 68–69, 109, 125, 127, 139

Hodge, Jim, 76

homemakers, 24

homogenization, 2, 14, 16, 18, 55, 58, 70–71, 94, 107, 109, 122, 135, 157

Hong, Grace Kyungwon, 7–8, 104

hooks, bell, 114, 116

Horne, Lena, 104

hot desking, 42, 166n12

Howard University, 56

Huerta, Dolores, 114

human as praxis, 39

human-computer interaction (HCI), 66

humanism, 30, 48, 52, 68, 73, 85, 91, 106, 121

human-machine, 28, 34–35, 62, 68, 106, 119

Pennsylvania: Philadelphia, 83

Perry, Sondra, 161n5

personhood, 28, 31–32, 39, 54, 57, 58, 139, 147, 158, 161n5; in Alma Thomas's work, 73; in Charles Gaines's work, 110–11, 117, 119–21; graphical, 11, 33; and GUI, 4, 10–11; in Jack Whitten's work, 75, 77, 81, 85–86, 94–95, 97; liberal, 4, 18, 47, 70, 109; racialized, 1, 10, 18, 33, 35–36, 38, 73, 85, 97, 104, 106, 110–11, 159

phenomenology, 67, 70, 90, 93, 108, 137, 144, 168n32

Pindell, Howardena, 3, 32, 93, 102, 160; *Untitled*, 1, plate 1; *Video Drawings: Swimming*, 2, plate 2

Piper, Adrian, 3, 115

pixelation, 81, 113

pixels, 2–3, 34, 59, 69, 81, 95; in Alma Thomas's work, 66; in Charles Gaines's work, 113, 115, 117; in Jack Whitten's work, 78, 86–87, 97, 99, 104, 107; in Julie Mehretu's work, 139

police violence, 5, 98, 154–56

political content *vs.* aesthetic form, 68

Pollock, Jackson, 43, 104–5, 145, 166n13

postexpressionism, 101

postmodernism, 45, 49

postnaturalism, 168n34

postracialism, 6, 11, 18, 27, 31, 54, 59, 138, 155. *See also* color-blindness

predatory lending, 153–55, 158

predictiveness, 41, 43, 133, 135, 139, 153, 158

preemption, 168n34

procedural image, 73, 75, 95–96

proprioception, 26

Quashie, Kevin Everod, 34

queerness, 45, 85

queer theory, 119

question of standing, 150–60, 176n28

quiet (Quashie), 34

Ra, Sun, 65

racial formation, 9, 27

racialism, 18

racialization, 5, 22, 32, 34, 49, 53–55, 73, 88, 153, 157–58, 173n3; and augmentation, 65; and autonomy, 84–85, 94, 156; and choice, 84, 104, 106, 155; and citizenship, 10, 155; and collectivity/collectivism, 2–3, 15, 19, 32, 76, 81–84, 98–101, 104–5; and computation, 6, 38, 76, 122, 162n23; and data, 5–6, 43–44, 83–84, 91, 158, 167n25; and democracy, 6, 10, 53; and discretization, 11; and GUI, 10–12, 27, 30; and liberalism, 8, 25, 119, 123, 129, 174n31; and management, 14–18, 20, 22, 44; and modernism, 9, 33, 68, 94; and personhood, 1, 10, 18, 33, 35–36, 38, 73, 85, 97, 104, 106, 110–11, 159. *See also* blackness; whiteness

racial liberalism, 8

racial warfare, 30

racism, 3, 57, 68, 72, 76, 119, 122, 129; crypto-, 158; NextGen, 155. *See also* white supremacy

RAM. *See* random-access computer memory (RAM)

random-access computer memory (RAM), 69, 95

random access image, 69, 80, 95–97, 101

Rankine, Claudia, 32

raster, 33, 35, 59, 86–87, 95, 106, 121, 175n42; in Alma Thomas's work, 55, 66; in Charles Gaines's work, 3, 111, 113–18, 123; and GUI, 4, 26, 71; in Howardena Pindell's work, 1–2; in Jack Whitten's work, 97, 105, 108

rationalism, 3, 140; techno-, 5

Rauschenberg, Robert, 42, 48, 67, 93; *Chairs*, 41; *Factum I* and *II*, 94

realism, 61, 70, 129, 144

Red Decade, 150

redlining, 28, 155

referentiality, 78, 80, 132, 136, 141, 145. *See also* nonreferentiality

Remote Viewing, 131

reparative reading, 34

representation, 44

representational politics, 9, 44, 45–47, 68, 70, 123, 157–59; and the differend, 167n31. *See also* nonrepresentational logics

Reuters, 144

Ricco, John Paul, 171n28

Robbins, Christa Noel, 167n16

Robinson, Cedric, 158

time management, 14–17
Tinder, 44
Tomkins, Calvin, 150
Turner, Fred, 12, 16–22, 25, 31, 104, 118–20, 162n18, 174n25
Turrell, James, 107–8
Twitter/X, 8

universalism, 30–31, 40, 67, 78, 85, 91, 93–94, 119, 120; and GUI, 27; racialized, 11, 18, 53–54, 81, 123
University of Utah, 28; Computer Science Laboratory, 12
user friendliness, 26, 65, 69
US House of Representatives, 85
US South, 78–79

Väliaho, Pasi, 31
Vietnam War, 43, 52
violence, 3, 9, 11, 21, 82, 90, 100, 113, 119, 140, 143, 164n56; anti-black, 30, 46, 53–54, 65, 79, 91, 96–98, 111, 123, 154–56, 158–59; and freedom, 3, 72, 101; police, 5, 98, 154–56. *See also* fungibility

wake work, 96
Warhol, Andy, 42, 48, 105
Washington, DC, 60
whiteness, 4, 33, 35, 47, 92, 111, 140, 159–60, 167n24; and autonomy, 155–56; and blackness, 57, 98, 119, 157; and collectivity, 32; and fungibility, 123, 174n31; gendered, 43, 163n43, 166n13; geometry of, 21; and GUI, 11, 25, 27, 88; history of, 2; and individuality, 94; and management, 14–18, 20, 22; and mathematics, 44; and modernism, 75; and personal computer, 6–11, 54; and personhood, 36, 40, 73, 83, 104, 106,

110; and postracialism, 59, 138; as a problem, 165n78; and space program, 52–54, 65; surround of, 3, 5, 17–30; violence of, 3, 5, 98, 164n56
white supremacy, 46, 123. *See also* anti-blackness; racism
Whitney Biennial, 133
Whitney Museum of American Art, 57
Whitten, Jack, 3, 10, 25, 32–35, 42, 48, 51, 72, 121, 127, 133, 144, 160, 170n1, 171n28, 173n63; *Apps for Obama*, 76–80, 99, 141, *plate 10*; *April's Shark*, 88–89, 92, *plate 12*; *Black Monolith III for Barbara Jordan*, 84–87, *plate 11*; *Black Monolith IV for Jacob Lawrence*, 97–98, *plate 14*; *Black Monolith series*, 76–82, 84–87, 97–98, 99, 141, *plate 11*, *plate 14*; *Greek Alphabet series*, 82, 90; *Heads*, 82, 106–8, *plate 15*; *Mee I*, 88–92, *plate 13*; and nonrelationality, 74–109; *Pink Psyche Queen*, 89–90; *Second Testing (Slab)*, 102; *Untitled*, 101–2
Wilderson, Frank, III, 44, 65, 120, 170n24
William, Pat Ward: *Accused, Blowtorch, Padlock*, 154
Williams, William T., 3, 161n5
windowing, 177n39
windows, 4–5, 11, 13, 25–26, 29, 118–19, 126, 139, 142, 151, 175n14; Microsoft Windows, 12, 27
World War II, 6, 11, 17, 26, 30, 54, 125, 159
Wynter, Sylvia, 8–9

X (studio assistants), 35, 124–28, 130, 139, 152–53, 159–60, 175n1
Xerox Corporation, 25, 82, 89, 91; PARC, 12, 27, 28–29